THE CAUSES OF WARS

and other essays

MICHAEL HOWARD

TEMPLE SMITH · LONDON

First published in Great Britain in 1983 by
Maurice Temple Smith Ltd
Gloucester Mansions, Cambridge Circus
London WC2H 8HD

© 1983 Michael Howard

British Library Cataloguing in Publication Data

Howard, Michael, 1922–
    The causes of wars and other essays.
    1. War
    I. Title
    355'.027   U21.2
ISBN 0-85117-222-9

Typeset, printed and bound at
The Camelot Press Limited, Southampton

Contents

Introduction

THIS volume contains a selection of articles, lectures and essays mainly written during the past decade. Twelve years ago in 1970 I published a similar volume of pieces written during the 1960s under the title *Studies in War and Peace*. Re-reading my introduction to that work I came across the following passage:

There is little cause for surprise in the failure of the innumerable studies devoted to the subject of disarmament to do much more than reveal its complexity. What is more strange is the equanimity with which that failure has been accepted by the groups which were once most urgent and anguished in their pursuit of peace. All but a tiny minority of those who once marched, demonstrated, and sat down to ban the bomb have learned to live with it. Their successors take the balance of terror very much for granted.

No one could write those words today. During the past two years the 'Peace Movement' has revived in redoubled strength, and at the moment of writing it is a force to be reckoned with not only on the British but on the Continental political scene. It may prove a political phenomenon as short-lived as its predecessor of twenty years ago, but it is one that deserves serious attention; especially since the leaders of the movement have not only attacked the existing structure of nuclear deterrence, but the whole practice of strategic studies as it has developed over the past twenty-five years.

All successful political campaigns have deeper motivations than the specific programme that unites them, and the current campaign for nuclear disarmament is no exception. It requires no subtlety of insight to see in it a generational protest, a largely emotional rejection of systems and values associated with an older generation against whom the young feel the need to assert their independence. No less obvious is

1

the role of the movement as a catalyst for all the discontents arising from the inability of governments so to manage their affairs as to provide full employment and a satisfying life-style for their peoples – particularly at a time when expectations have been aroused, by the mechanisms of a consumer-oriented economy, far beyond the capacity of any system to satisfy. But beyond this there are the real and justifiable fears aroused by the prospect of the nuclear holocaust, the possibility of which all governments accept, with apparent equanimity, as a necessary part of their security systems. There is understandable resentment at the continuing and in some cases mounting expenditure which, in a period of economic hardship, is devoted to maintaining the whole apparatus of nuclear deterrence; and there is anger at the callousness with which some strategic specia-lists, especially in the United States, appear to contemplate the prospect, if not indeed the necessity, of mass destruction on an unimaginable scale as part of the process of fighting a nuclear war.

One of the most significant and deplorable developments of the past decade has been the erosion of the consensus reached in the early 1960s, which not only reconciled the often conflicting perspectives from Europe and from the United States, but which bridged the gulf between those who believed that the problems of the world could be solved only by general disarmament, and those whose more prudent assessment of the state of international relations led them to demand the continued maintenance of adequate national defence and deterrent capabilities. This consensus recog-nized both the advantages and the dangers of the existence of nuclear weapons in a world of sovereign states pursuing their own interests and inspired by powerful and conflicting ideologies. It believed in the possibility of a stability achieved by sensible co-operation in the management of weapons-systems. And most important of all, it considered that the Soviet Union, with all its military power and its unremitting ideological hostility, might yet be turned into an *interlocuteur valable* by a shared perception of a common interest, leading to agreements that would make mutual nuclear deterrence a solid basis for peace from which more far-reaching arrangements might gradually be developed.

In explaining the collapse of these modest hopes it is impossible to avoid taking sides in a current and bitter controversy. The evidence is susceptible to conflicting interpretations which I discuss in some of the pieces in the following pages. For one school of thought, which has become increasingly dominant in the United States, the hopes were always illusory. They were deliberately encouraged by the Soviet Union to disarm the West while she continued to arm herself, to extend her influence in the Third World, and generally to pursue her long-term aim of world domination. The analogy was constantly drawn with the expanding power of Nazi Germany in the 1930s – almost the only event in international affairs before 1941 to which protagonists of this school ever refer. For the opponents of this school, who command wide support in Europe and with whom I do not conceal my own sympathy, the growth of Soviet military power, however formidable, is the result of a whole complex of reasons, in part reactive to the external situation, in part driven by internal processes; but in general the Soviet Union is to be seen as aspiring to maintain its status rather than aiming at world hegemony. Behind the façade of military strength, this school sees the economic weakness, the corruption, the inefficiency and the insoluble internal problems that obsess the Soviet leadership. Whereas the American hawks interpret the Soviet intervention in Afghanistan as a planned step in world conquest, the European doves see in it a botched military attempt to retrieve political failure, and one that augurs ill for further attempts at intervention in the Third World. Moreover the feeling is general in Western Europe that American perceptions of the Soviet threat owe as much to internal factors in American policy – military-industrial pressures and, even more important, the need to rediscover national self-confidence after the humiliations of Vietnam and Watergate – as they do to the actual behaviour of the Soviet Union. On this side of the Atlantic the historical analogy most often quoted is not that of 1939; it is that, more sombre and more ambiguous, of 1914.

To this extent the Peace Movement in Europe is only expressing, in greatly magnified form, many of the doubts about American policy that have arisen in the minds of less vociferous commentators and officials since the election of President Reagan in November 1980. But it is also reacting against the whole trend of official strategic thinking, on both sides of the Atlantic, that I have analysed in the article, 'The Forgotten Dimensions of Strategy', reprinted in this volume. In their analyses strategic thinkers have increasingly ignored the three most important factors they need to take into account: first, the political circumstances out of which conflicts might arise and that should determine their conduct; secondly, the problems that would present themselves to commanders in the theatre of war; and third, most important of all, the reactions of the peoples concerned, particularly those whose territory was being threatened or defended. The work of Clausewitz is often quoted, usually partially and inaccurately. Seldom if ever is reference made to the sentence in which he sums up the essence of his doctrine:

As a total phenomenon its dominant tendencies always make war a remarkable trinity – composed of primordial violence, hatred and enmity, which are to be regarded as a blind natural force; of the play of chance and probability, within which the creative spirit is free to roam; and of its element of subordination, as an instrument of policy, which makes it subject to reason alone.

The first of these aspects mainly concerns the people; the second, the commander and his army; the third, the government. . . These three tendencies are like different codes of law, deep-rooted in their subject and yet variable in their relationship to one another. *A theory that ignores any one of them or seeks to fix an arbitrary relationship between them would conflict with reality to such an extent that for this reason alone it would be totally useless.*[1]

Too many nuclear strategists have done precisely this, and separated themselves from reality to an extent that would be absurd if it were not so dangerous. It is all the easier to do this if one adopts a purely geopolitical approach to

1. Karl von Clausewitz, *On War* (Princeton University Press, 1976), p. 89. My italics.

4

strategic analysis; and if one regards the Soviet Union, not as one element in a complex and changing world – dangerous certainly, but itself beset by almost insuperable problems of political and economic management – but as a simple embodiment of evil power bent on world conquest; to be resisted and ultimately overthrown. It is natural enough therefore that exponents of this type of strategic analysis should enjoy high favour with the Reagan Administration, and equally natural that their influence should be greeted in Europe with varying degrees of alarm.

No less unrealistic, however, are those leaders of the Peace Movement who believe, as have their predecessors for two hundred years, that the problems of power in international relations would not exist if it were not for the vested interests of the governing classes that created them; that weapons-systems are not created to serve real security needs but only to gratify the interests of 'militarists' and their industrial backers; and that popular pressure can sweep away the whole tangled web of international rivalries and suspicions like so many cobwebs left over from the past. In several of the essays in this volume I explain why I cannot accept this view; why I believe that the system of states within which we operate is inescapable and not indeed undesirable, even though the system demands the constant management of conflict and can never be without a finite risk of war.

This is not a creed likely to rally massive popular enthusiasm, but neither is it necessarily a pessimistic one. The worst may happen, but it need not; and it will not if statesmen conduct the affairs of the world with reasonable caution and common sense. A prudent assessment of the dangers posed by hostile military power need not degenerate into paranoia. Defensive preparations can and should be based on assessments of probabilities rather than on worst-case analysis. The development by a potential adversary of a particular weapons-system is not in itself a good reason for seeking to match it. We must understand the problems of our opponents even if we have no sympathy with them. One can continue indefinitely with this list of platitudes, but the effort would not be wasted if it did something to recall military thinkers and political leaders from the divergent and equally misguided courses charted by the Committee on the Present Danger in the United States on the one hand, and the Campaign for European Nuclear Disarmament in this continent on the other.

To my academic colleagues I have to apologize for my continuing involvement in these current controversies. I can only hope that at least some of them will share my own view that a *Weltanschauung* formed by a study of the past can usefully supplement the more numerous and influential analyses of current world events based on disciplines which, however rigorous in their method, suffer from a notable lack of historical data. And I am sorry if some of the contents of this book seem over-dogmatic and insufficiently scholarly. Many of them were originally lectures, and were delivered before a wide variety of audiences. But I make no apology for any contradictions or inconsistencies that may be found in them. Those who do not change their minds in the course of a decade have probably stopped thinking altogether.

Oxford, 1982

The Causes of Wars

No one can describe the topic that I have chosen to discuss as a neglected and understudied one. How much ink has been spilled about it, how many library shelves have been filled with works on the subject, since the days of Thucydides! How many scholars from how many specialities have applied their expertise to this intractable problem! Mathematicians, meteorologists, sociologists, anthropologists, geographers, physicists, political scientists, philosophers, theologians and lawyers are only the most obvious of the categories that come to mind when one surveys the ranks of those who have sought some formula for perpetual peace, or who have at least hoped to reduce the complexities of international conflict to some orderly structure, to develop a theory that will enable us to explain, to understand and to control a phenomenon which, if we fail to abolish it, might well abolish us.

Yet it is not a problem that has aroused a great deal of interest in the historical profession. The causes of specific wars, yes: these provide unending material for analysis and interpretation, usually fuelled by plenty of documents and starkly conflicting prejudices on the part of the scholars themselves. But the phenomenon of war as a continuing activity within human society is one that as a profession we take very much for granted. The alternation of war and peace has been the very stuff of the past. War has been throughout history a normal way of conducting disputes between political groups. Few of us, probably, would go along with those socio-biologists who claim that this has been so because man is 'innately aggressive'. The calculations of advantage and risk, sometimes careful, sometimes crude, that statesmen make before committing their countries to war are very remotely linked, if at all, to the displays of tribal *machismo* that we witness today in football crowds.

7

Since the use or threat of physical force is the most elementary way of asserting power and controlling one's environment, the fact that men have frequently had recourse to it does not cause the historian a great deal of surprise. Force, or the threat of it, may not settle arguments, but it does play a considerable part in determining the structure of the world in which we live.

Indeed historians are usually less interested in the causes of war than they are in the causes of peace; in the way in which peaceful communities, controlled by legitimized authorities, have developed and sustained themselves at all. The great scholars who a hundred years ago gained the study of history its primacy of place in British universities, men such as Stubbs, Maitland and Tout, devoted themselves to discovering how a society so peaceful and so law-abiding as that within which they lived had come into existence. They examined the interaction between power and consent, freedom and obligation, State and community, that has made possible the emergence of that humdrum condition of political life that we know as peace. In international affairs the occasions for rivalries, whether dynastic, religious, economic, political or ideological, have been so self-evident that historians have found it more interesting to study the work of those statesmen whose skill *avoided* conflict – the Castlereaghs, the Cannings, the Salis-burys, even the Palmerstons – than those whose ineptitude failed to prevent it. The breakdown of international order does not, on the whole, strike us as a pathological aberration from the norm. On the contrary, the maintenance of that order and its peaceful adjustment to changing circumstances appears as a task presenting a continuous challenge to human ingenuity, and our wonder, like Dr Johnson's at women preaching, is not that it is done so imperfectly, but that it is under the circumstances ever done at all.

I spoke a moment ago about the multiplicity of books that have been written about the causes of war since the time of Thucydides. In fact I think we would find that the vast majority of them had been written since 1914, and that the degree of intellectual concern about the causes of war to which we have become accustomed has existed only since the First World War. In view of the damage which that war did to the social and political structure of Europe, this is understandable enough. But there has been a tendency to argue that because that war caused such great and lasting damage, because it destroyed three great empires and nearly beggared a fourth, it must have arisen from causes of peculiar complexity and profundity, from the neuroses of nations, from the widening class struggle, from a crisis in industrial society. I have argued this myself, taking issue with Mr A. J. P. Taylor on the subject,[1] but now I wonder whether on this, as on so many other matters, I was not wrong and he was not right.

It is true, and it is important to bear in mind in examining the problems of that period, that before 1914 war was almost universally considered an acceptable, perhaps an inevitable and for many people a desirable way of settling international differences, and that the war generally foreseen was expected to be, if not exactly *frisch und fröhlich*, then certainly brief; no longer, certainly, than the war of 1870 that was consciously or unconsciously taken by that generation as a model. Had it not been so generally felt that war was an acceptable and tolerable way of solving international disputes, statesmen and soldiers would no doubt have approached the crisis of 1914 in a very different fashion.

But there was nothing new about this attitude to war. Statesmen had always been able to assume that war would be acceptable at least to those sections of their populations whose opinion mattered to them, and in this respect the decision to go to war in 1914 – for Continental statesmen at least – in no way differed from those taken by their predecessors of earlier generations. The causes of the Great War are thus in essence no more complex or profound than those of any previous European war, or indeed than those described by Thucydides[2] as underlying the Peloponnesian

1. See 'Reflections on The First World War' in my *Studies in War and Peace* (Temple Smith, 1970), p. 99.
2. *History of the Peloponnesian War* (trans. Rex Warner, Penguin, 1954), p. 25.

War: 'What made war inevitable was the growth of Athenian power and the fear this caused in Sparta.' In Central Europe there was the German fear that the disintegration of the Habsburg Empire would result in an enormous enhancement of Russian power – power already becoming formidable as French-financed industries and railways put Russian manpower at the service of her military machine. In Western Europe there was the traditional British fear that Germany might establish a hegemony over Europe which, even more than that of Napoleon, would place at risk the security of Britain and her own possessions; a fear fuelled by the knowledge that there was within Germany a widespread determination to achieve a world status comparable with her latent power. Consideration of this kind had caused wars in Europe often enough before. Was there really anything different about 1914?

Ever since the eighteenth century, war had been blamed by intellectuals upon the stupidity or the self-interest of governing elites (as it is now blamed upon 'military-industrial complexes'), with the implicit or explicit assumption that if the control of state affairs was in the hands of sensible men – businessmen, as Cobden thought, the workers, as Jean Jaurès thought – then wars would be no more. By the twentieth century the growth of the social and biological sciences was producing alternative explanations. As Quincy Wright expressed it in his massive *Study of War*, 'Scientific investigators . . . tended to attribute war to immaturities in social knowledge and control, as one might attribute epidemics to insufficient medical knowledge or to inadequate public health services.' The Social Darwinian acceptance of the inevitability of struggle, indeed of its desirability if mankind was to progress, the view, expressed by the elder Moltke but very widely shared at the turn of the century, that perpetual peace was a dream and not even a beautiful dream, did not survive the Great War in those countries where the bourgeois-liberal culture was dominant, Britain and the United States. The failure of these nations to appreciate that such bellicist views, or variants of

1. Quincy Wright, *A Study of War* (Chicago 1941) vol. II, p. 733.

them, were still widespread in other areas of the world, those dominated by Fascism and by Marxism-Leninism, were to cause embarrassing misunderstandings, and possibly still do.

For liberal intellectuals war was so self-evidently a pathological aberration from the norm, at best a ghastly mistake, at worst a crime. Those who initiated wars must in their view have been criminal, or sick, or the victims of forces beyond their power to control. Those who were so accused disclaimed responsibility for the events of 1914, throwing it on others or saying the whole thing was a terrible mistake for which no one was to blame. None of them, with their societies in ruins around them and tens of millions dead, were prepared to say courageously: 'We only acted as statesmen always have in the past. In the circumstances then prevailing, war seemed to us to be the best way of protecting or forwarding the national interests for which we were responsible. There was an element of risk, certainly, but the risk might have been greater had we postponed the issue. Our real guilt does not lie in the fact that we started the war. It lies in our mistaken belief that we could win it.'

The trouble is that if we are to regard war as pathological and abnormal, then all conflict must be similarly regarded; for war is only a particular kind of conflict between a particular category of social groups, sovereign states. It is, as Clausewitz put it, 'a clash between major interests that is resolved by bloodshed – that is the only way in which it differs from other conflicts'.[1] If one had no sovereign states one would have no wars, as Rousseau rightly pointed out – but, as Hobbes equally rightly pointed out, we would probably have no peace either. As states acquire a monopoly of violence, war becomes the only remaining form of conflict that may legitimately be settled by physical force. The mechanism of legitimization of authority and of social control that makes it possible for the state to moderate or eliminate conflicts within its borders or at very least to

1. Karl von Clausewitz, *On War* (Princeton University Press, 1976), p. 149.

ensure that these are not conducted by competitive violence – the mechanism to the study of which historians have quite properly devoted so much attention – makes possible the conduct of armed conflict with other states, and on occasion – if the state is to survive – it makes it necessary. These conflicts arise from conflicting claims, or interests, or ideologies, or perceptions; and these perceptions may indeed be fuelled by social or psychological drives that we do not fully understand and that one day we may learn rather better how to control. But the problem is the control of social conflict *as such*; not simply or war. However inchoate or disreputable the motives for war may be, its initiation is almost by definition a deliberate and carefully considered act and its conduct, at least at the more advanced levels of social development, a matter of very precise central control. If history shows any record of 'accidental' wars, I have yet to find them. Certainly statesmen have sometimes been surprised by the nature of the war they have unleashed, and it is reasonable to assume that in at least fifty per cent of the cases they got a result they did not expect. But that is not the same as a war begun by mistake and continued with no political purpose.

Statesmen in fact go to war to achieve very specific ends, and the reasons for which states have fought one another have been categorized and recategorized innumerable times. Vattel the lawyer divided them into the necessary, the customary, the rational and the capricious. Jomini the strategist identified ideological, economic and popular wars, wars to defend the balance of power, wars to assist allies, wars to assert or to defend rights. Quincy Wright the political scientist divided them into the idealistic, the psychological, the political and the juridical. Bernard Brodie in our own times has refused to discriminate: 'Any theory of the causes of war in general or any war in particular that is not inherently eclectic and comprehensive,' he stated, '. . . is bound for that very reason to be wrong.'[1] Another contemporary analyst, Geoffrey Blainey, is on the

1. Bernard Brodie, *War and Politics* (Macmillan, New York, 1973), p. 339.

contrary unashamedly reductionist. All war-aims, he wrote, 'are simply varieties of power. The vanity of nationalism, the will to spread an ideology, the protection of kinsmen in an adjacent land, the desire for more territory . . . all these represent power in different wrappings. The conflicting aims of rival nations are always conflicts of power.'[1]

In principle I am sure that Bernard Brodie was right: no single explanation for conflict between states, any more than for conflict between any other social groups, is likely to stand up to critical examination. But Blainey is right as well. Quincy Wright provided us with a useful indicator when he suggested that 'while animal war is a function of instinct and primitive war of the *mores*, civilized war is primarily a function of state politics'.[2] Medievalists will perhaps bridle at the application of the term 'primitive' to the sophisticated and subtle societies of the Middle Ages, for whom war was also a 'function of the mores', a way of life that often demanded only the most banal of justifications. As a way of life it persisted in Europe well into the seventeenth century, if no later. For Louis XIV and his court war was, in his early years at least, little more than a seasonal variation on hunting. But by the eighteenth century the mood had changed. For Frederick the Great war was to be pre-eminently a function of *Staatspolitik*, and so it has remained ever since. And although statesmen can be as emotional or as prejudiced in their judgements as any other group of human beings, it is very seldom that their attitudes, their perceptions and their decisions are not related, however remotely, to the fundamental issues of *power*; that capacity to control their environment on which the independent existence of their states and often the cultural values of their societies depend.

And here perhaps we do find a factor that sets inter-state conflict somewhat apart from other forms of social rivalry. States may fight – indeed as often as not they do fight – not over any specific issue such as might otherwise have been resolved by peaceful means, but in order to acquire, to

1. Geoffrey Blainey, *The Causes of War* (London, 1973), p. 149.
2. Wright, *op. cit.* II, 144.

enhance or to preserve their capacity to function as independent actors in the international system at all. 'The stakes of war,' as Raymond Aron has reminded us, 'are the existence, the creation or the elimination of States.'[1] It is a sombre analysis, but one which the historical record very amply bears out.

It is here that those analysts who come to the study of war from the disciplines of the natural sciences, particularly the biological sciences, tend, it seems to me, to go astray. The conflicts between states which have usually led to war have normally arisen, not from any irrational and emotive drives, but from almost a superabundance of analytic rationality. Sophisticated communities (one hesitates to apply to them Quicy Wright's word, 'civilized') do not react simply to immediate threats. Their intelligence (and I use the term in its double sense) enables them to assess the implications that any event taking place anywhere in the world, however remote, may have for their own capacity, immediately to exert influence, ultimately perhaps to survive. In the later Middle Ages and the Early Modern period every child born to every prince anywhere in Europe was registered on the delicate seismographs that monitored the shifts in dynastic power. Every marriage was a diplomatic triumph or disaster. Every stillbirth, as Henry VIII knew, could presage political catastrophe. Today the key events may be different, the pattern remains the same. A malfunction in the political mechanism of some remote African community, a *coup d'état* in a miniscule Caribbean republic, an insurrection deep in the hinterland of South-East Asia, an assassination in some emirate in the Middle East – all these will be subjected to the kind of anxious examination and calculation that was devoted a hundred years ago to the news of comparable events in the Balkans: an insurrection in Philippopolis, a *coup d'état* in Constantinople, an assassination in Belgrade. To whose advantage will this ultimately redound, asked the worried diplomats, ours or *theirs*? Little enough in itself, perhaps, but will it not precipitate or strengthen a trend, set in motion a

1. Raymond Aron, *Peace and War: a Theory of International Relations* (London, 1966), p. 7.

tide whose melancholy withdrawing roar will strip us of our friends and influence and leave us isolated in a world dominated by adversaries deeply hostile to us and all that we stand for?

There have certainly been occasions when states have gone to war in a mood of ideological fervour like the French in 1792; or of swaggering aggression like the Americans against Spain in 1898 or the British against the Boers a year later; or to make more money, as did the British in the War of Jenkins' Ear in 1739; or in a generous desire to help peoples of similar creed or race, as perhaps the Russians did in 1877 and the British dominions certainly did in 1914 and 1939. But in general men have fought during the past two hundred years neither because they are aggressive nor because they are acquisitive animals, but because they are reasoning ones: because they discern, or believe that they can discern, dangers before they become immediate, the possibility of threats before they are made.

The Habsburg Monarchy might have shattered into a dozen pieces, the Russian railway system might have linked every corner of the Empire with rapid transit communications, without a single Bavarian farmer or Ruhr factory-hand necessarily having his way of life disturbed. But were German statesmen and soldiers being totally paranoid in their fear that, in a Europe where the Russians could deploy so vast a superiority of military power and were supported not only by France but by a string of client Slav successor states in the Balkans, those farmers and factory-hands would indeed be very seriously at risk? And if our answer is that they were indeed being paranoid, and that that paranoia was induced, as many historians would now have us believe, by internal social tensions, what are we to say about British perceptions of German power in the 1930s? Why should the British people of that generation have felt disturbed by the revival of German military capabilities and the extension of their hegemony over Eastern Europe when German leaders were at the time quite sincerely disclaiming any intention of threatening either Britain herself or her control over her Empire? Was this also paranoia? Those historians who have suggested that it was are not popular with their colleagues.

But be this as it may, in 1914 many of the German people, and in 1939 nearly all the British, felt justified in going to war, not over any specific issue that could have been settled by negotiation, but *to maintain their power*; and to do so while it was still possible, before they found themselves so isolated, so impotent, that they had no power left to maintain and had to accept a subordinate position within an international system dominated by their adversaries. 'What made war inevitable was the growth of Athenian power and the fear this caused in Sparta.' Or, to quote another grimly apt passage from Thucydides:

The Athenians made their Empire more and more strong . . . [until] finally the point was reached when Athenian strength attained a peak plain for all to see and the Athenians began to encroach upon Sparta's allies. It was at this point that Sparta felt the position to be no longer tolerable and decided by starting the present war to employ all her energies in attacking and if possible destroying the power of Athens.[1]

You can vary the names of the actors, but the model remains a valid one for the purposes of our analysis. I am rather afraid that it still does.

Something that has changed since the time of Thucydides, however, is the nature of the power that appears so threatening. From the time of Thucydides until that of Louis XIV there was basically only one source of political and military power – control of territory, with all the resources in wealth and manpower that this provided. This control might come through conquest, or through alliance, or through marriage, or through purchase, but the power of princes could be very exactly computed in terms of the extent of their territories and the number of men they could put under arms.

In seventeenth-century Europe this began to change. Extent of territory remained important, but no less important was the effectiveness with which the resources of that territory could be exploited. Initially there were the bureau-

1. Thucydides, op. cit., p. 77.

cratic and fiscal mechanisms that transformed loose coagulations of territorial authority into highly structured centralized states whose armed forces, though not necessarily large, were permanent, disciplined and paid. Then came the political transformations of the revolutionary era which made available to these state-systems the entire manpower of their country; or at least as much of it as the administrators were able to handle. And finally came the revolution in transport, the railways of the nineteenth century that turned the revolutionary ideal of the 'Nation in Arms' into a reality. By the early twentieth century military power – on the Continent of Europe, at least – was seen as a simple combination of military manpower and railways. The quality of armaments was of secondary importance, and political intentions were virtually excluded from account. The growth of power was measured in terms of the growth of populations and of communications; of the number of men who could be put under arms and transported to the battlefield to make their weight felt in the initial and presumably decisive battles. It was the mutual perception of threat in those terms that turned Europe before 1914 into an armed camp, and it was their calculations within this framework that reduced German staff officers increasingly to despair and launched their leaders on their catastrophic gamble in 1914.

But already the development of weapon technology had introduced yet another element into the international power calculus, one that has in our own age become dominant. It was only in the course of the nineteenth century that technology began to produce weapons-systems – initially in the form of naval vessels – that could be seen as likely in themselves to prove decisive, through their qualitative and quantitative superiority, in the event of conflict. But as war became increasingly a matter of competing technologies rather than competing armies, so there developed that escalatory process known as the 'arms race'. As a title the phrase, like so many coined by journalists to catch the eye, is misleading. 'Arms races' are in fact continuing and open-ended attempts to match power for power. They are as much means of achieving stable or, if possible, favourable power balances as were the dynastic marriage policies of Valois and Habsburg. To suggest that they in themselves are causes of war implies a naïve if not totally mistaken view of the relationship between the two phenomena. The causes of war remain rooted, as much as they were in the pre-industrial age, in perceptions by statesmen of the growth of hostile power and the fears for the restriction, if not the extinction, of their own. The threat, or rather the fear, has not changed, whether it comes from aggregations of territory or from dreadnoughts, from the numbers of men under arms or from missile systems. The means which states employ to sustain or to extend their power may have been transformed, but their objectives and preoccupations remain the same.

'Arms races' can no more be isolated than wars themselves from the political circumstances that give rise to them, and like wars they will take as many different forms as political circumstances dictate. They may be no more than a process of competitive modernization, of maintaining a *status quo* that commands general support but in which no participant wishes, whether from reasons of pride or of prudence, to fall behind in keeping his armoury up to date. If there are no political causes for fear or rivalry this process need not in itself be a destabilizing factor in international relations. But they may on the other hand be the result of a quite deliberate assertion of an intention to *change* the *status quo*, as was, for example, the German naval challenge to Britain at the beginning of this century.

This challenge was an explicit attempt by Tirpitz and his associates to destroy the hegemonial position at sea which Britain saw as essential to her security, and, not inconceivably, to replace it with one of their own. As British and indeed German diplomats repeatedly explained to the German government, it was not the German naval programme in itself that gave rise to so much alarm in Britain. It was the intention that lay behind it. If the *status quo* was to be maintained, the German challenge had to be met.

The naval race could quite easily have been ended on one of two conditions. Either the Germans could have abandoned their challenge, as had the French in the previous century, and acquiesced in British naval supremacy; or the British could have yielded as gracefully as they did, a decade or so later, to the United States, and abandoned a status they no longer had the capacity, or the will, to maintain. As it was, they saw the German challenge as one to which they could and should respond, and their power position as one which they were prepared if necessary to use force to preserve. The British naval programme was thus, like that of the Germans, a signal of political intent; and that intent, that refusal to acquiesce in a fundamental transformation of the power balance, was indeed a major element among the causes of the war. The naval competition provided a very accurate indication and measurement of political rivalries and tensions, but it did not cause them; nor could it have been abated unless the rivalries themselves had been abandoned.

It was the general perception of the growth of German power that was awakened by the naval challenge, and the fear that a German hegemony on the Continent would be the first step to a challenge to her own hegemony on the oceans, that led Britain to involve herself in the continental conflict on the side of France and Russia. 'What made war inevitable was the growth of *Spartan* power', to paraphrase Thucydides, 'and the fear which this caused in *Athens*.' In the Great War that followed, Germany was defeated, but survived with none of her latent power destroyed. A 'false hegemony' of Britain and France was established in Europe that could last only so long as Germany did not again mobilize her resources to challenge it. German rearmament in the 1930s did not of itself mean that Hitler wanted war (though one has to ignore his entire philosophy if one is to believe that he did not); but it did mean that he was determined, with a great deal of popular support, to obtain a free hand on the international scene, *so oder so*, as he was in the habit of saying. With that free hand he intended to establish German power on an irreversible basis; this was the message conveyed by his armament programme. The armament programme which the British reluctantly adopted in reply was intended to show that, rather than submit to the hegemonial aspirations they feared from such a revival of German power, they would fight to preserve their own freedom of action. Once again to paraphrase Thucydides:

Finally the point was reached when German strength attained a peak plain for all to see, and the Germans began to encroach upon Britain's allies. It was at this point that Britain felt the position to be no longer tolerable and decided by starting this present war to employ all her energies in attacking and if possible destroying the power of Germany.

What the Second World War established was not a new British hegemony, but a Soviet hegemony over the Euro-Asian land mass from the Elbe to Vladivostok; and what was seen, at least from Moscow, as an American hegemony over the rest of the world; one freely accepted in Western Europe as a preferable alternative to being absorbed by the rival hegemony. Rival armaments were developed to define and preserve the new territorial boundaries, and the present arms competition began. But in considering the present situation, historical experience suggests that we must ask the fundamental question: *what kind of competition is it?* Is it one between powers which accept the *status quo*, are satisfied with the existing power-relationship, and are concerned simply to modernize their armaments in order to preserve it? Or does it reflect an underlying instability in the system?

My own perception, I am afraid, is that it is the latter. There was a period for a decade after the war when the Soviet Union was probably a *status quo* power but the West was not; that is, the Russians were not seriously concerned to challenge the American global hegemony, but the West did not accept that of the Russians in Eastern Europe. Then there was a decade of relative mutual acceptance between 1955 and 1965; and it was no accident that this was the heyday of disarmament/arms-control negotiations. But thereafter the Soviet Union has shown itself increasingly unwilling to accept the Western global hegemony, if only because many other peoples in the world have been unwilling to do so either. Reaction against Western dominance has

brought the Soviet Union some allies and many opportunities in the global arena, and she has developed naval power
to be able to assist the former and exploit the latter. She has
aspired in fact to global power status, as did Germany before
1914; and if the West complains, as did Britain about
Germany, that the Russians do not *need* a Navy for defence
purposes, the Soviet Union can retort, as did Germany, that
she needs it to make clear to the world the status to which she
aspires; that is, so that she can operate on the world scene by
virtue of her own power and not by permission of anyone
else. Like Germany, she is determined to be treated as an
equal, and armed strength has appeared the only way to
achieve that status.

The trouble is that what is seen by one party as the
breaking of an alien hegemony and the establishment of
equal status will be seen by the incumbent powers as a
striving for the establishment of an alternate hegemony, and
they are not necessarily wrong. In international politics, the
appetite often comes with eating; and there really may be no
way to check an aspiring rival except by the mobilization of
stronger military power. An arms race then becomes almost
a necessary surrogate for war, a test of national will and
strength; and arms control becomes possible only when the
underlying power balance has been mutually agreed.

We would be blind therefore if we did not recognize that
the causes which have produced war in the past are
operating in our own day as powerfully as at any time in
history. It is by no means impossible that a thousand years
hence a historian will write – if any historians survive, and
there are any records for them to write history from – 'What
made war inevitable was the growth of Soviet power and the
fear which this caused in the United States.' But times *have*
changed since Thucydides. They have changed even since
1914. These were, as we have seen, bellicist societies in
which war was a normal, acceptable, even a desirable way of
settling differences. The question that arises today is, how
widely and evenly spread is that intense revulsion against
war that at present characterizes our own society? For if war
is indeed now *universally* seen as being unacceptable as an

instrument of policy, then all analogies drawn from the past are misleading, and although power struggles may continue, they will be diverted into other channels. But if that revulsion is not evenly spread, societies which continue to see armed force as an acceptable means for attaining their political ends are likely to establish a dominance over those which do not. Indeed they will not necessarily have to fight for it.

My second and concluding point is this. Whatever may be the underlying causes of international conflict, even if we accept the role of atavistic militarism or of military-industrial complexes or of socio-biological drives or of domestic tensions in fuelling it, wars begin with conscious and reasoned decisions based on the calculation, made by *both* parties, that they can achieve more by going to war than by remaining at peace.[1] Even in the most bellicist of societies this kind of calculation has to be made and it has never even for them been an easy one. When the decision to go to war involves the likelihood, if not the certainty, that the conflict will take the form of an exchange of nuclear weapons from which one's own territory cannot be immune, then even for the most bellicist of leaders, even for those most insulated from the pressures of public opinion, the calculation that they have more to gain from going to war than by remaining at peace and pursuing their policies by other means will, to put it mildly, not be self-evident. The odds against such a course benefiting their state or themselves or their cause will be greater, and more *evidently* greater, than in any situation that history has ever had to record. Society may have accepted killing as a legitimate instrument of state policy, but not, as yet, suicide. For that reason I find it hard to believe that the abolition of nuclear weapons, even if it were possible, would be an unmixed blessing. Nothing that makes it easier for statesmen to regard war as a feasible instrument of state policy, one from which they stand to gain rather than lose, is likely to contribute to a lasting peace.

1. See Blainey, *op. cit.*, p. 128.

War and the Nation State

THE occupants of the Chichele Chair of the History of War at Oxford,[1] were men of very diverse if equally distinguished qualities, but all shared a common perception of their duties of a kind unusual in academics. To a greater or lesser degree they all saw the teaching of their subject as a means of serving the State. For Spenser Wilkinson (1909–25) this was the purpose of the University as a whole: 'the training of servants for the nation, a training for citizenship and for that statesmanship which is but citizenship raised to a higher power . . . If we are to turn out citizens or statesmen equipped for functions in the actual State [he declared] we are bound to teach the nature of War.' Professor Sir Ernest Swinton (1925–46) in his Inaugural Lecture suggested that 'If [Oxford men] go forth into the world after ordered reflection on the nature of war and with a true conception of how the State may best prepare for it, avoid it, or meet it if and when it comes, they will be equipped to help their country at a time when help is most required.' Swinton also suggested, with great shrewdness, that 'the greatest service which the study [of the History of War] can render is to prevent our stumbling into hostilities because we do not recognize the signs nor appreciate the implications of their approach'.

Twenty years later in 1946 Professor Cyril Falls looked back over the smoking ruins of another world war and drew the same conclusion. If public opinion in the 1930s had been blind, weak, and obstinate, he argued, 'the weakness, the obstinacy, is to be found in part in a lack of historical background, in a failure to understand the nature of war or how or why wars come about'. 'There are', he said, 'not many positive services which the historian can do for the State and in a wider sense for the world, higher than that of tracing the causes of wars, describing the means by which they were

1. This chapter is based on an inaugural lecture in the Chichele Chair of the History of War delivered in Oxford in 1977.

23

fought, ascertaining the reasons which led to victory on one side or the other, describing the effects, and estimating the conditions likely to produce future wars and in which they would be fought.' And finally, Professor Norman Gibbs (1955–77) concluded his own Inaugural Lecture with the hope that the lessons to be derived from it would 'have taught our friends [in the North Atlantic Alliance] and not our enemies the secret of losing all battles except the last one'.

But although a common thread runs through the thinking of all those teachers, the change of emphasis in that thinking is yet more remarkable. Spenser Wilkinson saw war in terms derived from Hegel and Darwin, 'the struggle of a society for self-realization, its peculiar form being that of violent conflict with another society, its rival or enemy'. It was an activity to which positive value attached, one in which the individual realized his full potential in service to his State: 'To make the citizen a soldier', wrote Wilkinson in a work published in the year he took up his duties as a Professor,[1] 'is to give him a sense of duty to the country and that consciousness of doing it which, if spread through the whole population, will convert it into what is required – a nation.' For his post-war successors, it was not so easy to rhapsodize about war. The problem was, in the face of a violent reaction against the ideals professed by Spenser Wilkinson and his generation, to preserve a balanced attitude, in order at least as much to prevent war as to fight it. The lesson they preached, I think with increasing success, was that summed up in the words of one of the foremost thinkers about war in this century, Liddell Hart, who wrote: 'if you want peace, *understand* war'. Or as it was more comprehensively expounded by Carl Friedrich in his study of Kant, *Inevitable Peace*, 'It is not usually recognized by people who discourse upon war and peace that any general theory of war implies a general view of history. Nor have they always been aware of the fact that you cannot usefully discuss the problems of how to maintain peace if you have no theory of war.'[2]

1. *Britain at Bay* (London, 1909), p. 191.
2. C. J. Friedrich, *Inevitable Peace* (Harvard, 1948), p. 54.

Still, although war was a disagreeable phenomenon to be studied in order to be avoided, the events of the 1930s seemed to bear out Professor Swinton's warning that it was easier to avoid it if one was prepared for it. That preparation need no longer take the form of 'the Nation in Arms'; of a great outburst of national energy such as Wilkinson and Roberts tried unsuccessfully to create in Edwardian England but which occurred almost overnight in 1914. It required drier, more intricate organization of the kind dissected by Professor Gibbs in his Inaugural lecture on the Committee of Imperial Defence. It did not demand that young Oxonians should lead men into battle: they could render equal and perhaps even better service no further afield than the Government Code and Cypher School at Bletchley Park. But the basic assumption remained, that the State did in its hour of need command the total loyalty of its citizens. If one no longer felt that the individual reached his or her highest fulfilment in the service of the State, it seemed reasonable to suppose, in confrontation with totalitarian societies, that only by serving the State at that particular moment in its history would it be possible to remain an individual at all.

It is hard to deny that war is inherent in the very structure of the State. States historically identify themselves by their relationship with one another, asserting their existence and defining their boundaries by the use of force or the immanent threat of force; and so long as the international community consists of sovereign states, war between them remains a *possibility*, of which all governments have to take reasonable account. It was the great hope of liberal thinkers in the eighteenth and nineteenth centuries that once control of the State system had been taken out of the hands of monarchs and the feudal ruling classes who, it was thought, had so self-evidently a vested interest in war; once democratic control of states had been universally established through the creation of *Nations*, self-conscious peoples in control of their own destinies; then wars would cease. Because Providence had ordained that the interests of mankind should be harmoniously disposed, or were at least not beyond the capacity of reasoned discourse to reconcile, war could then, they hoped, be relegated, like slavery, to a remote and barbarous past.

The history of mankind chronicles few more cruel disillusions than that which these hopes suffered during the nineteenth and twentieth centuries. 'It is no accident', as the Marxists say, that the French Revolution ushered in an era of wars ever greater in their savagery and their scope. The French nation, or those who spoke in its name, initially asserted its rights and independence against the Crown; but it rapidly extended its hostility to the foreign associates of the Crown and those who took up arms on their behalf. It proclaimed war only against Princes and peace to peoples, and in invading their territory the French nation claimed to come as liberators. But those so liberated did not share this view. Not for the last time, what appeared to the donors as a liberating universalism was seen by the recipients as an alien imperialism, evoking a counter-nationalism. By the end of the nineteenth century such nationalism had spread throughout Europe. By the second half of the twentieth it had circled the globe. And it was a movement whose demands were total. Loyalty to the Crown was always to some degree contractual: an evil prince could be disowned, allegiance could be renounced or limited. But how could this be done with a *Nation* which was simply *you* and your own general will? What the Nation willed was its own justification: there were no limits to the demands it might make on its members.

Further this nationalism was almost invariably characterized by militarism. Self-identification as a Nation implies almost by definition alienation from other communities, and the most memorable incidents in the group-memory consisted in conflict with and triumph over other communities. France *was* Marengo, Austerlitz and Jena: military triumph set the seal on the new-found national consciousness. Britain *was* Trafalgar – but it had been a nation for four hundred years, since those earlier battles Creçy and Agincourt. Russia *was* the triumph of 1812. Germany *was* Gravelotte and Sedan. Italy *was* Garibaldi and the Thousand (and there remained perhaps a frustrated sense among the Italians of the Giolitti period that it had been all too easy, that there had not been enough fighting, that Italy had not fully proved herself). Could a Nation, in any true sense of the word, really be born without war? Certainly in the writings of nineteenth-century theorists of nationalism, Mazzini in Italy, Fichte, Hegel, and Treitschke in Germany, war was explicitly identified as a positive value, part of a natural process of struggle whereby mankind evolved to ever higher forms of political organization. This was the dialectic that Marx, by substituting the class-struggle for the struggle of nations, turned on its side rather than on its head. And in the latter part of the century this politico-philosophic doctrine was reinforced by Social Darwinian concepts of the survival of the fittest. The purely historical concept of the Nation merged into the biological one of the Race.

All this filtered down into the national educational systems for which the State was everywhere in Western Europe taking over responsibility from private eleemosynary or ecclesiastical bodies. A great deal of research remains to be done in this important field, but an impressionistic survey based on evidence selected very much at random would suggest that one of the explicit criteria of national education after 1870 in most West European countries was to produce generations physically fit for and psychologically attuned to war. It was a necessary part of citizenship. The history of one's country was depicted by writers both of school textbooks and of popular works as the history of its military triumphs. One identified other nations according to one's military relations with them: foreigners were people with whom one went to war and almost always defeated – and if one had not done so last time, one certainly would the next. Service to the Nation was ultimately seen in terms of military service; personal fulfilment lay in making 'the supreme sacrifice'. At a certain level of literary sophistication the spirit of militaristic nationalism blended into the Gothic revivalism, the medieval imagery of knighthood depicted in Bernard Partridge's cartoons in *Punch* and some of the poems of Henry Newbolt; an imagery enhanced by all the ritual and the liturgy of the Christian Churches. When the young men of Europe went out in 1914 to die in their millions, they did so for an ideal epitomized in the three words, God, King, and Country; and for those who recognized neither God nor King, *La Patrie* provided an adequate substitute for both. In 1914, in a historical moment of incandescent passion, the Nation almost in its entirety was fused with the State.

It is hard to speak of these events without emotion, and I do not think that we should try to do so. It is only if we comprehend and to some extent share these emotions that we can understand how the tragedy of 1914 occurred. The explanation is not to be found, as some distinguished historians would have us believe, in diplomatic blue books or railway timetables or even the balance sheets of international bankers or manufacturers of arms. Statesmen and soldiers could not have functioned as they did if they did not command, and were indeed driven on by, massive popular enthusiasms. We are also better placed to understand the depth of the revulsion, of betrayed idealism, that after 1918 led so many of the finest minds of a new generation to regard 'King and Country' as dirty words; explicitly, in a famous debate in the Oxford Union, to renounce them; to commit themselves to causes, especially to communism, which denied the validity of the Nation State altogether; and to consider military history, not as an essential study for statesmen and citizens, but as an arcane and disagreeable speciality like the history of pornography, not to be encouraged in any self-respecting university.

We can now take a rather more balanced view of these matters. The later nineteenth-century apotheosis of the Nation State, together with the glorification of war which accompanied it, is for most Europeans a historical curiosity, almost impossible to conceive of today. The violent reaction which followed in the 1920s and 1930s was moderated by the experience of the Second World War, when it was discovered that if one was to deal effectively with the grotesque and evil exaggerations of militaristic nationalism which survived in

Germany and elsewhere, the traditional national values as well as the traditional military virtues and skills really had a great deal to be said for them. When their existence as communities appeared to be threatened, both British liberals and Russian communists reverted to nationalism of a highly traditional type, and were grateful for such moral strength as they could draw from that discredited source. Between 1939 and 1945, war evoked nationalism no less surely than, before 1914, nationalism had provoked war.

After 1945, as after 1918, there was again a reaction, but of a different kind. The Second World War, like the First, had called forth a massive degree of popular participation in the war effort, but in this country and the United States (unlike the Soviet Union) it did not this time take the form of a mass slaughter, an *effort du sang*. A comparatively small number of names had to be added to the war memorials which testify, in every parish church in the country, to the depth of the wounds inflicted on British society between 1914 and 1918. When a new generation came critically to scrutinize the conduct of that war, it focused therefore less on the sacrifices which had been suffered by their own societies than on the destruction that had been inflicted on others; especially on the moral problems involved in strategic bombing in general, and the use of nuclear weapons in particular.

When the western nations declared that in future they proposed to rely primarily upon such means for the preservation of their liberties, these doubts grew. The victors in the Second World War, like their enemies, may have drawn strength from the ideology of nationalism; but as the war progressed they proclaimed with increasing emphasis that they were fighting also for the vindication of international public law and the creation of a new international order in which no transgressor nation would go unpunished. The Second World War may have ended with the destruction of Dresden and Hiroshima, but it ended also with the Nuremberg Trials and the Declaration on Human Rights. It was difficult to maintain in the post-war world that national loyalties absolved the citizen from the obligation of individual moral choice.

It was in Britain that protests against nuclear war, and a State apparatus involved in preparation for nuclear war, made themselves most strongly felt. In the United States protest was to take a different form. The belligerents during the Second World War had not only developed weapons of mass-destruction: they had also developed methods of strategem, subversion, and psychological warfare which afterwards remained in their arsenals and became, as it were, institutionalized. In the ideological confrontation which developed after the war and with which we still have to live, honourable men of great ability served their countries by engaging in activities of a kind unjustifiable by any criteria other than the most brutal kind of *raison d'état*, and by the argument that their adversaries were doing the same.

It may be that clandestine activities of this kind arise as inevitably from the nature of the international system as do nuclear and other advanced weapons-systems from the development of scientific knowledge and its technological exploitation, and that it is naïve not to accept it. But whatever their justification, such clandestine activities, like the development of nuclear weapons, have the effect of alienating, in the precise sense of that much-misused word, the State from the people. Governments have to keep their preparations for nuclear warfare and the clandestine activities connected with ideological confrontation as secret from their own peoples as from their putative enemies. There can be no sense of mass participation by citizen-soldiers in nuclear or clandestine warfare as there was in the great military acts of the two World Wars. It is not easy even for the most sympathetic of citizens to identify themselves with such activities. It is much more natural to be appalled by them. The almost insoluble problems of command and control which are posed by the use of nuclear weapons, or those, no less intractible, of constitutional responsibility for the operations of clandestine services, only epitomize the difficulty of legitimizing such actions of the State through the normal operation of the constitutional process. The State *apparat* becomes isolated from the body politic, a severed head continuing to function automatically, conducting its intercourse with other severed heads according to its own laws.

The effect of these developments can also be alienation in the more vulgar sense of the word; alienation especially of a new generation with no tradition of passive acquiescence in the automatic functioning of the State machine. It was not simply the initiation and conduct of the war in Vietnam which aroused such disquiet in American and other universities; it was the revelation of the clandestine activities, the domestic deception and the oblique morality which the government of the United States felt to be justified by that war and the circumstances that surrounded it. So grave did this situation become that for a terrible period the executive arm in the United States felt itself to be almost a beleaguered garrison surrounded by a hostile population against which any means were legitimate in order to ensure its own survival. The apparatus of the State seemed not only severed from the body of the Nation it was supposed to lead: at times indeed its activities appeared almost to be directed *against* that Nation.

This was not a purely American phenomenon. All democratic states (states, that is, where people can freely express their views) have suffered and are still suffering from the same sense of alienation. Among many universities in this country there is an instinctive reluctance – and not only among their junior members – to have anything to do with such organs of State power as the armed forces, the intelligence or the security services. In a letter to *The Times* of 30 September 1977 a group of scholars of high distinction, including some of the most respected senior members of this University, implied that association by academics with the national intelligence services was almost by definition reprehensible. Clearly we have travelled a long way since 1945, when so many senior members of this University returned to Oxford after serving in those intelligence services; and it is by no means clear where the direction in which we have travelled is likely to take us.

It can certainly be argued that manifestations such as these are symptomatic of no more than that robust Whiggery which should be the life-blood of any free society; which is the strongest guarantee against the creeping advance of totalitarianism, of the Servile State, and which during the last sixty years has run far too thinly in our veins. I would certainly not contest the view that mistrust of the State and its activities is the beginning of political wisdom. It is difficult to look back on that apotheosis of the Nation State, which many of us in our own lifetime experienced, without amazement and incredulity that such absurdities should have been proclaimed, and such crimes should have been committed, by all peoples, in its name. It is natural enough that men of independent spirit and intellect should now scrutinize all traditional claims on their loyalties with suspicion. It is not only natural but positively desirable that all concerned with political studies should seek for patterns of world politics which would make possible new and wider loyalties of an international, trans-national, or supra-national kind; loyalties which would dissolve the old system of states which has apparently produced no more than an apparently endless series of increasingly destructive wars. What the conservative pessimist sees as the disintegration of the only system which made orderly government and political intercourse possible, the liberal optimist sees as the first stage in the reintegration of mankind in new political patterns which will transcend the old 'war system' and make possible perpetual peace.

I have however three difficulties with this approach. The first is that, with all its problems and imperfections, the Nation State still remains the only mechanism by which the ordinary man and woman achieves some sense, however limited, of participation in, and responsibility for, the ordering of their own societies and the conduct of the affairs of the world as a whole. It is a mechanism sometimes so imperfect that its members may feel that only devolution, revolution, or even outright secession can make it work successfully: but the fact remains that most of the serious political movements of our time, however radical, are concerned with remodelling nation states, if necessary creating new ones, rather than with abolishing them. Furthermore, among the peoples of the 'Third World', the achievement of effective statehood, even on the most miniscule scale, is seen as an essential condition for making their voices heard and their interests respected within the international community. There may be almost insoluble difficulties about adjusting or structuring states to make them responsive to the wills of the communities for which they claim to speak, or in creating states to speak for communities at present voiceless; but that does not mean that the Nation State itself no longer serves an essential purpose in the ordering of the affairs of mankind, and most therefore continue to make large claims on the loyalty of their citizens. The withering away of the Nation State at present remains a dream and, in the eyes of the masses of the peoples of the world, not even a beautiful dream.

And nowhere does the Nation State show fewer signs of withering away than among those peoples whose leaders profess the philosophy of Marxism-Leninism. This is my second difficulty, and I hope it will not seem a parochial or a paranoid one. In communist societies eminent academics do not consider relations with the intelligence and security services to be reprehensible, or if they do they do not say so out loud. The Armed Forces and the activities associated with them are not starved for lack of government appropriations and popular support. The Soviet Armed Forces, to quote a recent Soviet textbook on the subject, are seen as 'an army of liberated working people and peasants and a tool for defending their revolutionary achievements',[1] and they are accorded the appropriate prestige and financial support within their society. The armies and peoples of the Soviet Union, if one is to believe the consensus of accounts, are motivated less by Marxist-Leninist ideology than by robust patriotism of rather an old-fashioned kind. One does not have to assume nefarious and aggressive intentions on the

1. A. A. Grechko, *The Armed Forces of the Soviet State* (Moscow, 1975: translated and published under the auspices of the US Air Force, Washington, 1977).

part of the Soviet leadership to recognize that the immense military power of the Soviet Union, a community where there is little evidence of any serious attempt to question the loyalty due from citizens to the State, presents a phenomenon that we cannot ignore when we come to assess what developments we see as desirable and what undesirable within our own societies in the West.

Finally, I have a more general difficulty. The State is a body which has by definition a legitimate monopoly of the use of violence, or, as it is usually termed under such conditions, armed force. It is legitimate in that it represents or is held to represent the entire community, and when it does resort to force it does so as the agent of the community expressing its will through agreed constitutional processes. Force can be used only on the authorization of responsible political leaders by trained men under the strictest possible discipline in accordance with the dictates of both military and constitutional law. This politically legitimized monopoly of force is the primary characteristic of any State worthy of the name. It is a monopoly which has all too often been abused: there can be few countries – and our own is not one of them – where responsible citizens have not at one time or another been appalled at the use to which their Armed Forces have been put. But the erosion of that monopoly can lead to nothing but a return to barbarism. Small groups of men using violence to forward their own interests and political objectives may eventually by their very success achieve legitimacy. But the generalized use of violence in pursuit of such objectives by groups recognizing no legitimacy save that created by their own aspirations can only create such disorder, such fear, such resentment, and such vindictiveness that even the most Whiggish of us finds a Tory inside him, kicking and screaming to be let out. When the bonds of social cohesion are loosed to this extent, Whiggery becomes a luxury which even the most fortunately placed members of our society find too expensive to afford.

We live today in times which are sufficiently troubling to force most of us to wonder, if only fleetingly, how we can justify our activities in terms of the social, the political, and the economic trials through which our own society, in common with the whole of the Western world, is at present passing. Here I can repeat and endorse the words of Spenser Wilkinson, that an understanding of the causes and the nature of war is a necessary characteristic of the educated citizen; and those of Ernest Swinton and Cyril Falls, that the deeper such understanding is, the less likely is war to occur. But I would add that such an understanding is more urgent than ever today. This is not just because misunderstanding can now produce disaster for mankind on a scale that no human language contains words adequate to describe. It is because the misperceptions, the mistrust, and the failures to communicate within our societies which arise from such misunderstanding are among the most significant factors which, in free societies, divide men of affairs from intellectuals, governments from peoples, and worst of all, generation from generation.

Academic studies can by themselves no more prevent wars than they can teach people how to fight them. They cannot resolve honest disagreements; indeed it is more often their function to provoke them. But, whether their field lies in the humanities or in the natural or the social sciences, academic studies can provide the knowledge, the insight, and the analytic skills which provide the necessary basis, first for reasoned discussion, and then for action. They provide a forum, and breed the qualities, which enable the student, the teacher, the politician, the civil servant, the moral philosopher, and not least the soldier to reach a common understanding of the problems which confront them, even if, inevitably, there is disagreement about the solutions. This dialogue is what civilization is all about. Without it, societies disintegrate. It is to maintain it that universities exist. And if there is a field where it is more urgently needed than that which concerns the nature of war in the nuclear age and its implications, not only for international relations but for the structure of the State itself, I have yet to find out what it is.

35

The Strategic Approach to International Relations

SINCE the term 'strategy' is now generally used to describe the use of available resources to gain any objective, from winning at bridge to selling soap, it is necessary to make clear that I shall use it in the traditional sense only: that is, as meaning the art of the *strategon*, or military commander. 'The strategic approach' is thus one which takes account of the part which is played by force, or the threat of force, in the international system. It is descriptive in so far as it analyses the extent to which political units have the capacity to use or to threaten the use of armed force to impose their will on other units; whether to compel them to do some things, to deter them from doing others, or if need be to destroy them as independent communities altogether. It is prescriptive in so far as it recommends policies which will enable such units to operate in an international system which is subject to such conditions and constraints.

The strategic approach derives from two characteristics of the international system. The first is the instability of the actors themselves. States may be treated as persons in international law and deal with each other as such in diplomatic negotiation, but they are in fact corporations which do not exist in the precise and finite sense that an individual human being exists. International law may recognize and legitimize their existence, but it can neither create them nor preserve them. They come into being and have their geographical extent delineated as the result of political processes in which the actual or potential use of force often plays a considerable part; and similar processes may dissolve and destroy them. The 'Germany' of 1871–1945 is an interesting example of a state which came into existence as the result of a series of successful wars from the seventeenth to the nineteenth centuries and disappeared as the result of unsuccessful wars in the twentieth. The United States exists as a predominantly Anglo-Saxon unit because of a war fought between 1740 and 1763; as a sovereign unit because of a war fought between 1776 and 1783; as a geographical unit embracing California and other south-western States because of a war fought in 1846; and as a unit at all because of a war fought between 1861 and 1865. The Soviet Union's frontiers extend to Rumania, Poland and the Baltic as a result of wars fought between 1918–21 and 1941–5. Ukraine, Latvia, Esthonia and Lithuania, for the same reasons, have no such sovereign independence. The frontiers and at times the very existence of such states as Poland and Israel have been determined by wars. The list can be extended almost indefinitely.

This is not of course universally and necessarily the case. The peaceful birth of the Kingdom of Norway is an attractive example to the contrary, and many states have come into existence without conflict over the past twenty-five years. Even so, this peaceful evolution was in many cases possible only because the communities concerned made clear their will and capacity to assert their independence by force if they were debarred from attaining it by any other means. The cost of holding a rebellious India – or indeed a rebellious Ireland – in check indefinitely was rated by the British as being impracticably high, and other colonial powers came ultimately to the same conclusion. Angola and Mozambique have taken their places as independent actors on the international scene very largely as a result of the ability of the 'freedom fighters' in those countries to put the Portuguese Government under comparable strain.

There is, unfortunately, little reason to suppose that this process, of creating and preserving states by the use or threat of armed force, belongs to a bygone era from which no conclusions can be derived applicable to the contemporary international system. Israel owes her existence as a state, not to recognition by the United Nations, but to her victories in the wars of 1949 and 1967. Biafra's non-existence is due equally to military causes. Bangladesh emerged as a sovereign political community as the outcome of a military struggle, and the future of the unhappy people of Northern Ireland may ultimately be determined in the same way. Armed force may today be deployed at different levels and utilize different means than in the past, but it remains an element in international relations which it is dishonest descriptively and unwise prescriptively to ignore.

The second aspect of international politics on which the strategic approach lays emphasis is the function of the State as the guardian of certain value-systems; or, as David Easton has put it, its function in 'the authoritative allocation of values for a society'. Communities seek independence when they consider that their value-systems are no longer taken sufficiently into account by the society of which they have hitherto formed part and the élites which rule it. The symbols of sovereignty which they adopt may epitomize traditional value-systems, or the defiant introduction of new ones, or sometimes (as with the French tricolour) an amalgamation of both. The difference between the value-systems and cultural patterns characteristic of these various communities may be as minimal and *nuancé* as those which distinguish Canada from the United States, or Australia from New Zealand, a matter sometimes more of aesthetics than of politics; but equally they may be profound; and the very survival of a value-system may depend on the capacity of the political community which has adopted it to maintain its independence in the face of outside attack.

It is, for example, difficult to see how the Soviet Union could have developed a society on Marxist principles if it had not successfully resisted the attempts of various groups, backed by foreign powers, to restore the *ancien régime* in 1918–19. Further, it was the military incapacity of the nations of eastern Europe to resist Soviet political domination in 1945 that led to their adoption of Marxist value-systems rather than those of the pluralistic Western communities. This paper would be rather different in style if published in the Soviet Union, and very different indeed if the Nazis had won the Second World War and been able to impose their value-system on western Europe. Western liberal academics need constantly to remind themselves of certain factors in their own situation which Marxists, to their credit, never forget. Our attitudes and aspirations, our desire to eliminate war and create a peaceful and orderly world society, our interest in applying scientific or legal methodology in order to do so, the very processes of the physical and social sciences themselves, all are the fruit of a cultural environment rooted in and protected by a certain kind of political system about which we must remember two things. First, its values are not universal: societies have existed in the recent past which have regarded war and violence not simply as acceptable but as positively desirable social activities, and the condition of the world is not yet such that the permanent disappearance of such attitudes can be taken for granted. Secondly, the political system which makes possible our cultural activities and aspirations is not immortal. It is as vulnerable as any other in history to destruction from without and disruption from within. A scholar's awareness of this situation is likely to be the more acute if his formative years were passed in Europe – especially central Europe – between 1919 and 1939. The strategic approach to international relations is rooted in this consciousness of the vulnerability of the cultural and political base from which the political scientist operates. He may need the soldier and the policeman to creat a favourable environment in which he can discover how to dispense with their services.

The problem of the control and legitimization of military power has been a central concern of writers on international relations since Grotius wrote his *De Jure Pacis et Belli* at the beginning of the seventeenth century. It was in general accepted that if states wished to maintain their independence they needed weapons for their protection and that a military capability was a central element in their power both to protect themselves and to affect the processes of international society. By the nineteenth century it was widely assumed among both practitioners and theorists of international relations that the preservation of peace was a matter of ensuring a stable balance of power, although this was a doctrine from which liberal thinkers were already beginning very explicitly to dissent. The experiences of 1914–18 brought into dominance a largely Anglo-American group of thinkers and statesmen – Lowes Dickinson, Lord Hugh Cecil, President Wilson, James Shotwell – who considered the old assumptions and prescriptions of power politics to be totally discredited and who hoped to substitute for its erratic procedures a firm system of international law and organization preserving peace by a system of collective security not unlike the Common Law device of the *posse comitatus*: all members of the international community being bound to assist in the repression of felony – *i.e.* aggression – in whatever quarter it occurred.

This attempt to transfer the concepts and processes of domestic law to the international scene both oversimplified the origins of armed conflicts by the assumption that they were always initiated by simple and felonious 'aggression', and overestimated the readiness of certain major or potentially major states to accept as final the distribution of power, influence and territory of the post-war settlements. Further, how were states which accepted law and organization as the basis for international society to deal with groups which professed a blatantly militaristic philosophy, which used force without restraint to impose their will both in internal and international affairs, and which saw international relations in terms of war, subordination and conquest? Law could be no substitute for power, for without power there could be no law; but power involved precisely those strategic considerations of force-levels, arms procurement, alliances, staff-talks and availability of bases for military operations which enthusiastic protagonists of the League of Nations were so determined to avoid. It was significant that one of the slogans of the British Labour Party in the 1930s was 'Against War and Fascism' and that few people saw anything self-contradictory about this until it was almost too late.

Thus whereas the First World War was considered by liberal thinkers to have discredited the power-oriented approach to international relations, the Second World War was widely believed to justify it. A new direction was given to a subject hitherto considered primarily in terms of international law and organization by the contribution of scholars who had seen and sometimes suffered at first hand the operations of unchecked power operating in support of an alien value-system, notably such eminent European emigrés to the United States as Hans Morgenthau, Arnold Wolfers and Klaus Knorr. In Britain E. H. Carr in his *Twenty Years Crisis* drew a sharp distinction between 'Realists' and 'Utopians' in the study of international relations: between analysing the international system as it worked in practice, and creating a model which, however desirable, bore little relation to the realities of power.

This reaction was probably an over-reaction. The 'Utopians' of the League of Nations did not ignore the factor of military power but were anxious to organize it on a more stable basis than that provided by the separate and incompatible ambitions of mutually antagonistic sovereign states. The 'Realists', at least in their earlier writings, tended to equate 'Power' with military power, or at least military potential, at the expense of the capacity to influence the actions of others through diplomatic skills, cultural affinities, and ideological drives. Such an emphasis between 1940 and 1944 was not altogether surprising. Not is it surprising that by the end of the war such 'Realist' political thinkers as Nicholas Spykman, Arnold Wolfers and Hans Morgenthau had established flourishing schools in American universities which were taking as their bases the very concepts of the national interest, military capabilities and the balance of power on which American political scientists had turned their backs twenty-five years earlier. Nor, finally, is it surprising that the political leaders, East and West, responsible for reorganizing the post-war world should have seen their task in precisely these terms. Mao was not the only statesman of this epoch who believed that power grew out of the barrel of a gun.

British and Soviet leaders found little difficulty in visualizing the post-war world as one divided into 'spheres of interest' with appropriate military power to define and maintain them. The United States was less willing to abandon the ecumenical concepts of the Wilson era. The cautious warnings of such professional diplomats as George Kennan, that Soviet power must be recognized, accepted and contained, had to contend with moralistic and legalistic views based on a monist rather than a pluralist view of the world, which saw the Soviet Union not as a power to be treated with firmness and caution, a potential adversary yet also a potential partner, but as a dangerous criminal outside the world community, to be punished for its crimes against 'peace'. Such crimes were to be deterred and if need be punished by a United States which this time would not, as it had in 1919, abdicate its responsibility for acting as the policeman of the world.

From 1948 onwards the United States thus adopted the 'strategic approach' to international relations which the Soviet Union had probably never abandoned. It visualized the world in terms of possible armed conflict and so conducted its policy as to maximize its military effectiveness in the event of such a conflict; much as the Powers of Europe had done between 1870 and 1914. It wooed and armed allies, attempted to intimidate neutrals and set itself the task of building up and maintaining a nuclear strike capability which would enable it to retaliate massively, at times and places of its own choosing, to Soviet aggression anywhere in the world. To this course of action west European governments, conscious of the presence of Soviet power a few miles from their borders and unwilling to share the destiny of their east European neighbours, saw no cause to object.

As to whether this policy was necessary in order to balance Soviet power and create a stable world-system, or whether it was the result of paranoid misperceptions of intent, historians are not likely to agree, and they would be foolish to attempt a definitive judgement until they have examined the Soviet archives. Anyhow, given the absolutist traditions of American foreign policy and the natural and legitimate fears of their western European allies, it was entirely understandable. The Russians found it as difficult as the Americans to accept the possibility and the necessity of the peaceful co-existence of their two conflicting value-systems, and it was easier for both to do so if they could rely on the security of their own bases. It was also easier for them to do so if they could be sure that any major conflict between them was likely to result in the total destruction of both.

This indeed was the situation in the mid 1950s, once both powers had developed thermonuclear weapons and an inter-continental capability for delivering them. It was a development which compelled strategic thinkers to re-examine their presuppositions more closely than ever before. Did it any longer make sense to talk of 'fighting' a thermonuclear war? How could one deter a potential adversary from inflicting on one's own community inescap-able and unacceptable destruction except by maintaining the capacity to retaliate if he did; and how could such a capability be maintained? Could one credibly threaten the use of nuclear weapons except in retaliation for the use of nuclear weapons, and if not, did one not need a large conventional capability as well? Could nuclear weapons be used selectively to avoid civilian targets? Could they be used in anything short of all-out war? How could their use be controlled especially in alliances? Could they be legislated out of existence and if so how?

These and cognate matters were exhaustively analysed and discussed in the ten years between 1955 and 1965 by a group of largely American thinkers: Albert Wohlstetter, Herman Kahn, Bernard Brodie, Henry Kissinger, Robert Osgood and Thomas Schelling foremost among them. Although most devoted themselves largely to technical questions, and perhaps only Kissinger and Osgood would claim to be political theorists dealing in universally valid concepts of international relations, a common attitude is apparent among them that marks them as the successors to the 'Realist' thinkers of the 1940s. Unlike the 'Utopians' of both the Wilson and the Dulles eras, they accepted the bipolarity if not the multipolarity of the world-system and considered that its stability was dependent on adequate power balances. Such a power balance, they considered, might now be constructed at a far higher level of stability than ever before by the development of second-strike nuclear weapons capable of retaliating against a pre-emptive blow. Such systems were irrelevant to the low-level and peripheral conflicts which must be expected in a complex world, and appropriate armed forces must be available to deter and if necessary to fight these without recourse to nuclear weapons. Finally, although States would continue to need weapons-systems of various kinds to ensure their own security, such defences were always liable to be seen as a threat by potential adversaries, while technological innovation was likely to lead to competitive developments as expensive as they were destabilizing. Agreements, tacit or explicit, on arms control were therefore a necessary element in international stability.

This group contained thinkers whose views often conflicted sharply, but in general they saw their roles as being to make weapons-systems in general, and nuclear weapons in particular, contribute to the stability of a multipolar world as well as to the defence of their own community and its value-system. As aids to clear thinking some of them used techniques of game-theory and systems analysis which were sometimes useful, sometimes not. Their success in gaining the attention of influential political and military leaders brought for many of them a degree of involvement in the formulation of US government policy which naturally earned them the odium of those, such as Professor Noam Chomsky, who disliked that policy and its results. But they were also attacked by those who, like Professor Anatole Rapoport, condemned their acceptance of terms of reference which contained the possible use of nuclear weapons at all, and who denied that the 'game' of power politics was worth playing.

Much of this controversy was concerned too narrowly with the problems and options of the United States to contribute greatly to a general theory of international relations. But the critics of these strategic theorists tended to bypass the continuing dilemma: how, if one foreswears the use of nuclear weapons, does one avoid being at the mercy of those who do not; and if one abandons the game of power politics (which is anyhow not so much a game as a continuous and inescapable process of intercourse), how does one in the long run preserve, against those who do not share them, the values which led one to abdicate in the first place? A solution to this dilemma needed to be as valid for the Czechs and the Israelis as for the United States.

Criticism of United States policy naturally focused on American actions in Vietnam. But such criticisms came as much from within the strategic community as from without. Such 'Realists' as Hans Morgenthau condemned from the very beginning so grandiose a vision of where American interests and frontiers lay. Others agreed with the Administration that American interests demanded a stable and friendly government in South Vietnam and that armed assistance was probably necessary to protect it against invasion from outside and subversion from within; but they considered the military methods used for this delicate task to be about as appropriate as stopping a decaying tooth with a bulldozer. 'Vietnam' has become as emotive a term for this generation as 'Munich' or 'Pearl Harbor' was for the last, and there is a grave danger that from this experience, as from those, hasty conclusions will be drawn and given a universal validity which subsequent experience will show to be entirely spurious. Nevertheless it was a strategic approach to international relations, a desire to deny an area of potential significance to an adversary, a determination to prevent the balance of power tilting to their disadvantage, that led to the American involvement in Vietnam; and that involvement illustrates very clearly certain dangers inherent in the strategic approach.

The first danger is paranoia. This originates in the quite justifiable perception that security is seldom attainable by purely passive, territorial defence. It is always desirable to have friendly territory beyond one's borders or the capacity to control the seas around one's coasts to prevent the accumulation of overwhelming forces for assault or the imposition of a blockade. If the surrounding territory is not friendly but neutral or negative, security considerations dictate that one should have the capacity to prevent a possible adversary from controlling it, if necessary by doing so oneself. So imperceptibly one may extend along a gamut, from the *microdefence* which is the defence of one's own territory to concepts of *megadefence*, which may appear to others to involve little short of world conquest. In 1918, for instance, the British General Staff were recommending the permanent occupation of the area between the Black Sea and the Caspian in order to protect the frontiers of India. The German General Staff at the same period were insisting on war aims involving the permanent occupation of Belgium and the French coast to the mouth of the Somme as well as the Baltic coast as far as Finland to enable them to defend Germany in a Second World War. President Eisenhower's view, that the integrity of Laos was essential to the security of the United States, was an identical example of the same process at work.

The second danger is a solipsism which takes account of other communities only as agents or patients in one's own strategic plans. The Soviet Union is interested in Czechoslovakia only as an element in her own security system, and will permit only such internal developments in that society as do not conflict with that role. For seventy years, from 1882 until 1952, the United Kingdom treated Egypt in precisely the same fashion, as an element in her Imperial Defence System rather than as a community with legitimate interests and aspirations of its own. In the same way successive American governments saw Vietnam as a pawn – or, rather, a domino – in a global strategic confrontation, an area to be defended whether the people concerned desired it or not and whose governments were to be supported or abandoned only in so far as they were prepared to co-operate in that defence. The interests of the Vietnamese people themselves became subordinated to American concepts of global security.

Finally the Vietnam conflict underlined the greatest danger of all, that in fighting to defend a system of values one loses sight of the very values one is fighting to defend. This was no problem for societies which accept war as an intrinsic element in political life, for Nazis who quite frankly elevated brutality and violence to the status of virtues, and for those Marxists who believe equally frankly that the cause of the revolution creates its own value-system and that actions are permissible or otherwise only in so far as they serve, or fail to serve, the historical dialectic. But for those Christians and humanists who believe their values to be absolute the problem is inescapable. What is or is not permissible in war, what causes justify recourse to war, *jus in bello* and *jus ad bellum*, have perplexed them since the days of Augustine of Hippo. The development of nuclear weapons has sharpened this perplexity to the point of anguish. What cause, even survival itself, can justify the infliction of death and suffering on so cataclysmic a scale? The horrifying prospect of nuclear war indeed tended to make people forget the perfectly adequate horrors of conventional war, and perhaps the worst horror which it involves: not what can happen to the victims but what can happen to the victors: their progressive brutalization, their growing contempt for human life, their alienation from the standards they are in principle fighting to defend. Who fights with Dragons, said Nietzsche, shall himself become a Dragon.

All these dangers of the strategic approach to international relations have led men of the highest intellectual ability and academic attainments to condemn it as a totally immoral and counterproductive attitude to international politics. Those who do so, however, merely impose themselves firmly on the other horn of the dilemma: he who does not fight with Dragons may be devoured by them. A failure to adopt the strategic approach may place one at the disposition of somebody who does. One's community may become willy-nilly part of somebody else's security system, or an area contested between two rivals. The values one professes may be eliminated as inconvenient irrelevances by groups with the will and the power to do so (and those who maintain that this cannot happen have to ignore a depressingly large number of examples, historical and contemporary, to the contrary). Statesmen are normally expected to provide for the security of their communities, and those who in the past have failed to do so have not earned the gratitude of

47

posterity. The path of strategic wisdom may lead them to a policy of neutrality or non-alignment. It may lead them into alliances. It may lead them, as it has Israel and Jugoslavia, into a posture of self-reliance. But no statesmen – not even those of India, in spite of Mr Nehru's pristine hopes of doing so – have yet found it possible to abandon the strategic approach altogether.

The thesis of this paper may therefore be summed up as follows:

Value-systems, including those which seek the peaceful resolution of international conflict, do not have a self-evident and universal validity, but are the outcome of peculiar cultural and political conditions prevalent in certain types of communities.

These communities are vulnerable to violent intimidation, dispersal and physical destruction.

Statesmen are expected by the communities which they guide to take whatever measures appear necessary to ensure their protection against such dangers. Unless carefully controlled, the measures they adopt may be seen by other communities as threats and therefore prove dysfunctional. They may also be destructive of the value-systems they are designed to protect.

A strategic *approach* to international relations, as one approach among several being simultaneously adopted, is inevitable and necessary, so long as it is constantly qualified by other factors. A strategic *system* of international relations, that is a system oriented entirely towards conflict, is (except of course for cultures which set a high value on conflict) counter-productive since it is likely to produce conflicts rather than avert them.

A strategic approach may be necessary to produce conditions of stability which will make possible continuing peace; but other, more positive measures, are needed to create peace itself.

Ethics and Power in International Policy

THERE has perhaps been no teacher in the field of international politics in our time whose approach to his subject was more deeply serious than that of Martin Wight – more serious, or more erudite. There have been many specialists more influential, more articulate and more prolific in their publications. Wight left behind him a lamentably small number of writings, enough to give only a glimpse of the qualities which so awed his pupils, his colleagues and his friends. It is thus all the more necessary that those of us who did have the privilege of knowing him should recall and retail as much as we can of his personality – of the moral force which he brought to intellectual questions, of the profound, sombre questioning which characterized his work.

Wight was a philosopher in the oldest and best sense of the word: a man who sought and loved wisdom. He was also a scholar in the oldest and best sense: a man who loved learning. He was above all a deeply committed Christian. He never forgot – and I think quite literally never for a moment forgot – that in the field of international politics one is dealing with the very fundamentals of life and death: with the beliefs, the habits, the structures which shape moral communities and for which it is considered appropriate to die – and, worse, to kill. He saw his subject neither as the interaction of abstract State-entities nor as the equally abstract legal and structural problems of international organizations, but as the exercise of crushing responsibilities by statesmen in an infinitely complex world; the conduct of policies for which the ultimate sanction might have to be war. And war was no matter of heroics or war-gaming, but the deliberate infliction, and endurance, of extremes of suffering as the ultimate test of the validity of human institutions and beliefs. The work of some American 'behaviourists', who sought to reduce the vast and tragic tapestry of human affairs to elegant mathematical formulae, was not simply repellent to him. It was unintelligible. He could not understand how people could do such things. He refused even to discuss it. For him, International Relations did not consist of a succession of problems to be solved in conformity with any overarching theory. Rather, like the whole of human life, it was a predicament: one to be intelligently analysed, where possible to be mitigated, but if necessary to be endured – and the more easily mitigated and endured if it could be understood. In his acceptance of the ineluctably tragic nature of human destiny he was a thinker in a European tradition going back to that classical antiquity in which his own learning was so deeply rooted.

To superficial appearances Wight presented something of a contradiction. He accepted the fact, as he saw it, of 'Power Politics'. The study which he wrote under this title is an almost defiantly traditional work, disdainful both of Liberal Utopianism and of the contributions of the behavioural scientists to the subject. It expounds the mechanisms of power politics in the international system without praise or condemnation: this is the way it has been, he implies, and there is no reason to suppose it could be otherwise. But at the same time he was a Christian pacifist and a conscientious objector, and no one who met him could be in any doubt of the profundity and the unshakeable firmness of the convictions on which his pacifism rested.

In actuality there was for him no contradiction. In a world of evil one must face the fact of evil and the need, in face of that fact, for the unfortunate Children of Darkness to be wise in their generation. In such a world statesmen and soldiers have responsibilities and duties which they cannot and should not seek to evade. Nevertheless in such a world it is the duty of some Christians to bear witness to a transcendent loyalty; and those on whom this duty is laid will know it in their inmost conscience and must fulfil it, irrespective of consequent embarrassment or hardship. Martin Wight's burning sincerity fused the apparent contradiction – not, probably, without much inner anguish – into a single coherent philosophy; one which provided an analysis of the world predicament as much as a guide to his own actions.

Wight was in fact a Christian pessimist, as were so many of that generation which had seen the hopes of the Locarno era wither, and who grew to maturity under the shadow of the vast menaces of the 1930s. Even the menaces of the 1950s, the perils, as they appeared at the time, of nuclear holocaust, never loomed so large in the eyes of contemporary observers. Those perils could be, and indeed have been, kept at bay by prudent statesmanship. The nuclear danger is predictable and controllable. But the 1930s saw the emergence of forces of irrationality which it would be neither inappropriate nor hyperbolic to call forces of *evil*: unpredictable, uncontrollable, still only partially understood. These forces fitted into the world picture neither of the liberal humanists nor the Marxists. Both of these schools were children of eighteenth-century rationalism and nineteenth-century radicalism. Each believed in its own way in inevitable progress towards world democratic systems and had welcomed the overthrow of the militarist autocracies of Central Europe as obstacles to the gradual convergence of mankind towards unity and peace. But in Fascism one was dealing with something consciously beyond reason and defiant to reason – something of which no secular ideology had hitherto taken account.

Christianity, unlike Liberalism or Marxism, did provide an explanation; not the cheerful liberal humanitarian Christian teaching which read little into the Bible except the Nativity and the Sermon on the Mount, but the teaching which digested all the implications of the Old Testament, including the Prophetic books, before turning to the New, which emphasised that the Gospels themselves were full of uncompromisingly dark passages, and which faced the fact that at the centre of the Christian religion, as of no other great world religion, was the symbol of agonizing and unavoidable suffering. The Christian eschatology, long disdained by liberal humanists even within the Church itself, once again became terrifyingly relevant to human affairs. The works of Charles Williams, of C. S. Lewis, and – drawing on yet wider sources of Manichean myth – of J. R. Tolkien were deservedly popular as allegorical commentaries on the events of the time. And the teachers who best provided an adequate framework for understanding were the philosophers and the theologians – Niebuhr, Bonhoeffer, Karl Barth, Tillich – who accepted uncomplainingly the remoteness, the inscrutability of God, who saw the focus of Christianity as the Passion rather than the Sermon on the Mount; men for whom the march of humanitarian, utilitarian liberalism, including its change of gear into Marxian socialism, had simply been a long excursion into the desert in pursuit of a mirage.

In the light of such a philosophy the accepted explanations of the problems of international politics and the causes of war all appeared inadequate to the point of superficiality. The received wisdom among liberal thinkers of the 1920s was that wars in general, and the First World War in particular, had been caused precisely by the operation of 'power politics' which in their turn reflected the prejudices of a militaristic ruling class and the interests of capitalist investors and armaments manufacturers. The solution lay in the abandonment of power politics conducted by means of secret diplomacy, and the adoption instead of programmes of collective security, arbitration, disarmament and the resolution of differences through open and reasoned discussion at the League of Nations. The problems which called for solution were those arising from the inequities of the Paris Peace Settlement, which was far too tainted with the evils of the old system. If only Germany could be reconciled and the injustices done to it undone, then a new world order, a new era in the history of mankind, might be expected to dawn.

These ideas were reiterated in a deliberately simplistic form by publicists – E. D. Morel, Goldsworthy Lowes Dickinson, H. N. Brailsford, Leonard Woolf – who with some reason saw their first duty as the re-education of that public opinion on which they relied to make their dreams come true, but which had repeatedly shown itself vulnerable to stubborn fits of atavistic xenophobia. Few of them were as naïve as sometimes appears from their writings. The complexity of the problems of international politics was certainly not underrated by the founders of Chatham House.[1] This group included not only such outstanding idealists as Lord Robert Cecil and Philip Noel-Baker but 'realists' of the stamp of Eyre Crowe and Neil Malcolm and such scholarly specialists as James Headlam-Morley and Arnold Toynbee; men who had discovered at Paris how terribly under-equipped the Allied statesmen were to deal with the tangled problems which victory had dumped in their laps, how vast was the distance which separated popular expectations from practical realities, and how important it was for the future peace of mankind that judgment on foreign affairs should be formulated on a basis of widely-shared expert knowledge.

Yet in broad terms these men certainly shared the aspirations of the liberal idealists. There was a broad ethical consensus that international politics should be conducted, not with the aim of maximizing the national interest, but in order to enable mankind to live in a community of mutual tolerance and respect, settling its differences rationally, resolving its conflicts by peaceful means. This could best be achieved by the creation and management of international institutions, in particular the League of Nations; and by the education of public opinion in loyalties wider than narrow, old-fashioned patriotism. And finally Britain's own national affairs should be conducted in accordance with a Kantian categorical imperative, to provide an example for other nations and to smooth the path towards the development of a higher national community based on the rule of law. They would have accepted that it was their task to transcend the old order based on national power and to create a new one based on consent.

But what this generation did not fully appreciate was how far these values, the fine flower of Victorian Liberalism, were tied up with a social order and national institutions which might continue to need power, and in the last resort *military*

1. Where this lecture was delivered in January 1977.

power, for their survival. All had supported the Allied cause during the Great War on the not unwarranted assumption that its defeat would be a catastrophic setback to the progress of liberal ideas. All believed that responsibility for the war rested very largely with the militaristic ideology rooted in the quasifeudal monarchical social order in Central Europe whose destruction had removed a serious obstacle to world peace. What was harder for them to appreciate was that the destruction of that order would not make easier the work of the peace-loving bourgeoisie such as themselves, but infinitely more difficult: that it would create a vacuum to be filled by warring forces of revolution and counter-revolution out of which regimes would arise far more ferocious than those they had replaced – regimes even less susceptible to reason or enamoured of an order based on consent. It was the tragedy of the League of Nations, that consummation of a century of striving and dreaming, that it was founded at a moment when it could not hope to operate successfully except as the executive organ of a group of like-minded nations prepared in the last resort to enforce their decisions by precisely those mechanisms of military power which its very existence was intended to render obsolete.

The lesson was not lost on the men who had to reconstruct the international system after the Second World War. They were more modest in their aspirations – more modest also, it must be admitted, in their talents. The new generation, at least in Britain, produced no one to equal the vigour and vision of the surviving veterans, Toynbee, Webster, Lionel Curtis, Philip Noel-Baker. The officials and the statesmen – Strang, Jebb, Cadogan, Bevin – were the equals if not the superiors of their predecessors; but there were no seers to inspire them, no prophets of a new order. Only one new academic figure of any eminence had been tempted by wartime experience to reflect with any degree of profundity on the state of the world – Herbert Butterfield; and he did so in terms which echoed the teaching of Reinhold Niebuhr across the Atlantic, and which were to provide a continuing influence on Martin Wight. There were certainly no British thinkers who felt the world was now theirs to mould; who would claim, as Dean Acheson was to claim, that they were present at the Creation. Perhaps the failure of the first creation was too fresh in all their minds. But what *was* dominant in their consciousness was the impotence, almost one might say the irrelevance, of ethical aspirations in international politics in the absence of that factor to which so little attention had been devoted by their more eminent predecessors, to which indeed so many of them had been instinctively hostile – military power: power not necessarily to impose their standards upon others (though that, in the re-education of the defeated enemy, was not irrelevant) but simply to ensure the survival of the societies in which those ethical values were maintained. And to the vulnerability of such societies and their value systems a sad procession of emigré scholars and statesmen from Central and Eastern Europe bore eloquent witness – both before and after 1945.

This realization of the impotence of ethical principle to operate unaided in a world of power does much to explain the speed with which the world rearmed after 1950. The spirit of historical irony will record that it was Mr Attlee and his colleagues, not excepting Sir Stafford Cripps, the men who had voted and spoken so eloquently in the 1930s against power politics and great national armaments, who now took the decision to equip the United Kingdom as a nuclear power; that the Minister of Supply responsible for the construction of the atomic bomb was Mr John Wilmot – the same John Wilmot whose election for the constituency of East Fulham in 1934 had convinced Stanley Baldwin of the impossibility of persuading the country to accept a major rearmament programme; and that the Secretary of State for Air in 1947, when the Air Ministry began to design the V-bombers which would deliver the bombs, was that most tireless and dedicated advocate of disarmament, Mr Philip Noel-Baker. And in the United States liberals of equally impeccable antecedents, men who had throughout their lives fought against American entanglement in the old world of power politics, now helped to build up an armoury of terrifying strength in order to 'defend the Free World'.

It is easy enough either to deplore this apparent volte-face as a shameful betrayal of principle, or to sneer at it as a belated acceptance of the facts of life. But both reactions arise from an attitude towards political morality – indeed, towards social action as a whole – which has, although very widely shared, proved throughout history to be misleading. According to this view, actions are to be judged against a single scale which runs from the pole of 'power politics' at one end to that of 'ethical action' at the other. Ethical considerations are held *automatically* to enfeeble power; considerations of power are regarded as unavoidably sullying ethics. It is an attitude no less popular with professed 'men of the world' and 'realists' than it is with idealists and reformers. The reluctance of liberal critics seriously to examine the technical problems faced by the military – a reluctance as evident today as it was in the 1930s – is paralleled by the scepticism with which a substantial number of officials, soldiers and 'defence experts' regard the relevance of ethical factors to the problems which they face. War, they say, is war. Business is business. What needs to be done, has to be done.[1]

The assumption that the exercise of coercive power is in itself fundamentally immoral, and that involvement in power relationships automatically vitiates ethical behaviour, is natural enough. How can good ends be served by evil means? How can one get peace by preparing for war? How can all the mechanisms of military power – the disciplining of soldiers, the development of weapons, the training to kill, the posing of threats, to say nothing of the awful actuality of warfare, shocking enough in the pre-nuclear age, inconceivable today – how can such activities

1. Although in my experience, in this country at least, defence specialists are more likely to be concerned about questions of ethics than are 'peace researchers' and liberal reformers about the problems, either fundamental or technical, of military or any other kind of power. It is significant that association by universities with the Ministry of Defence in this country, or with the Pentagon or the Central Intelligence Agency in the Unites States, is regarded by many students as being immoral almost by definition, and one is regarded as extremely naïve if one ventures to ask why.

conceivably contribute to ethical goals? Is not the whole 'power system' alien to and irreconcilable with any ethical objectives except those of the barbarian – and in adopting it even to fight barbarians, is one not becoming a barbarian oneself? To adopt the methods of coercive power – and economic can be as debasing as military power – is *in itself* considered to be unethical, to debase the cause which those methods are intended to serve.

Are ethics and power in fact such poles apart? Most of us in practice do not consider that they are, and within our own experience we can normally reconcile them without too much difficulty. But this may simply be the result of our own moral obtuseness and intellectual laziness. To provide a satisfactory conceptual synthesis is not so easy. The long debate over *raison d'état* has never been properly concluded. The tradition that led through Plato and Machiavelli to Hegel, by which all contradictions were resolved in service to a State which was itself the highest value since it made possible all other values, disastrously popular as it became in Germany, has never been acceptable to Anglo-Saxon Liberals – although the Marxist variant which for 'State' would substitute 'Revolution' succeeded in attracting some of them in the 1930s. But perhaps a clue to a more satisfactory formula can be found in the work of another German thinker, albeit one who is seldom regarded as an authority on ethical questions: Karl von Clausewitz.

Clausewitz did not indeed deal with ethical questions as such. He did not fundamentally question the crude Machiavellianism of eighteenth-century politics: the Grotian Laws of Nations he dismissed as 'certain self-imposed, imperceptible limitations hardly worth mentioning, known as international law and custom'. But on the relationship between war and politics he did, as we know, have interesting and original things to say; and these may provide useful guidance in any consideration of the relationship between power and ethics.

Clausewitz's theory was teleological. In warfare, every engagement was planned to serve a tactical purpose. These tactical purposes were determined by the requirements of strategy. The requirements of strategy were determined by the object of the war; and the object of the war was determined by State policy, the State being the highest embodiment of the values and the interests of the community. Thus the objectives of State policy ultimately dominated and determined military means the whole way down the hierarchy of strategy and tactics. War was not an independent entity with a value-system of its own.

For Clausewitz State policy was the ultimate mover and justification, the criterion by which all other actions were to be judged – which in itself would make his doctrine as it stands unacceptable to the liberal. But what if one introduces one further, and ultimate, step in the hierarchy, to which State policy itself should be subordinated – the ethical goal? The State itself then becomes not an end but the means to an end. It has a dual role. It exists primarily to enable its own citizens to realize their ethical values; but it exists also to make possible an *international* community of mankind, whose values and interests are ultimately determinant, not only of State policy as such, but of all the means, military and otherwise, that are used to implement State policy.

Such a pattern goes beyond the 'Grotian' concept of international relations, for although in the Grotian formulation States are governed by a 'Law of Nations' which is based partly on a reflection of the divine order and partly on prudential considerations of self-preservation, they need no justification for their policy beyond the requirements of their own existence. They accept a law of nations as man accepts the laws of a just society: because his own needs dictate that he should do so. But in the Clausewitzian formulation, as we have elaborated it, State policy would be determined by and judged according to the needs of the international community. In the same way as war, if it were not directed by State policy, would be 'a senseless thing without an object', so State interests and State policy would make no sense and have no justification if they were not shaped in accordance with the overriding needs of mankind. As military power is subordinated to and guided by State policy, so State power should be subordinated to and guided by ethical norms. The relationship would then become one, not of irreconcilable opposition between mutually exclusive poles, but of hierarchical subordination of means to ends.

That all sounds very fine as a theory. In practice, unfortunately, it settles very little. Having stated his own theory, Clausewitz identified the fundamental problem about its application. The military means should always by definition be subordinated to the political object, true: but the military had its own requirements. It had to work according to its own inner necessities. Only the military specialist could determine whether the goals set by policy were attainable, and if so what the requirements were for attaining them. Military affairs had, as Clausewitz put it, their own grammar, even if they were subordinated to political logic; and the grammar was intricate and ineluctable. Armed forces require bases, and those bases may only be available in countries with which one would, for ethical reasons, prefer not to be allied. National industry, on which military capacity is based, may require access to raw materials available only from countries which are equally politically embarrassing. The successful conduct of the most just and defensive of wars may demand alliance with states whose price is the support of war aims which flatly contradict all one's own normative values – as did those of Italy in the Treaty of London in 1915, that notorious example of power politics and secret diplomacy. Yet rather than yield to Italian demands on Slav territory, would it have been *morally* preferable to have waived the Italian alliance, leaving the Central Powers with their hands free to deal with Russia, and thus prolonging the war if not risking outright defeat?

One can multiply examples endlessly; let me concentrate simply on one. In 1935 there occurred a superb opportunity for Britain to shape its policy in the service of an ethical objective: the implementation of its obligations under the Covenant of the League of Nations by imposing penal sanctions upon Italy in order to deter or punish its aggression against Abyssinia. Not only was the crime unambiguous: the criminal was highly vulnerable. Public opinion, in the 'Peace Ballot', had recently expressed itself in favour of mandatory sanctions, even at the risk of war. The case might have been deliberately created to test the effectiveness of that new system of collective security and the rule of law which had been brought into being since 1918 to replace the old chaotic system of power politics. It would have been a perfect example of the use of coercive means to attain political ends.

We can see that there were many reasons why the British government flinched from the test; but certainly not the least was the uncompromising and unanimous opposition of those experts in military grammar, the Chiefs of Staff. Within the power structure which it was their duty to operate there were two far more serious threats, not simply to the rule of law in international politics, but to the security of Britain and its Empire: the growing power of Nazi Germany and the increasingly open aggression of Japan. To risk even successful war against Italy would have been to enfeeble the already pathetically weak fleet available to deter Japanese attack in the Far East, and to antagonize a potential ally whose help was, in the eyes of France if not of Britain, indispensable in containing the German threat. The military grammar appeared unanswerable; it was to be that, rather than the ethical imperatives of collective security, which determined State policy.

In retrospect one can say that even in their own terms the military grammarians may have got it wrong. Faced with the real prospect of war Mussolini might very easily have retreated; his catastrophic humiliation would probably have imposed a high degree of caution both on Germany and Japan; a pattern of peace-keeping would have been successfully established. But the arguments of the grammarians could not simply be overridden. The ethical imperative could not be, in Clausewitz's words, 'a despotic lawgiver'. In the last resort the statesmen were, as ever, faced with a balance of imponderables, with problems to which there were no clear-cut ethical solutions.

To say, therefore, that State policy should be subordinated to the ethical imperative as strategic considerations should be subordinated to State policy does not get us very far. The world of power remains stubbornly autonomous; the suzerainty of ethics may be of quite Merovingian ineffectiveness. Moreover such a formulation can lend itself to the crudest of casuistical justification of all coercive means in terms of the ethical end – of police torture of political dissidents in order to preserve a stable and orderly society, of the Soviet invasion of Czechoslovakia in 1968 in order to preserve the stability of Eastern Europe, of the 'destabiliz- ation' of Chile to maintain the stability of the Western hemisphere, of the secret bombing of Cambodia to maintain the independence of South Vietnam. Because such actions may be dictated by the grammar of coercive power, they cannot – any more than can terroristic destruction of life and property or intimidatory guerilla massacres – be *justified*, i.e. made in themselves ethical, by an ethical object. The dimensions of power and of ethics remain stubbornly different.

But if we think of power and ethics in terms of *dimensions*, we may not go too far wrong. Dimensions do not contradict one another, nor can they be subordinated to one another. They are mutually complementary. Political activity takes place in a two-dimensional field – a field which can be defined by the two co-ordinates of ethics and power. The ethical co-ordinate (which we may appropriately conceive as vertical) indicates the purposes which should govern polit- ical action: the achievement of a harmonious society of mankind in which conflicts can be peacefully resolved and a community of cultures peacefully co-exist within which every individual can find fulfilment. The horizontal co- ordinate measures the capacity of each actor to impose his will on his environment, whether by economic, military or psychological pressures. Movement along this co-ordinate, the increase or decrease in coercive capability, has *as such* no dimension of morality, any more than does any elevation of moral standards necessarily involve an increase in one's power to implement them.

Effective political action needs to take constant account of both dimensions. To concern oneself with ethical values to the total exclusion of any practical activity in the dimension of power is to abdicate responsibility for shaping the course of affairs. To accumulate coercive power without concern for its ethical ends is the course of the gangster, of St Augustine's robber bands. Indeed it could be argued that each of these unidimensional courses is self-defeating; that the co-ordinates, if indefinitely prolonged, become circular. Obsession with ethical values with no concern for their implementation is ultimately unethical in its lack of *practical* concern for the course taken by society. Concern for coercive capability without the legitimization of moral acceptance leads ultimately to impotence, and disaster at the hands of an indignant and alienated world. Thus political action, whether in the international or any other sphere of activity, needs to be *diagonal*. Ethical goals should become more ambitious as political capability increases. The political actor, whether statesman or soldier, needs to grow in moral awareness and responsibility as he grows in power. The moralist must accept that his teaching will not reach beyond the page on which it is written or the lectern from which it is expounded without a massive amount of complex activity by men of affairs operating on the plane of their own expertise. The more ambitious and wide-ranging the ethical goals, the greater the power-mechanisms required to achieve them.

In pursuing his diagonal course the statesman is like a pilot reading a compass-bearing from which he must not diverge in either direction if he is to achieve his goal. Too rigorous a concern for moral absolutes may reduce or destroy his capacity for effective action. Yet to ignore such norms entirely may gain him short-term advantages at the cost of ultimately reducing his capacity to operate effectively in a world made up, not of robber bands but of states functioning as moral as well as military entities, whose authority is as dependent on moral acceptibility as on coercive capability. He may have to commit or authorize acts which, as a private citizen, he would deeply deplore. No one involved, for example, in the repatriation of Soviet troops from British-occupied Europe to Russia immediately after the Second World War should have felt anything other than distress bordering on misery at the need for such action. But in the political dimension the object of maintaining friendly relations with the Soviet Union in order to achieve yet wider ethical objectives – the peaceful settlement of Europe and of the world as a whole – had to be regarded as mandatory. To call attention to the ethical problems created by such actions is appropriate and necessary; but they cannot be condemned on such grounds unless account is taken of the political dimension as well.

Acton was being less than fair to the world of politics when he declared that power tends to corrupt. What does tend to happen, as I suggested earlier, is that the grammar of power, so intricate, so compelling, becomes for those who operate it a universe in itself – as indeed for the moralist and the reformer, the ethical objective can become an exclusive obsession which makes him disdain the tedious and murky problem of how to attain it. Yet perhaps there is a kind of gravitational force against which statesmen have consciously to fight, which keeps their activities always closer to the horizontal co-ordinate of power than to the vertical one of ethics, which constantly weighs down their efforts to maintain the diagonal. Overloaded political decision-makers and members of huge bureaucracies have enough to contend with in day-to-day management of affairs without constantly searching their consciences as to the ethical implications of their actions. That makes it all the more important that their ethical perceptions should be internalized and operate automatically and continuously. Government departments seldom carry a chaplain on the establishment to provide an ethical input into policy-making.

The appropriate response of the political moralist to the world of power must therefore be not to condemn but to enlighten, to understand, and to acknowledge and accept that the Children of Darkness have a painfully-learned wisdom in their own generation which is deserving of genuine respect. As Niebuhr put it, 'Politics will, to the end of history, be an area where conscience and power meet, where the ethical and coercive factors of human life will interpenetrate and work out their tentative and uneasy

63

compromises.'[1] As a thinker whose ideas were deeply rooted in ethical values, Martin Wight knew that even he could make no serious contribution to the study of international politics without first attaining a full understanding of the coercive factors operating within it. But he never ceased to look beyond these 'uneasy compromises' to the ultimate goal of full and final reconciliation.

1. Reinhold Niebuhr, *Moral Man and Immoral Society: A Study in Ethics and Politics* (Scribner, New York, 1949; first publ. 1932), p.4.

Social Change and
the Defence of the West

IN the nineteenth century Western society entered one of the greatest transitions in the history of mankind. For a thousand years its economy had been predominantly agrarian. Now it became increasingly industrial; and with the change in the means of production, as Marx was not alone in observing, there came a fundamental shift in societal values. One of the questions which particularly interested social and political thinkers throughout the century was whether industrial societies would be any less prone to warfare than their feudally-structured predecessors. Liberal sociologists such as Augustus Comte suggested that industrialization would bring about an end to war altogether. War, they maintained, had been an activity peculiar to feudal, agrarian civilizations and their nomadic predecessors. In the new industrial age it would serve no purpose. The new social structures and patterns of behaviour would not accommodate themselves to it as an institution; so inevitably it would disappear. And what these liberal thinkers hoped, conservative leaders feared. Throughout Western Europe the spread of bourgeois pacifism and materialism created, among military men, something like horror. War indeed was to be welcomed as an antidote to it. In Imperial Germany the Army did its best to confine recruitment to the reliable inhabitants of country districts, regarding the cities of the Rhineland and the Ruhr as hotbeds of pacifism and socialism. In Britain, Edwardian statesmen were appalled by the physical unfitness of recruits from the urban slums and wondered how 'a street-bred people' could endure in the struggle for national survival which, in that era of Social Darwinianism, seemed increasingly probable. Whether with pleasure or apprehension, the view was widely held that the

65

products of industrial societies would be neither able nor willing to fight.

But able and willing they were, and fight they did. When war came in 1914 the city-bred peoples of Western Europe showed no lack of capacity to adjust to it. Units raised from urban areas – in Britain from the industrialized Midlands, in Germany from Silesia and the Ruhr – fought as courageously and perhaps rather more skilfully than did those from such traditional military areas as the West Country or the Mark Brandenburg. Furthermore, without the organizational and technical skill of the bourgeois entrepreneurial classes (once the military leadership could bring itself to make use of it) the war could never have been sustained at all. Finally, the morale of the 'street-bred people' on both sides remained heroically staunch through five terrible years. It was in the backward, still largely agrarian Russian Empire that revolution came, not in the highly industrialized West. And the experience of the Second World War was to provide yet stronger evidence of the capacity of industrialized societies to endure the most terrible of hardships and ordeals and still provide loyal and efficient armed forces.

Why did Comte and his followers prove so wrong? Why did industrial societies prove quite as apt at warfare as their agrarian predecessors? Two schools of thought arose to give an explanation. The Marxists maintained that Comte and other bourgeois sociologists had quite simply failed to perceive that war was as inherent in the capitalist order of society as it was in the feudal. It was a continuation of industrial competition by other means; and so far from unfitting the population for war, industrial society, through the disciplines it imposed through factory modes of production, turned it into more docile and malleable cannon fodder. Capitalism and militarism were interdependent, indeed indistinguishable; so only the overthrow of capitalism would bring about the end of war.

There were, however, other sociologists who tried to salvage something of their predecessors' hopes. Schumpeter in Europe, Veblen in the United States, attributed the successful militarization of industrial society not to the inherent nature of capitalism as such but to the atavistic survival of feudal attitudes, structures and ideologies; not only in Imperial Germany and Japan but to some extent also, Veblen pointed out, in the social structure of England. The effectiveness with which these most advanced of industrial societies adapted themselves to war was due, they considered, to the continuing habit of deference to, and emulation of, a military ruling class; one whose survival, so far from being necessary to the capitalist leaders of industrial society as the Marxists maintained, was positively harmful to them. Veblen indeed expressed the hope that the war would go on for long enough for the English officer-class to kill itself off completely, so that a more equitable, efficient and peace-loving society could grow over their graves.

Both schools of thought gave partial explanations of a highly complex phenomenon. Certainly in both British and German society continuing patterns of social deference, the acceptance of the leadership of a traditional and notionally landed ruling class did much to preserve both military discipline and social cohesion.[1] But even before the First World War ended a new kind of militarism was emerging which owed nothing to pre-industrial survivals and indeed reacted violently against them. This was based not on subordination and obedience to traditional authority but on demotic values: individual toughness, group-cohesion on an egalitarian basis, personal rather than class leadership qualities, combined with an understanding and mastery of technology. This was the spirit of the American and Australian Armed Forces. It was that of the new Air Forces of all nations. It was that of the new storm-troops who spearheaded the German attacks in 1918 and who were to transmit it through the *Freikorps* to a new generation of German soldiers. It was not, as good socialists would have wished, a proletarian spirit, but it was *classless*, and that gave it a far wider appeal.

1. But not in France, an exception which limits the validity of Veblen's analysis as well (in view of the agrarian structure of much of French society in 1914–18) as that of the Marxists.

This new militarism, entirely indigenous to advanced industrial societies, was to provide much of the appeal of Fascism everywhere. It combined the glamour of new technology with the promise of escape from the drab confines of bourgeois morality into a colourful and heroic world in which violence was not only permissible but *legitimized*. It reached its apogee in Nazi Germany, but it was latent throughout Western civilization and to some extent still is. In the form of the comic strip it was to penetrate and perhaps mould the consciousness of the very young. The fighter-pilot, the Panzer leader, the resistance group, above all the *para*, that international symbol of *machismo*, these were to become the military archetypes with which adventurous adolescents could identify themselves, and who provide so much more dramatic an image of war than do the patient, invisible navies, the bureaucratized mass-armies and the disciplined destructiveness of the bomber fleets whose operations were actually decisive in the Second World War.

That such a military spirit still exists in the West will not come as much of a surprise to anyone who has to deal with adolescent or prepubescent males, or even to anyone passing a well-stocked toyshop; though obsession with the Second World War itself probably nowhere reaches the levels characteristic of the United Kingdom. In a more generalized fashion this emphasis on ruggedness, masculinity and physical endurance is far more typical of the younger generation in the West than is the soft hedonism which older generations invariably fear to be sapping the fibre of their national strength. There may have been, during the two decades immediately following the Second World War, an understandable emphasis on the restoration and improvement of material standards, which combined with an equally understandable search for social equity to dominate the values of the post-war generation. But such emphasis on material welfare usually breeds its own antidote. In the 1890s the desire to escape from the intolerable stuffiness of bourgeois society led, among other things, to the spread of *volkisch* youth movements and sports clubs, which were ultimately to prove seed-beds of the new militarism described above. The same spirit has in our own day produced a revolt against 'consumerism' that is widespread throughout Western society and that now, as then, sometimes takes bizarre and even violent forms.

There is thus on the face of it no more reason why the societies of Western Europe and North America should today be any less able to adapt themselves to military activity than they have been at any time during the past hundred years, even though changes in social *mores* may impose on that activity new forms to which traditionally-minded military professionals may find it difficult to adjust. There would be major economic and political difficulties involved in any such adaptation, but there always were. The military profession as such is not popular, but outside the Kingdom of Prussia it never was. The increasing difficulty of recruitment as the growing diversification of society created alternative and more lucrative occupations was observed by Clausewitz in the early part of the last century. It is true that the military now require a far higher proportion of trained specialists whose skills are better rewarded by other sectors of the economy, but this is a problem of resource-allocation common to all advanced countries; and although the West does not have the social-control mechanisms available to its adversaries it has, in this as in other respects, a proportionately greater abundance of such skills. National Service in Continental countries is accepted without enthusiasm, but accepted it is, and there does not appear at present to be any great pressure to abolish it. Even in Britain, when National Service was abandoned in 1958, this was done for economic reasons which owed nothing to social or political protests. In the United States hostility to the draft became politically significant only as the result of compulsion to serve in a peculiarly unpopular and morally ambiguous war. Now as in the past military institutions are accepted by the great majority of the population as a disagreeable necessity, and they leave it to governments to decide what their size and shape may be.

On these governments there do of course come short-term economic and political pressures of varying intensity; and it is these, rather than any deeper social patterns, that limit the military effectiveness of the West. And it is here that the invalidity of the Marxian doctrine, of the inevitably militaristic nature of monopoly capitalism, becomes fully evident. In the first place there is an inherent resistance on the part of the possessing classes to public expenditure in any form and a preference for money to be left to fructify in their own pockets; and here defence suffers from the same disabilities as any other activity of government. In the second, there is the economic diversification we have already noted, that creates so highly competitive a market both for labour and for investment. And in the third place, the representative nature of the pluralist democracy which is the normal political form of advanced capitalistic societies gives an urgency to pressures which in command-economies are mediated through the bureaucratic process. There is no reason to suppose that in communist regimes there is any less demand for lower taxes, better schools, more easily-accessible welfare systems and greater investment both in heavy and consumer-oriented industries than there is in the West. What these regimes lack, however, are those institutions, above all a free press and openly elected responsible representative bodies, which prevent resources from being allocated entirely according to priorities determined by closed bureaucratic and political élites. And it is precisely the existence of these institutions, as I understand it, that we in the West are concerned to preserve. They present us with problems, but of a kind that very few other societies are privileged to enjoy.

The difficulties that we experience in creating a militarily effective defence posture in the West thus arise not from any moral deficiency in our societies but from precisely those characteristics in them that we wish to defend and that our adversaries would wish to eliminate. Nor can those difficulties be blamed on any deep *political* divisions within Western Europe; much less on any skilful subversion by our adversaries. Indeed, given the profound social and political cleavages that have divided the societies of Western Europe during the past hundred years, it is remarkable how much support NATO has commanded across the whole political spectrum. It must be admitted that this is due less to any skilful political management by the statesmen of the West than to the brutality and blunders of the Soviet Union, which have effectively destroyed the very powerful appeal that it exercised in the 1930s, as an ideal alternative society. The Soviet brand of Marxism-Leninism now commands the allegiance only of small and isolated minorities within Western Communist Parties, while the mainstream of the socialist movement has turned its back on it altogether. That does not mean that left-wing parties in the West are necessarily any less hostile to what they see as 'monopoly capitalism' and the imperialist neo-colonialism which they believe to be so closely associated with it. The Marxist creed seems to them none the less valid because of the perversions inflicted on it by Stalin, and even by Lenin. But in terms of political action this does not lead them to regard the Soviet Union as an ally for whose protection they would wish to exchange that of the United States. The position of the Communist Parties of Eastern Europe can have a limited appeal for Señor Carillo, Signor Berlinguer or even M. Georges Marchais. To talk of 'Eurocommunism' is a totally misleading oversimplification, but all the effective Communist Parties in Western Europe are deeply rooted within national political systems which they show few signs of wishing to exchange for a Moscow-dominated hegemony. Some, like the PCF, are neutralist, embracing with enthusiasm the idea of *défense à tous azimuths* and staunchly supporting the *force de frappe*. Others, like the PCI, accord the Alliance a grumbling acquiescence. All use it as a convenient whipping boy; but it remains remarkable how little trouble these parties have caused the Alliance over the past thirty years.

Opposition to and doubts about the Alliance extend of course far beyond the official Communist Parties. A liberal, pacifistic tradition is a continuing, inevitable, and to my mind admirable element in the Western political system, and its influence, in Northern Europe and the Netherlands in particular, has probably caused more problems to NATO leaders than any amount of communist activity. Those influenced by it range from saintly men of penetrating intelligence to mindless fanatics impervious to reasoned argument, but it would be morally disreputable as well as politically foolish to treat them simply as a nuisance, far less as enemies. More often than not, the questions they raise and the criticisms they make about Western defence postures are entirely legitimate. They furnish our societies not only with a conscience but also with a critical intelligence. If sometimes they deal with society not as it is but as we would all wish it to be, at least they save us from the cynical *immobilisme* that is the besetting sin of bureaucrats and the academics who tend to associate with them. They are the 'philosophers' whose freedom of expression Kant modestly claimed to be a condition of Perpetual Peace, and with whom a dialogue is the essential prerequisite of a free society.

So the Alliance must continue to live with and take notice of its critics, as it must continue to accept the political legitimacy of left-wing, including communist, parties in Western Europe. Nothing would bring the Alliance more quickly into disarray than if it could convincingly be depicted as the creature of the Right, a new Holy Alliance directed not at maintaining the political and territorial sovereignty of its members but at preserving a particular structure of society about whose merits there was deeply felt disagreement. It is a military alliance to defend its members against external aggression; not an instrument for the suppression of social change, either in Western Europe or anywhere else in the world. That NATO should be championed by the more right-wing elements in Western Europe, those groups who not only have the greatest stake in the existing order but are temperamentally most concerned about questions of national defence, is natural enough. But if it had not also been supported by those parties of organized labour which represent the true centre of gravity in industrial societies, especially the Labour Party in Britain and the SDP in Germany, it would have disintegrated long ago.

The support of organized Labour is the more important in the light of a problem which is particularly severe in Britain but which might in the event of a prolonged economic recession become more widespread. Like so many of our difficulties, there is nothing very new about it. It consists in the *ungovernability* of key elements in society; the arbitrary determination of certain groups to pursue their own short-term economic interests without concern for the rest of the community. Lightning strikes by civilian workers for purely parochial causes – usually without any deeper political motivation – can create havoc in delicate defence systems, and they are impossible to deal with unless the government enjoys the support, or least the acquiescence, of organized labour as a whole. More widespread *dirigiste* measures of a kind essential in a serious military emergency would also be inconceivable without full labour support; and labour support, in Europe, means the backing of full-blooded socialists and, in many cases, communists. Such support can be relied on, as it could in 1914 and in 1939, only for the most basic and obvious of emergencies: the defence of one's own territory or that of one's neighbours against a threat to national survival. It is this minimalist definition of the Alliance's goals that is likely to maintain the consensus behind it, whatever the temptations might be to extend its objectives whether ideologically or geographically. Any actions, however strategically desirable, by which the Alliance appeared to be extending its support to oppressive regimes elsewhere in the world, would have seriously divisive consequences within the Western European political community.

The problem is, of course, to convince the peoples of Western Europe that there is, or plausibly might be, a 'threat to national survival'. It is a concept that the generation which had no experience of the Second World War and its immediate aftermath has some difficulty in assimilating. For the military, it may be enough to indicate the strength and dispositions of the armed forces of the Soviet Union, those alarming capabilities which might one day tempt the Soviet leadership into the disastrous course of applying military means to solve their political problems. But the military specialist does not have to concern himself with the reasons why another state may wish to attack his own. It is enough that it should have the capacity to do so, and it is his job to see that the costs of such an action would be so high as to clearly outweigh any possible benefits. But this can be done only by an allocation of resources which involves his own society in heavy and continuing costs; and to make such costs acceptable to a sceptical and now profoundly undeferential public opinion, it is necessary to demonstrate a strong possibility that the Soviet leadership intend, or one day might intend, to use their military strength to overrun Western Europe. Soviet military capability *as such* is no more evidence of aggressive intent than is that of the United States. Although it is no doubt true that it greatly exceeds what our own military leaders would consider adequate for the territorial defence of the Soviet Union, there are too many alternative explanations – atavistic Soviet suspicions of the outside world, the growing collusion of Soviet adversaries East and West, the primacy enjoyed by the military in Soviet bureaucratic processes, a determination to demonstrate super-power status in the only way open to her, above all an understandable determination that any future conflict will be fought out on the soil of her adversaries rather than her own – for this to be accepted as *prima facie* evidence of aggressive intentions. Indeed Western perceptions of Soviet strength bear a strong family resemblance to the fears expressed by the German General Staff about the growing might of the Russian Empire before 1914; yet as we know, the intentions of that Empire, though certainly not purely defensive, were far from predatory. As Clausewitz indicated, military grammar does not necessarily dictate political logic.

This military imbalance is thus not in itself likely to be enough to persuade the peoples of Western Europe that a plausible threat exists to their national survival which can be countered only by the acceptance of considerable additional costs. The people of Mexico and Canada, after all, co-exist quite happily with the military power of the United States. It is necessary to show what lawyers would call *mens rea*, aggressive intentions. For a sceptical generation that would far rather spend its money on something else the question has to be answered, *Why* should the Soviet Union wish to attack Western Europe? Or is it, like Hitler's Germany, the kind of militarized society that regards war and conquest not as an instrument of policy but as a way of life?

It is now necessary to say something about the nature of 'the threat'; for if indeed the Russians have the same kind of predatory intentions towards us as Hitler had towards them, a determination to conquer our territories and remould our societies as servile dependencies, then there is indeed an overwhelming case for evoking the latent military elements in the West and, at whatever the economic and social cost, creating Nations in Arms to defend our independence; which would require not simply well-equipped professional armed forces to take the first shock of the Soviet attack but well-trained and highly-motivated reservists, disciplined 'stay-behind' guerilla forces, and above all an elaborate and convincing system of civil defence against nuclear attack. That this can be done in face of a clear and present danger even by the most bourgeois and pacific of societies was demonstrated by the United Kingdom in 1940. The fact that it has *not* been done, but that Western Europe remains free none the less, will be attributed by some to the benignity of Soviet intentions, by others to the effectiveness of nuclear deterrence. Obviously over the past thirty years the Soviet leadership has calculated that the costs of any attack on the West would outweight any possible benefits, but the same could be said about Western intentions towards the Soviet Union. Did the Russians ever wish to attack us anyway, and do they now?

This is the question that must be convincingly answered, and comparative figures of military strengths are simply not enough. Between the two conflicting views of the Soviet Union, one as an implacable predator, the other as a society obsessed with internal problems, paranoid about the external world and driven reluctantly into an arms race by the competition of far wealthier and more sophisticated adversaries, there is room for a wide range of opinions. The first of these is more general, oddly enough, in the United States than it is in Western Europe; not because Europeans have any greater confidence than have their American allies in Soviet benevolence, but perhaps because they have a livelier appreciation of the weaknesses of the Soviet Union and see in much of her behaviour a familiar if disagreeable pattern that has changed little since the days of Peter the Great.[1] Without taking sides in this classic debate, beyond suggesting that the two concepts are not mutually exclusive, it can be suggested that, barring further self-inflicted wounds such as the Soviet leaders delivered against their cause in the 'Prague Summer' of 1968, the image of the Russians as predators may be one that Western peoples may find it increasingly difficult to accept; at least so far as their own territories are concerned. Historians are beginning to scrutinize with some care the stock explanations of the origins of the Cold War, and to question the validity of those fears of Soviet aggressive intentions which were used to justify the creation of the Alliance thirty years ago. The original extreme and iconoclastic form of this 'revisionism' as set out in the works of such writers as Gar Alperovitz and Gabriel Kolko has now been substantially modified, but few students of the period would now accept the simplistic views of the Soviet threat which were current in the early fifties. A doctrine rejected by the bulk of the academic community is not likely to remain tenable for very long by those school teachers and publicists who mould public opinion. Too many documents have been released and too many memoirs written for the simple and heroic certainties of a quarter of a century ago to be acceptable to a new and properly sceptical generation. And if we were wrong about 'the threat' then, they will quite rightly ask, are we any more likely to be right now?

The danger is that in rejecting the simple and exaggerated

1. There is also a greater readiness to accept Russia as historically part of the European community, to regret her self-imposed alienation and to welcome any indications that she wants to be reconciled. That this applies even more strongly to the captive nations of Eastern Europe goes without saying. It is perhaps significant that Europeans tend, however inaccurately, to speak of 'the Russians' rather than 'the Soviets'; seeing them as a people rather than as a regime.

fears of the post-war era, the intellectual leaders of Western society will fail to appreciate the more solidly-based anxieties that underlay them. Those who cried 'Wolf!' in 1948–53 may have been the victims of their own fears, but they were quite right in perceiving that, whether they were really threatened by a Soviet attack or not, the international environment was such that a stable and prosperous society could be built in Western Europe only on a basis of military security convincing enough to reassure its own members and discourage those who wished, by whatever means and for whatever motives, to disrupt it.

For whether they had predatory intentions or not, the cold hostility of the Soviet leadership to the West was made unmistakably clear after the Second World War, and there is no sign that it has ever abated. Whether or no Stalin had any plans for military attack during the last six years of his life, there is no doubt that he would have liked to absorb the whole of Germany into the Soviet system, and weaken the remaining states of Western Europe by every means in his power. These means would have been political, at least initially. Even in Germany the role of the Red Army would have been to enable the spearhead of the proletariat, the KPD, to complete the revolution begun by Karl Liebknecht and Rosa Luxembourg without foreign-backed intervention. It is a basic principle of Marx-Leninism that the revolution cannot be carried abroad on the points of foreign bayonets, but where the workers are defending their revolution against the forces of reaction, whether indigenous or foreign, Soviet Armed Forces could not be expected to fold their hands and sit idly by. And it was by no means clear to anyone that there was not a 'revolutionary situation' in Western Europe in the chaotic aftermath of the Second World War, which would enable the communists to complete the work begun, and interrupted, after the First. The Communist Parties of Western Europe, furthermore, were loyal to Moscow. The links forged before 1939 had been strengthened by the admirable performance of the Soviet peoples during the war which enabled the Soviet Union to project itself, with good reason, as the true rescuers of the peoples of Europe from the

77

menace of Fascism. It is not surprising that the Russians had many friends in high places in the West as well as low.

It is seldom that empires grow as a matter of settled policy. More often they expand, as did the British in India, reluctantly and piecemeal, with repeated and sincere disclaimers of predatory intent. Every step of Soviet expansion westwards could be justified by impeccable considerations of national defence. It was highly desirable, if not essential, that the whole of Germany should be controlled; how else could the Soviet Union feel safe from the invasions which had devastated her in two world wars? But with Germany under control, Russian suzerainty over Scandinavia would need to be assured, and defence facilities could reasonably be demanded at Copenhagen and the North Cape. The rest of Western Europe might be left alone on the strict understanding that it afforded no kind of toehold to the military power of the United States, but its governments would have to give firm guarantees of good behaviour and of course do nothing to impede the historic development of socialism within their borders. An inverse Monroe Doctrine, in short, would have been proclaimed for Europe, excluding all intervention by the powers, or rather the Power, of the Western hemisphere.

This was the real danger that faced the statesmen of the West after the war. They had no reason to suppose that Stalin's Russia would not act exactly as all great powers (their own included) had always acted when they had the chance, and even less to suppose that they had abandoned the fundamental principles of Marx-Leninism which made it impossible for them to see the pattern of world politics as anything other than a Hobbesian state of war or to view capitalist states as anything other than long-term enemies bent on their destruction. So even if the myth of an imminent Soviet attack on Western Europe, deterred only by an American commitment to her defence, does not stand up to scholarly analysis of the documents, it was, like all myths, a dramatic representation of an underlying truth.

Does it remain true after thirty years? All the above arguments may be convincing, but that was a full generation ago, and an enormous amount has now changed, in Soviet society as well as our own. In the first place, alarming as many of the developments in Western society may seem, no serious Marxist thinker would maintain that they add up to a classic 'revolutionary situation'. Least of all is this evident in Western Germany, the country of most immediate concern to the Soviet Union. Indeed it has been the total absence of any signs of such a situation ever developing, thanks to the *embourgeoisement* of the proletariat and the revisionism of the official Communist Parties, that has driven the idealists of the New Left either to nihilistic terrorism or to abandon orthodox politics altogether in favour of ecological and kindred protest movements. Further, if a revolutionary situation *were* to develop in the West out of an economic recession compounded by an energy crisis leading to massive unemployment and a drastic fall in the standard of living, it is doubtful whether the leaders it would throw up would look to Moscow for guidance, or whether the Soviet government would see it as being in their best interests, economically and politically, to exploit such a situation. To embarrass and weaken the economy of Western Europe is one thing; to cause its total collapse, with all the implications that would have for the well-being of Eastern Europe, is quite another. In any case, the precedents of the 1930s suggests that in mature capitalist economies such catastrophes strengthen the parties of the extreme Right rather than the extreme Left. It is notable that the appeal of extreme left-wing policies in Western Europe has steadily waned as the economic situation has grown worse.[1]

Further, it is only fair to recognize that the present generation of Soviet leaders is quite unlike that of Stalin, Molotov and Vishinsky. They are unamiable men, but they have not fought their way to power through the thickets and quagmires of revolutionary conspiracy. They have come up through the established hierarchies of political and economic management, and their successors are likely to do the same. They are likely, as 'scientific' Marxists, to

1. Those words were written in 1979. Events may yet belie them.

view Western Europe in terms of cold calculation. What would the costs be of conquering us, and where would be the benefits? There is no revolutionary situation to exploit. The proletariat of the West is now by Marxist-Leninist standards hopelessly corrupt. The Communist Parties are divided between revisionists and adventurists, neither of whom would provide docile instruments of Soviet control. The advantages which the Soviet Union at present gains from East-West trade depend on a flourishing capitalist economy in the West, and it is doubtful whether anyone in the Soviet leadership is under any illusions about this. Why should the Soviet leaders wish to turn a prosperous, productive and relatively friendly Western Europe into another group of fractious and hostile dependencies?

These are the questions being posed by intelligent and well-informed young sceptics, and we cannot deny their force. Whatever opportunities of expansion and control the Soviet leaders may see elsewhere in the world (and the sceptics have something to say about that as well) it is very doubtful whether they see any in Western Europe or are likely to in the foreseeable future. This cautious Soviet attitude towards its Western neighbours is an essential panel in a diptych of which the other half certainly consists of the armed strength of the Alliance. It would be quite unrealistic to assume that the Russians have been deterred from attacking us solely by their perception of the military costs involved or by fear of nuclear retaliation. It is probably many years since Western Europe presented itself to them as an attractive, even if an attainable, prize. It is not only the strength of the locks on their doors that protect ageing spinsters from rape.

We may accept therefore that there is at present little in the nature of Soviet society[1] or Soviet political intentions to

---

1. To deal with social and cultural patterns within the Soviet Union would far exceed the bounds of this paper and the capacity of its author. But it would be generally agreed that while Soviet society remains docile to its leaders and has an old-fashioned respect for its armed forces, it shows little tendency towards the kind of irrational militarism which might distort its government's calculations of *Realpolitik*.

justify the ringing of alarm-bells in the West, the evocation of the militaristic elements in our society and the conversion of the nations of Western Europe into garrison states. Indeed, to do anything of the kind could easily make the situation more dangerous rather than less. The Soviet leadership is no more prone than we are ourselves to accept that the military preparations of its neighbours are purely defensive, and to refrain from responding in kind. But we should be wary of drawing too much comfort from the best-case analysis presented above. It has to be pointed out that in disorderly societies elderly spinsters *do* get raped. Further, the record tends to show that states, especially powerful states, have seldom calculated their self-interest so coolly and correctly as political scientists could do on their behalf. (On any calculation of self-interest, would the United States have got herself involved in Vietnam?) The Soviet leadership has not abandoned its doctrinaire hostility to the West; Soviet publicists are commendably frank in explaining that 'peaceful co-existence' does not mean the end of an ideological struggle which they could not terminate even if they wanted to. Whatever short-term accommodations may be made and however long they last, they remain in a Hobbesian state of war with us, and there is nothing that can be done about it. And it requires very few dealings with Soviet officials to bring home to the most starry-eyed of Western intellectuals how glacial and impermeable remains the permafrost beneath the shallow top-soil of official 'peaceful co-existence'.

Most important of all, it has to be pointed out that wars in Europe have not always begun with a settled intention of conquest on the part of the aggressor. To say that the Soviet Union today is not like Hitler's Germany, or even Stalin's Russia, may be quite true, but it is of limited relevance to our problems. When Germany attacked France through Belgium in 1914, it was with no plan of conquest and settlement. Even in 1940 Hitler had, at least initially, no plans for transforming the *societies* of Western Europe; only of neutralizing the military power of their *states*. Social transformation followed only in so far as it was necessary to ensure the continued subordination of the defeated adversary. Both in 1914 and in 1940, Germany would have been happy to see Britain and France continue to flourish as prosperous and pacific communities with complete domestic freedom of action so long as they had neither the political will nor the military capacity to interfere with German intentions elsewhere. Her intention was to eliminate the threat which French and British power posed to her freedom of action; not to conquer either of them.

This seems to me to be the appropriate analogy with the intentions of the Soviet Union towards Western Europe today. We are not a prey to be devoured. We are a potential threat which might have to be neutralized, reluctantly and *in extremis*, in full consciousness of all the social and political as well as military costs involved, and only if all else fails. The Soviet Union would undertake the invasion and occupation of Western Europe without enthusiasm, simply to destroy our military power and ensure our continued debellation. But as other countries have found in other circumstances, it is a lot easier to put troops into a defeated country than to take them out, and the Russians would then find, in spite of their very best intentions, that they had another chunk of ungovernable Empire on their hands. It is an embarrassment that we should do our very best to spare them.

It would be going far beyond the bounds of this chapter to suggest in any detail the circumstances in which the Soviet leadership might feel tempted to launch such an attack. (Indeed, in military exercises NATO leaders sometimes find it as difficult to sketch a convincing political scenario for a Russian invasion as to devise means of checking it if it were to come.) One might have to visualize a pre-emptive strike, on the analogy of the Schlieffen Plan, in an Armageddon triggered off by a crisis elsewhere in the world. Another and more plausible possibility would be a situation in Eastern Europe so explosive that the Russians felt unable to contain it unless the source of infection beyond the Iron Curtain could be eliminated; and the history of Empires, both Roman and British, provides plenty of precedents for such defensively-intended punitive strikes. In either case the attack would be improbable unless the Soviet military could promise rapid success without nuclear escalation, and the alternative appeared to be the disintegration of the Soviet Empire. But it is in precisely these circumstances that wars usually begin.

It would be pointless to multiply scenarios. Few wars, if indeed any, have started in any way foretold in advance, and none have ever pursued the course predicted for them. But whatever the circumstances it will remain the task of Western military leaders to ensure that their Soviet opposite numbers are never in a position to give such optimistic advice to their political masters, and their own political masters in the West must provide them with the means to do so.

This is the situation that must be explained to the sceptical peoples of our societies. The danger they have to face is not so likely to be one of invasion directed towards the conquest of our societies and the destruction of our liberties as of a disarming attack with strictly limited military objectives; though how secure our societies and liberties would be if such an attack were to succeed is another matter. Such a threat presents problems for military planners that it is beyond the scope of this chapter to discuss, but it may be remarked in passing that the distinction between such limited and total intentions is one that has not always been made in the works of Western strategists. A defence posture which is designed to deter the Soviet Union from a *Niederwerfungskrieg*, a war of total conquest, could be disastrously inapplicable if their intention was simply to destroy the bulk of our forward conventional capabilities, occupy a stretch of territory, and then offer generous peace terms long before the decision had been taken to initiate nuclear escalation.

What concerns us here are the implications of all this for our societies. These are simple, but they are neither reassuring nor new. The first, admittedly, is not without comfort for us: we do not confront a threat of totalitarian conquest such as could be countered only by a militarization of our societies. The second is that our security, our political freedom of action, and our stability in the event of a crisis depend on the provision of effective armed forces capable of deterring any attack by their evident capacity to impose immediate and intolerable costs on the attackers. And if this is *not* done, there are only three options open to us. The first is to continue to deter attack by the threat to initiate the use of nuclear weapons; but today this means accepting the use of nuclear weapons against us on at least a comparable scale. The second would be to back up our regular forces with sufficient reserves and territorials to fight a long and destructive war of attrition. The third would be to make the best terms with the adversary that we could get; and we must not be surprised or outraged if the political leaders of Western Europe, faced with so appalling a choice of options, were to opt for the last.

This then is the price that our societies have to pay, not perhaps for 'national survival', but to guarantee our continuing independence. It is a situation that has to be clearly and repeatedly expounded: only if adequate conventional forces are maintained will statesmen be spared the agonizing dilemma outlined above. The difficulties of maintaining these forces will be no less in the future than in the past. They will be all the greater if we allow ourselves to believe that, in an age of nuclear equivalence, nuclear deterrence any longer offers an easy way out, or that technology can somehow eliminate problems that can only be solved by trained, well-equipped fighting men. The military have the obligation to state their requirements with clarity and moderation. Like all demands for massive public expenditure they will, very properly, be contested and scrutinized. Vociferous minorities will remain stubbornly unconvinced of their necessity. But there is nothing inherent in the structure of our societies or the nature of our political systems to prevent them from being met.

The Relevance of
Traditional Strategy

I

IT is a sombre thought that, at a time when so large a proportion of the human race remains near starvation level, about six per cent of the world's resources, or something under $200 billion, is still being devoted to military expenditure [1973], with no serious likelihood of this situation fundamentally changing during the remainder of this century. Social scientists will continue to seek basic causes in the hope of offering total solutions, but at the political working level the explanation is simple enough. Any sovereign state – that is, any community which wishes to maintain a capacity for independent political action – may have to use or indicate its capacity and readiness to use force – functional and purposive violence – to protect itself against coercion by other states. Given the State system, peace is possible only when there is freedom from all fear of coercion; and in the absence of any supranational authority enforcing a universal rule of law, such freedom from fear still depends at least partly on independent or collective military capability. Such is the conventional wisdom which will continue to rule mankind until we develop a viable alternative, or until there develops so strong a global sense of community that coercion, the use of force to impose one's will on others, becomes literally unthinkable. At present, unfortunately, such coercion is by no means unthinkable even within the most stable of communities and the most powerful of sovereign states.

Military strategy is organized coercion. It can be defensive or offensive: either posture involves the use or threatened use of force to compel an adversary to abandon his preferred course of action and conform to one's will. The traditional object of military operations was to force one's opponent into a position where the only alternatives open to him were compliance with one's own demands or acceptance of an intolerable level of destruction, extending even to total annihilation – whether of his armed forces, or his social system, or both. Against a very weak adversary it might not be necessary to use serious strategy (the art of the *strategon*, or general) at all. Pure coercion was then possible at the level of 'gunboat diplomacy'. But since it is normally the object of any community to escape from such a condition of total vulnerability, whether by developing its own power or enlisting the support of an effective protector, the opportunities for such pure coercion in the international system tend constantly to diminish; and a state resorting to force as an instrument of policy will require a strategy appropriate for overcoming an opposing, and armed, will.

The development of strategy as an activity consciously studied, analysed and practised according to principles rationally deduced from experience went *pari passu* in Europe with the development of the State system itself; with the development, that is, of communities conscious of their identities and expecting from their governments protection against coercion by alien groups. Before the seventeenth century such protection was rarely possible. Outside such compact and defensible areas as the Low Countries and the Lombard Plain, warfare consisted often of no more than predatory raids whose object was to inflict the maximum damage on the peoples and possessions of one's adversary; it was a process of mutual and sometimes simultaneous coercion. The protection of territory against such raids by the creation of adequate, fixed defences and instantly available armed forces required a level of social mobilization and a control over economic resources such as European princes were only beginning to establish during the seventeenth century. Fortified frontiers and standing armies with their own supply systems were in fact an intrinsic part of the development of the State itself. Once direct coercion was no longer possible, serious strategy, the struggle to outwit and disarm the enemy, had to begin.

How strategy then developed from the eighteenth up to the twentieth centuries, how it was affected by technical transformations in transportation and weapons-systems and by the broadening of popular participation in national affairs, has been described too often for it to be necessary to say much about it here. An activity limited in the eighteenth century to professional forces absorbing a tiny proportion of national resources became, by the twentieth century, the concern of the whole community. Resources, enormously increased by industrial development, were made available in their entirety to governments by the expansion of their general administrative competence. Thus, strategic triumphs by limited forces over limited forces, such as had in Napoleon's time been accepted as politically decisive, were treated in the twentieth century as incidental reverses by governments which could draw on apparently limitless resources of money and manpower to repair the damage. Lightning military strokes might still be effective against physically or morally unprepared opponents, as the Germans found in 1939 and 1940, but in general the Second World War bore out the lesson of the First. Against a fully mobilized and determined adversary, nothing short of the erosion of his entire physical and moral resources to a point of virtual impotence could be effective in reducing him to a condition in which he could be truly 'coerced'.

II

The experience of the First World War made it clear, also, that the morale and cohesion of the community as a whole were at least as important an element in military effectiveness as weapons technology or expertise in generalship. Between the Wars there was much discussion of the possibility of reducing or even eliminating the need for military operations by concentrating on this factor – civilian morale – alone: whether by subversion and pyschological warfare, as Hitler often suggested, or by the direct use of air power, as Douhet, Trenchard and Mitchell believed. But the Second World War gave little comfort to either school of thought. Whatever the effectiveness of strategic bombing in other respects, civilian morale proved the last element affected. If anything, bombing intensified the solidarity between government and people in democracies and totalitarian states alike. As for subversion, this was a weapon of which great things were expected by belligerents when they were weak, but which they downgraded as soon as they were strong enough to do so. Hitler's alleged 'fifth column' successes against the West in 1939–40 were rather the result of his insight into the existing weaknesses of the democracies than of any specific measures he took to exploit them. Against the Soviet Union he disdained subversion altogether, and there is little evidence to suggest that the Soviet Union devoted any considerable resources to subversion within Germany. The British during their period of maximum weakness in 1940 and 1941 did indeed hope that subversion, together with bombing and blockade, might bring about the collapse of the Nazi empire, but with hindsight we can see how unrealistic such hopes were. Subversion had no serious place in US plans, and after 1942 even the British came to regard the European Resistance as purely ancillary to Allied military operations.

Traditional strategy, in short, assumed that in any conflict the antagonists were in complete control of their national resources and that their governments commanded a total consensus of national will. Violence between states was considered to be totally crystallized into those manifestations of it and controlled by governments. When this proved not to be so, professional fighting forces often reacted with anger and embarrassment, treating friendly partisans with suspicion and hostile ones with savagery. Partisan operations were for them a retrograde step to the sporadic and uncontrolled violence, the isolated and reciprocal atrocities, of which war had so largely consisted before the State had acquired a monopoly of force and channelled it along rational and purposive ends sanctioned and to some degree controlled by international law.

Such an attitude was natural enough in conflicts occurring within a settled social framework which both belligerents were concerned to preserve. But it was out of place in conflicts in which at least one of the belligerents was concerned not with preserving that framework but with destroying it. The Second World War was for some of its participants a struggle of this type, and so, of course, have been a large number of armed conflicts since. The revolutionary objective and its methods can exist within the pattern of traditional strategy. The Nazis sought to achieve military victory by orthodox methods before introducing their 'new order', but communist resistance movements in Western Europe, like that of Mao Tse-tung against Japan, were consciously making war and revolution at the same time. While eroding the power and authority of a foreign invader, it was all to the good if they could in the process discredit the established institutions and dispossess the native élites who were collaborating with him. So there developed within the womb of traditional strategy a new technique of revolutionary war: of growing from weakness to strength, of erosion from the periphery to the centre, of the use of violence to discredit and humiliate authority where it could not be overthrown directly, of substituting an alternative hierarchy of government with patently effective sanctions and rewards. All these techniques could be used against an unpopular invader. But they could be just as effective in a domestic situation – especially against a colonial occupier whose charisma had been destroyed by external defeat, or an indigenous regime which, in conditions of prolonged turbulence, had failed to establish its legitimacy. It was this kind of strategy which was being perfected in the middle years of the twentieth century. Its object was no longer the coercion of a community from outside; it was the transformation of its social and political structure from within.

The implications of this revolutionary strategy for international politics, considerable though they are, can be and have been overrated. Until now its effectiveness has been limited to the fragile structures of colonial, and the chaotic conditions of post-colonial and similar societies, and it has yet to be shown that it can really be an effective technique in international conflict between major powers. The tendency commented on earlier for subversion to be used by powers in their weakness and abandoned once they are strong certainly appears to apply to the Soviet Union, whose relations with revolutionary movements throughout the world have grown steadily cooler as it has established a position of respectable international strength. The Russians have had more opportunity than most to observe how seldom it is that successful insurgents make docile satellites, and the Chinese seem to have no illusions about this in Vietnam. Without underrating the skill and relish with which communist powers first trouble waters and then fish in them, one can now say with reasonable certainty that the successes of revolutionary warfare during the past quarter of a century have owed more to the peculiar circumstances of a postcolonial epoch than to any far-sighted strategy masterminded in Moscow or Peking.

Still, these historical circumstances – the 'objective conditions' so beloved by Marxists – have to be taken into account by any contemporary student of strategy. One must be properly cautious about extrapolating from the confused conditions of the Third World, where the impact of Western culture first shattered indigenous forms of authority and then abandoned those it had put in their place, to the more settled societies of the developed world, whose traditional value-systems give their governmental structures and established authorities deeper roots of legitimacy. But it is no longer possible to assume that any of these developed societies are inherently stable. Those in Continental Europe, from the Atlantic to the Urals, have been ravaged by war, occupation and revolution for over half a century. Beyond the Iron Curtain a precarious order is maintained only by totalitarian discipline. In Western Europe the political system impresses less by its stability than by its confusion. The Anglo-Saxon nations whose fortunate geographical circumstances enabled them to escape the worst ravages of the World Wars have their own problems in adjusting their institutions and their values to the bewilderingly rapid social transformation brought about by their very economic successes. In their dislocation only a very optimistic Marxist would see a situation which could be exploited to the point of take-over by revolutionary cadres. But these societies are unhappy, confused and decreasingly responsive to traditional authority. Their complexity makes them highly vulnerable to the violence of ruthless minorities. And only a very optimistic patriot would hope that they could achieve the same degree of social mobilization, the same dedicated unanimity, that brought them all, on whichever side, through two World Wars. This is a factor which must be borne very much in mind when assessing the viability of strategies on the part of Western societies which involve the use of nuclear weapons and the credibility of nuclear threats.

III

Nuclear weapons could at first be seen simply as an extension of a long trend in military technology, which for a hundred years had been making armed forces capital-intensive rather than labour-intensive, so that firepower rather than manpower could be used to overthrow the opposing forces. Their timely development spared the United States the disagreeable necessity of deploying a massive conventional invasion force to complete the defeat of Japan. But when the further step was taken to the development of thermonuclear weapons with ballistic-missile delivery systems, it seemed that the entire apparatus of traditional strategic thought could now be discarded. The whole object of traditional strategy had been so to deploy armed force as to compel the enemy to face the inescapable alternatives of unacceptable destruction or compliance with one's will. Now thermonuclear weapons confronted him with these alternatives before a shot had been fired. Had not technology therefore replaced strategy altogether as a means of political coercion?

The answer could be 'yes' only if the state concerned did not face equally unacceptable destruction itself – which of course in a confrontation between nuclear powers, it did. The strategic situation had thus reverted to that of the sixteenth century and earlier epochs, when princes could not prevent their rivals from ravaging their territories but only deter them, by taking hostages or retaliating in kind. Governments again found themselves unable to protect their populations. Some early British strategic thinkers did indeed speak of the need for civilians to be prepared to 'take it' as they had taken the 1940 Blitz – an attitude which probably only increased the recruiting rates of the Campaign for Nuclear Disarmament. Well-intentioned American statesmen declared their resolve to shrink from no sacrifice in order to live up to their obligations; but behind the rhetoric lay the disagreeable fact that they were proposing to incur for the peoples for whose safety they were responsible a holocaust of horror inconceivably greater than anything suffered by the far more disciplined and cohesive societies which had endured the two World Wars. The political credibility of nuclear strategy indeed decreased in indirect ratio to its technical credibility, for it was precisely those technologically advanced societies best able to build sophisticated weapons-systems whose social and political structure made them least likely to be able to endure, or even seriously to contemplate, the costs of nuclear war.

Can it then be said that in the nuclear age traditional strategic concepts retain any validity at all?

Certainly these concepts have shown themselves to be still valid in conflicts between non-nuclear powers. In the wars between India and Pakistan and between Israel and her Arab neighbours, the techniques and even sometimes the weapons of the Second World War still showed themselves highly effective. But between these operations and those of 1939–45 we must note one major difference. Non-nuclear powers are, with obvious exceptions, poor powers. (An armed conflict between highly industrialized but non-nuclear states is, under existing world conditions, very difficult to visualize indeed.) Such powers lack the industrial base which enabled the belligerents in the World Wars to fight prolonged conflicts of attrition. The forces which they have *en présence* with their first-line reserves are often all the strength they possess. For that reason their strategy can revert to a

Napoleonic model. It is quite possible for them to destroy their enemy's entire available armed forces in a single battle or series of battles and leave him literally defenceless. At this level, war in the hands of skilful commanders and well-trained and equipped troops can still be a very effective instrument of policy.

It is highly doubtful whether the acquisition of nuclear weapons by such powers would make it any more effective, since it would then be subject to all the constraints and uncertainties of conflicts between nuclear powers considered below. The deterrent effect of nuclear weapons might be a reinforcement for those concerned to preserve the status quo, but 'nuclear blackmail' has yet to be shown to be an effective weapon in the hands of those who wish to change it. Not only would threats of nuclear action for offensive purposes depend on verbal credibility alone, in contrast to the visible deployment of conventional forces, but such a threat would cause reverberations throughout the international system whose outcome would be very difficult to assess. There are indeed national leaders in the Third World who might not be particularly interested in assessing them; but the strategist, like the economist, has to assume a degree of rationality for his calculations which is not always met with in the real world.

It may not be this kind of rationality which has deterred nuclear powers from using their nuclear capability to coerce non-nuclear parties (if we except Khrushchev's barely serious statements at the time of Suez) even when, as in the case of the United States and North Vietnam, they are in open military conflict with them. But this restraint may also be due not so much to rational calculation as to an almost instinctive feeling on the part of policy-makers that any short-term advantage which might be gained by the use of nuclear weapons, even against an adversary who had neither the capacity to retaliate nor allies willing to do so for him, would be rapidly swallowed up in the costs to the international system as a whole, and that those costs would be borne by the initiator in the long run as much as anyone else – not least in terms of his own internal social cohesion. But this sentiment derives from a value-system which is far from universally shared throughout the world, and it cannot be denied that the use of nuclear threats to coerce a non-nuclear state by a power with the technical capability and political will to implement them remains a finite, if at present remote, possibility.

IV

Today, however, nuclear powers see their nuclear capability almost wholly in terms of holding one another in check. Soon after nuclear parity emerged in the middle 1950s, a school of thought arose in the West which argued that since in effect the nuclear capabilities of the major powers now cancelled one another out, traditional strategic concepts would once again become valid, and conventional forces would be required to fulfil much the same role as before. This argument did not stand up to close analysis. However reluctant a state might be to use its nuclear forces at the beginning of a conflict with another nuclear power, this reluctance would be likely to diminish the closer it approached to defeat; and the prospects of its ultimately surrendering with its nuclear arsenal intact would be very slight indeed. Each side would therefore fight in the knowledge that its opponents might at any moment decide to introduce nuclear weapons into the struggle; and the greater the success of its own conventional forces in battle, the more likely would such a decision on the part of its opponent become. The temptation to pre-empt would thus be strong on both sides, and even if it were to be resisted non-nuclear forces would have to deploy and operate on the assumption that nuclear weapons might at any moment be used against them. Traditional strategic concepts thus have to be profoundly modified. The nuclear element can neither be left out of account altogether nor postponed to the later stages of an action. It is present from the very beginning of hostilities as an inescapable dimension affecting the calculations of both adversaries.

Under these conditions the task of conventional forces is

not to act according to traditional concepts as if nuclear weapons did not exist, but to operate so as to minimize the possibility of the adversary using his nuclear forces at all, and to maximize the credibility of the nuclear threat of their own government. The first role primarily required of conventional forces would be taking the offensive. If the opponent's nuclear weapons were small in quantity it might be possible to destroy them by a conventional surprise attack. If the object of the conflict was the control of disputed territory, conventional forces might seize the area by a rapid attack and force on their adversary the decision to use nuclear weapons to evict them. Even if such territory could not be easily seized, other hostages more vulnerable might be nearer to hand, as the population of West Berlin understands very well. Or a low-profile strategy might be adopted in which the attacker approached his objective by stages, each so slight that no nuclear reaction was credible. Under conditions of nuclear parity, the power which can force upon its adversary the decision to initiate the use of nuclear weapons enjoys an enormous strategic advantage. For the military planner must never leave out of his calculations the fundamental fact that his political masters, however brave their rhetoric, will grasp at every excuse not to authorize nuclear release, or to delay doing so for as long as they possibly can.

Can this nuclear threat indeed ever appear credible – especially when made by the leaders of pluralistic democracies with all their lack of social cohesion and political consensus? The question is one that haunts policy-makers. But we can take as our starting point the argument so frequently enunciated in the context of NATO by a former British Minister for Defence that it deserves to be known as 'Healey's Theorem': if there is one chance in a hundred of nuclear weapons being used, the odds would be sufficient to deter an aggressor even if they were not enough to reassure an ally. The nature of the stakes involved, which would make such a decision so appalling for those who have to take it, would make even the bare possibility that it might be taken equally dreadful for their adversary. When we discuss the question of nuclear credibility we are doing so on a quite unique scale of magnitude – or, if such a word exists, minitude. A microscopic degree of credibility, as of some hideously powerful poison, may be all that is needed to work effectively.

There are degrees, however, even of microscopic credibility. The credibility of a retaliatory second strike is far from microscopic: this indeed is a technical rather than a political problem. So long as it is technically feasible, there is little reason to question the credibility of a governmental decision to retaliate after its territory has been subjected to nuclear attack – or to build a system in advance to make such retaliation automatic. But once we start moving away from maximum credibility of this kind, the political problems multiply even if the technical difficulties diminish. It is considerably less credible that a state would initiate the use of nuclear weapons in response to an invasion of its territory by purely conventional forces. A decision to accept conquest rather than holocaust, to be Red rather than dead, would be an entirely rational one to take in the circumstances, and one which an aggressor might expect from societies preoccupied with material welfare and having a low degree of social cohesion. Even less credible would be a decision to use nuclear weapons in response to the invasion of anyone else's territory, given the possibility of nuclear retaliation against one's own. Beyond that, the likelihood of any state initiating the use of nuclear weapons in an offensive action against an adversary with an invulnerable second-strike capability becomes more remote still.

It is obvious enough that the credibility of nuclear use will be in direct ratio to the degree to which the actual territory of a state is under threat. The strategic problem is thus how to increase that credibility for politico-military objectives other than pure territorial defence – a problem which has preoccupied NATO planners for the past twenty-odd years. They have not been entirely unsuccessful in solving it, for the function of the conventional forces in Western Europe is precisely this: to maximize the credibility of a decision by the United States to initiate the use of nuclear weapons in response to an invasion of territory other than its own.

Within the European context this has become a familiar concept. The crude 'plate-glass window', 'trip-wire' or 'burglar-alarm' analogies of the 1950s, like the grandiose image of 'the sword and the shield' which was rather more popular in SHAPE, were discarded in the 1960s in favour of the concept, elastic in itself, of 'flexible response'. But even the most dedicated exponents of flexible response did not suggest that the conventional defence of Europe should be decoupled from American nuclear striking power. For them conventional forces were rather a kind of fuse which should be made as long as possible so that even when it was lit there would still be time to stamp out the flame before it reached the nuclear powder-barrel. Once fighting began, and particularly once American forces were involved, the decision to use nuclear weapons, at first on a small and local scale to prevent total military collapse, would become a highly credible option; and once low-yield nuclear weapons had been used, the way would be frighteningly clear for escalation up to almost any level. The object of strategy had remained unchanged since before the advent of the nuclear age – coercing one's opponent into abandoning his preferred course of action by posing the alternative of unacceptable punishment; but that object was now to be achieved less by manipulation of actual forces than by manipulation of risks.

A study of the possible confrontation of the superpowers in Europe, or indeed in Cuba, indicates two conclusions. First, to make a nuclear threat an effective instrument either of offensive or of defensive coercion, the engagement of conventional forces is a prior necessity – a detonator to the otherwise inert mass of nuclear credibility. The engagement of such forces produces a conflict-situation and a conflict mentality for which the decision to introduce nuclear weapons becomes, even for confused pluralistic societies, not simply an academic possibility but a horrible real-life probability. Precisely because of that linkage, the deployment of conventional forces, whether by land or sea, can therefore be a very effective instrument of policy indeed.

This was clearly the lesson which the Soviet Navy learned from Cuba, and this perhaps is the true significance of Soviet maritime expansion. It does not indicate, as has sometimes been suggested, that the Russians have read Mahan and are seeking 'command of the sea'. It shows rather that they have learned from an earlier age of naval history that the political effectiveness of warships lies, like that of a policeman on the beat, less in the force they can command themselves than in their capacity to represent and if need be to commit the total strength and interest of their State. They play the role of fuses which nobody in his right senses would wish to ignite.

The second point is this. The more remote a crisis or a country from the territory of a nuclear power, the more necessary it will be for that power to deploy conventional forces if it wishes to demonstrate the intensity of its interest in that area, and the less will be the significance of its bare nuclear strength. An American nuclear threat in the context of the Middle East would command little credibility unless it arose in the context of such a commitment of conventional forces. In the context of Cuba, however, a very much smaller commitment was needed: the intensity of American interest in that area required no emphasis. Conversely, the Soviet Union would have required a considerable commitment of conventional strength in the Caribbean to enhance the credibility of any nuclear threat it might have made. It is in the light of this principle that the presence of American forces in Western Europe must be considered. It could certainly be argued that American interest in that area is so evident that it no longer requires so massive a commitment of American forces to demonstrate it. But some commitment of forces there must be if the American nuclear guarantee is to remain credible either to the allies or to the adversaries of the United States. The reduction of existing American troop levels in Europe is not therefore necessarily to be seen as a lessening of American interest. But unless European forces are prepared to make up the balance, it could lead to a significant shortening of the conventional fuse leading to the ultimate nuclear holocaust.

In what sense, if at all, would these conventional forces of nuclear powers operate against one another in accordance with the principles of traditional strategy? Only to this extent: that it would be their function to confront their adversary at every point with the alternatives of withdrawal or facing the possibility of unacceptable punishment, by making the risk of nuclear release more probable with every step he took. Their object must be to make the use of nuclear weapons unnecessary while at the same time making the prospect of it convincing. As in the days of pre-Napoleonic strategy, the movement of forces once again becomes part of the bargaining process, an indicator of resolution or of willingness to consider accommodation. To that extent classical models have relevance for nuclear as for non-nuclear powers, but the models must be those, not that of Napoleon with his decisive battles nor those of Napoleon's successors with their total wars of attrition, but of Napoleon's eighteenth-century predecessors: men who had much to lose and little to gain from war, who fearfully committed their forces to battle and manoeuvred them cautiously; men with limited resources and often a divided public opinion within their domains.

V

But all such precedents must be considered with extreme caution. The historical conditions which made traditional strategy possible have now very largely disappeared. It is not simply that governments can no longer protect their populations against wholesale destruction by their enemies. The change goes deeper than this. The whole governmental control of violence which made military strategy possible at all – which indeed made peace possible at all – is being rapidly eroded. The state monopoly has been broken. Violence is being increasingly employed, whether against the international community as a whole by groups which pride themselves on standing outside the existing State system, or by groups with comparatively limited and local objectives, economic as well as political. The violence which was once concentrated into wars conducted by legitimate authorities with carefully identified forces according to agreed conventions is fast becoming as generalized as it was in the centuries before any State mechanism existed to maintain order and security by organized and legitimized coercion.

Yet this sinister development may have its advantages. It is not likely that any government feels sufficiently immune from its dangers to contemplate with much satisfaction the damage suffered by its rivals. It is even less likely that any government, however radical, feels confident of its ability systematically to manipulate these movements so as to advance its own State interests. If this generalized political violence were really to increase to a level at which it appeared seriously to threaten the structure of the international State system as it has developed over the past three hundred years, governments of every colour might find that they had a common interest which transcended their rivalries – much as the interest in survival transcends the ideological rivalries of the superpowers. Anarchy is little more attractive as a prospect than is nuclear holocaust. The development of common and co-operative procedures to maintain governmental authority could then increase yet further those transnational links which offer the best hope of creating a world community in which states will need neither to practise, nor to fear, nor to prepare for mutual coercion. Only then will traditional strategy be truly and, one hopes, permanently irrelevant.

The Forgotten Dimensions of Strategy

I

THE term 'strategy' needs continual definition. For most people, Clausewitz's formulation 'the use of engagements for the object of the war', or, as Liddell Hart paraphrased it, 'the art of distributing and applying military means to fulfil the ends of policy', is clear enough. Strategy concerns the deployment and use of armed forces to attain a given political objective. Histories of strategy usually consist of case studies, from Alexander the Great to MacArthur, of the way in which this was done. Nevertheless, the experience of the past century has shown this approach to be inadequate to the point of triviality. In the West the concept of 'grand strategy' was introduced to cover those industrial, financial, demographic, and societal aspects of war that have become so salient in the twentieth century. In communist states all strategic thought has to be validated by the holistic doctrines of Marxism-Leninism. Without discarding such established concepts, I shall offer here a somewhat different and perhaps slightly simpler framework for analysis, based on a study of the way in which both strategic doctrine and warfare itself have developed over the past 200 years. I shall also say something about the implications of this mode of analysis for the present strategic posture of the West.

II

Clausewitz's definition of strategy was deliberately and defiantly simplistic. It swept away virtually everything that had been written about war (which was a very great deal) over the previous 300 years. Earlier writers had concerned themselves almost exclusively with the enormous problems of raising, arming, equipping, moving, and maintaining armed forces in the field – an approach which Clausewitz dismissed as being as relevant to fighting as the skills of the sword-maker were to the art of fencing. None of this, he insisted, was significant for the actual conduct of war, and the inability of all previous writers to formulate an adequate theory had been due to their failure to distinguish between the *maintenance* of armed forces and their *use*.

By making this distinction between what I shall term the *logistical* and the *operational* dimensions in warfare, Clausewitz performed a major service to strategic thinking; but the conclusions he drew from that distinction were questionable and the consequences of those conclusions have been unfortunate. In the first place, even in his own day, the commanders he so much admired – Napoleon, Frederick the Great – could never have achieved their operational triumphs if they had not had a profound understanding of the whole range of military activities that Clausewitz excluded from consideration. In the second place, no campaign can be understood, and no valid conclusions drawn from it, unless its logistical problems are studied as thoroughly as the course of operations; and logistical factors have been ignored by ninety-nine military historians out of a hundred – an omission which has warped their judgments and made their conclusions in many cases wildly misleading.

Clausewitz's dogmatic assertion of priorities – his subordination of the logistical element in war to the operational – may have owed something to a prejudice common to all fighting soldiers in all eras. It certainly owed much to his reaction against the super-cautious 'scientific' generals whose operational ineptitude had led Prussia to defeat in 1806. But it cannot be denied that in the Napoleonic era it *was* operational skill rather than sound logistical planning that proved decisive in campaign after campaign. And since Napoleon's campaigns provided the basis for all strategic writings and thinking throughout the nineteenth century, 'strategy' became generally equated in the public mind with *operational* strategy.

But the inadequacy of this concept was made very clear, to those who studied it, by the course of the American Civil War. There the masters of operational strategy were to be found, not in the victorious armies of the North, but among the leaders of the South. Lee and Jackson handled their forces with a flexibility and an imaginativeness worthy of a Napoleon or a Frederick; nevertheless they lost. Their defeat was attributed by Liddell Hart, whose analyses seldom extended beyond the operational plane, primarily to operational factors, in particular, to the 'indirect approach' adopted by Sherman. But, fundamentally, the victory of the North was due not to the operational capabilities of its generals, but to its capacity to mobilize its superior industrial strength and manpower into armies which such leaders as Grant were able, thanks largely to road and river transport, to deploy in such strength that the operational skills of their adversaries were rendered almost irrelevant. Ultimately the latter were ground down in a conflict of attrition in which the *logistical* dimension of strategy proved more significant than the operational. What proved to be of the greatest importance was the capacity to bring the largest and best-equipped forces into the operational theatre and to maintain them there. It was an experience that has shaped the strategic doctrine of the US Armed Forces from that day to this.

But this capacity depended upon a third dimension of strategy, and one to which Clausewitz was the first major thinker to draw attention: the *social*, the attitude of the people upon whose commitment and readiness for self-denial this logistical power ultimately depended. Clausewitz had described war as 'a remarkable trinity', composed of its political objective, of its operational instruments, and of the popular passions, the social forces it expressed. It was the latter, he pointed out, that made the wars of the French Revolution so different in kind from those of Frederick the Great, and which would probably so distinguish any wars in the future. In this he was right.

With the end of the age of absolutism, limited wars of pure policy fought by dispassionate professionals became increasingly rare. Growing popular participation in government meant popular involvement in war, and so did the increasing size of the armed forces which nineteenth-century technology was making possible and therefore necessary. Management of, or compliance with, public opinion became an essential element in the conduct of war. Had the population of the North been as indifferent to the outcome of the Civil War as the leaders of the Confederacy had initially hoped, the operational victories of the South in the early years might have decisively tipped the scales. The logistical potential of the North would have been of negligible value without the determination to use it. But given equal resolution on both sides, the capacity of the North to mobilize superior forces ultimately became the decisive factor in the struggle. Again Clausewitz was proved right: *all other factors being equal*, numbers ultimately proved decisive.

III

In one respect, in particular, other factors were equal. The Civil War was fought with comparable if not identical weapons on both sides, as had been the revolutionary wars in Europe. The possibility of decisive *technological* superiority on one side or the other was so inconceivable that Clausewitz and his contemporaries had discounted it. But within a year of the conclusion of the American Civil War, just such a superiority made itself apparent in the realm of small arms, when the Prussian armies equipped with breech-loading rifles defeated Austrian armies which were not so equipped. Four years later, in 1870, the Prussians revealed an even more crushing superiority over their French adversaries thanks to their steel breech-loading artillery. This superiority was far from decisive: the Franco-Prussian War in particular was won, like the American Civil War, by superior logistical .capability based on a firm popular commitment. But technology, as an independent and significant dimension, could no longer be left out of account.

In naval warfare, the crucial importance of technological parity had been apparent since the dawn of the age of steam, and in colonial warfare the technological element was to prove quite decisive. During the latter part of the nineteenth century, the superiority of European weapons turned what had previously been a marginal technological advantage over indigenous forces, often counterbalanced by numerical inferiority, into a crushing military ascendancy, which made it possible for European forces to establish a new imperial dominance throughout the world over cultures incapable of responding in kind. As Hilaire Belloc's Captain Blood succinctly put it: 'Whatever happens, we have got/The Maxim gun, and they have not.' Military planners have been terrified of being caught without the contemporary equivalent of the Maxim gun from that day to this.

So by the beginning of this century, war was conducted in these four dimensions: the *operational*, the *logistical*, the *social*, and the *technological*. No successful strategy could be formulated that did not take account of them all, but under different circumstances, one or another of these dimensions might dominate. When, in 1914–15, the operational strategy of the Schlieffen Plan, for the one side, and of the Gallipoli campaign, for the other, failed to achieve the decisive results expected of them, then the logistical aspects of the war, and with them the social basis on which they depended, assumed even greater importance as the opposing armies tried to bleed each other to death. As in the American Civil War, victory was to go, not to the side with the most skilful generals and the most courageous troops, but to that which could mobilize the greatest mass of manpower and firepower and sustain it with the strongest popular support.

The inadequacy of mere numbers without social cohesion behind them was demonstrated by the collapse of the Russian Empire in 1917. But the vulnerability even of logistical and social power if the adversary could secure a decisive technological advantage was equally demonstrated by the success of the German submarine campaign in the spring of 1917, when the Allies came within measurable distance of defeat. The German Empire decided to gamble on a technological advantage to counter the logistical superiority which American participation gave to their enemies. But they lost.

IV

From the experiences of the First World War, different strategic thinkers derived different strategic lessons. In Western Europe, the most adventurous theorists considered that the technological dimension of war would predominate in the future. The protagonists of armoured warfare in particular believed that it might restore an operational decisiveness unknown since the days of Napoleon himself – the first two years of the Second World War were to prove them right. Skilfully led and well-trained armed forces operating against opponents who were both militarily and morally incapable of resisting them achieved spectacular results.

But another school of thinkers who placed their faith in technology fared less well. This school included those who believed that the development of air power would enable them to eliminate the operational dimension altogether and to strike directly at the roots of the enemy's *social* strength, at the will and capacity of the opposing society to carry on the war. Instead of wearing down the morale of the enemy civilians through the attrition of surface operations, air power, its protagonists believed, would be able to attack and pulverize it directly.

The events of the war were to disprove this theory. Technology was not yet sufficiently advanced to be able to eliminate the traditional requirements of operational and logistical strategy in this manner. Neither the morale of the British nor that of the German people was to be destroyed by air attack; indeed, such attack was found to demand an operational strategy of a new and complex kind in order to defeat the opposing air forces and to destroy their logistical support. But operational success in air warfare, aided by new technological developments, did eventually enable the Allied air forces to destroy the entire logistical framework that supported the German and Japanese war effort, and rendered the operational skills, in which the Germans excelled until the very end, as ineffective as those of Jackson and Lee.

Technology had not in fact transformed the nature of strategy. It of course remained of vital importance to keep abreast of one's adversary in all major aspects of military technology, but given that this was possible, the lessons of the Second World War seemed little different from those of the First. The social base had to be strong enough to resist the psychological impact of operational set-backs and to support the largest possible logistical build-up by land, sea and air. The forces thus raised had then to be used progressively to eliminate the operational options open to the enemy and ultimately to destroy his capacity to carry on the war.

V

The same conclusions, set out in somewhat more turgid prose, were reached by the strategic analysts of the Soviet Union – not least those who in the late 1940s and early 1950s were writing under the pen-name of J. V. Stalin. But Marxist military thinkers, without differing in essentials from their contemporaries in the West, naturally devoted greater attention to the social dimension of strategy – the structure and cohesiveness of the belligerent societies. For Soviet writers this involved, and still involves, little more than the imposition of a rigid stereotype on the societies they study. Their picture of a world in which oppressed peoples are kept in a state of backward subjection by a small group of exploitative imperialist powers, themselves domestically vulnerable to the revolutionary aspirations of a desperate proletariat, bears little resemblance to the complex reality, whatever its incontestable value as a propagandistic myth. As a result their analysis is often hilariously inaccurate, and their strategic prescriptions either erroneous or banal.

But the West is in no position to criticize. The stereotypes which we have imposed, consciously or unconsciously, on the political structures that surround us, have in the past been no less misleading. The Cold War image of a world which would evolve peacefully, if gradually, toward an Anglo-Saxon style of democracy under Western tutelage if only the global Soviet-directed Marxist conspiracy could be eradicated was at least as naïve and ill-informed as that of the Russian dogmatists. It was the inadequacy of the sociopolitical analysis of the societies with which we were dealing that lay at the root of the failure of the Western powers to cope more effectively with the revolutionary and insurgency movements that characterized the post-war era, from China in the 1940s to Vietnam in the 1960s. For in these, more perhaps than in any previous conflicts, war really was the continuation of political activity with an admixture of other means; and that political activity was itself the result of a huge social upheaval throughout the former colonial world which had been given an irresistible impetus by the events of the Second World War. Of the four dimensions of strategy, the social was here incomparably the most significant; and it was the perception of this that gave the work of Mao Tse-tung and his followers its abiding historical importance.

Military thinkers in the West, extrapolating from their experience of warfare between industrial states, naturally tended to seek a solution to what was essentially a conflict on the social plane either by developing operational techniques of 'counter-insurgency' or in the technological advantages provided by such developments as helicopters, sensors, or 'smart' bombs. When these techniques failed to produce victory, military leaders, both French and American, complained, as had the German military leaders in 1918, that the war had been 'won' militarily but 'lost' politically – as if these dimensions were not totally interdependent.

In fact, these operational techniques and technological tools were now as ancillary to the main socio-political conflict as the tools of psychological warfare had been to the central operational and logistical struggle in the two World Wars. In those conflicts, fought between remarkably cohesive societies, the issue was decided by logistic attrition. Propaganda and subversion had played a marginal role, and such successes as they achieved were strictly geared to those of the armed forces themselves. Conversely, in the conflicts of decolonization which culminated in Vietnam, operational and technological factors were subordinate to the socio-political struggle. If that was not conducted with skill and based on a realistic analysis of the societal situation, no amount of operational expertise, logistical back-up or technical know-how could possibly help.

VI

If the social dimension of strategy has become dominant in one form of conflict since 1945, in another it has, if one is to believe the strategic analysts, vanished completely. Works about nuclear war and deterrence normally treat their topic as an activity taking place almost entirely in the technological dimension. From their writings not only the socio-political but the operational elements have quite disappeared. The technological capabilities of nuclear arsenals are treated as being decisive in themselves, involving a calculation of risk and outcome so complete and discrete that neither the political motivation for the conflict nor the social factors involved in its conduct – nor indeed the military activity of fighting – are taken into account at all. In their models, governments are treated as being as absolute in their capacity to take and implement decisions, and the reaction of their societies are taken as little into account as were those of the subjects of the princes who conducted warfare in Europe in the eighteenth century. Professor Anatole Rapoport, in a rather idiosyncratic introduction to a truncated edition of Clausewitz's *On War*, called these thinkers 'Neo-Clausewitzians'. It is not easy to see why. Every one of the three elements that Clausewitz defined as being intrinsic to war – political motivation, operational activity and social participation – are completely absent from their calculations. Drained of political, social and operational content, such works resemble rather the studies of the eighteenth-century theorists whom Clausewitz was writing to confute, and whose influence he considered, with good reason, to have been so disastrous for his own times.

But the question insistently obtrudes itself: in the terrible eventuality of deterrence failing and hostilities breaking out between states armed with nuclear weapons, how will the peoples concerned react, and how will their reactions affect the will and the capacity of their governments to make decisions? And what form will military operations take? What, in short, will be the social and the operational dimensions of a nuclear war?

It is not, I think, simply an obsession with traditional problems that makes a European thinker seek an answer to these questions. If nuclear war breaks out at all, it is quite likely to break out here. And in Europe such a conflict would involve not simply an exchange of nuclear missiles at intercontinental range, but a struggle between armed forces for the control of territory, and rather thickly populated territory. The interest displayed by Soviet writers in the conduct of such a war, which some writers in the West find so sinister, seems to me no more than common sense. If such a war does occur, the operational and logistical problems it will pose will need to have been thoroughly thought through. It is not good enough to say that the strategy of the West is one of deterrence, or even of crisis management. It is the business of the strategist to think what to do if deterrence fails, and if Soviet strategists are doing their job and those in the West are not, it is not for us to complain about them.

But it is not only the operational and logistical dimensions that have to be taken into account; so also must the societal. Here the attention devoted by Soviet writers to the importance of the stability of the social structure of any state engaged in nuclear war also appears to me to be entirely justifiable, even if their conclusions about contemporary societies, both their own and ours, are ignorant caricatures.

About the operational dimension in nuclear war, Western analysts have until recently been both confused and defeatist. In spite of the activities of Defense Secretary Robert McNamara and his colleagues nearly twenty years ago, and in spite of the lip-service paid to the concept of 'flexible response', the military forces in Western Europe are still not regarded as a body of professionals, backed up where necessary by citizen-soldiers, whose task it will be to repel any attack upon their own territories and those of their allies. Rather they are considered as an expendable element in a complex mechanism for enhancing the credibility of nuclear response. Indeed, attempts to increase their operational effectiveness are still sometimes opposed on the grounds that to do so would be to reduce the credibility of nuclear retaliation.

But such credibility depends not simply on a perceived balance, or imbalance, of weapons-systems, but on perceptions of the nature of society whose leaders are threatening such retaliation. Peoples who are not prepared to make the effort necessary for operational defence are even less likely to support a decision to initiate a nuclear exchange from which they will themselves suffer almost inconceivable destruction, even if that decision is taken at the lowest possible level of nuclear escalation. And if such a decision were taken over their heads, they would be unlikely to remain sufficiently resolute and united to continue to function as a cohesive political and military entity in the aftermath. The maintenance of adequate armed forces in peacetime, and the will to deploy and support them operationally in war, is in fact a symbol of that social unity and political resolve which is as essential an element in nuclear deterrence as any invulnerable second-strike capability.

So although the technological dimension of strategy has certainly become of predominant importance in armed conflict between advanced societies in the second half of the twentieth century – as predominant as the logistical dimension was during the first half – the growing political self-awareness of those societies and, in the West at least, their insistence on political participation have made the social dimension too significant to be ignored. There can be little doubt that societies, such as those of the Soviet Union and the People's Republic of China, which have developed powerful mechanisms of social control, enjoy an apparent initial advantage over those of the West, which operate by a consensus reached by tolerating internal disagreements and conflicts; though how great that advantage would actually prove under pressure remains to be seen.

Whatever one's assessment of their strength, these are factors that cannot be left out of account in any strategic calculations. If we do take account of the social dimension of strategy in the nuclear age, we are likely to conclude that Western leaders might find it much more difficult to initiate nuclear war than would their Soviet counterparts – and, more important, would be perceived by their adversaries as finding it more difficult. If this is the case, and if on their side the conventional strength of the Soviet armed forces makes it unnecessary for their leaders to take such an initiative, the operational effectiveness of the armed forces of the West once more becomes a matter of major strategic importance, both in deterrence and in defence.

Most strategic scenarios today are based on the least probable of political circumstances – a totally unprovoked military assault by the Soviet Union, with no shadow of political justification, on Western Europe. But Providence is unlikely to provide us with anything so straightforward. Such an attack, if it occurred at all, would be likely to arise out of a political crisis in Central Europe over the rights and wrongs of which Western public opinion would be deeply and perhaps justifiably divided. Soviet military objectives would probably extend no farther than the Rhine, if indeed so far. Under such conditions, the political will of the West to initiate nuclear war might have to be discounted entirely, and the defence of West Germany would depend not on our nuclear arsenals but on the operational capabilities of our armed forces, fighting as best they could and for as long as they could without recourse to nuclear weapons of any kind. And it need hardly be said that hostilities breaking out elsewhere in the world are likely, as they did in Vietnam, to arise out of political situations involving an even greater degree of political ambiguity, in which our readiness to initiate nuclear war would appear even less credible.

The belief that technology has somehow eliminated the need for operational effectiveness is, in short, no more likely to be valid in the nuclear age than it was in the Second World War. Rather, as in that war, technology is likely to make its greatest contribution to strategy by improving operational weapons-systems and the logistical framework that makes their deployment possible. The transformation in weapons technology which is occurring under our eyes with the development of precision-guided munitions suggests that this is exactly what is now happening. The new weapons-systems hold out the possibility that operational skills will once more be enabled, as they were in 1940–1, to achieve decisive results, either positive in the attack or negative in the defence. But whether these initial operational decisions are then accepted as definitive by the societies concerned will depend, as they did in 1940–1 and in all previous wars, on the two other elements in Clausewitz's trinity: the importance of the political objective, and the readiness of the belligerent communities to endure the sacrifices involved in prolonging the war.

These sacrifices might or might not include the experience, on whatever scale, of nuclear war, but they would certainly involve living with the day-to-day, even the hour-to-hour, possibility that the war might 'go nuclear' at any moment. It is not easy to visualize a greater test of social cohesion than having to endure such a strain for a period of months, if not years, especially if no serious measures had been taken for the protection of the civil population.

Such measures were projected in the United States two decades ago, and they were abandoned for a mixture of motives. There was, on the one hand, the appreciation that not even the most far-reaching of preparations could prevent damage being inflicted on a scale unacceptable to the peoples of the West. On the other was the reluctance of those peoples to accept, in peacetime, the kind of social disruption and the diversion of resources which such measures would involve. The abandonment of these programmes was then rationalized by the doctrine of Mutually Assured Destruction. And any attempt by strategic thinkers to consider what protective measures might have to be taken if the war which everyone hoped to avoid actually came about was frowned on as a weakening of deterrence. But here again, there seem to have been no such inhibitions in the Soviet Union; and their civil defence programme, which some Western thinkers find so threatening, like that of the Chinese, seems to me no more than common sense. It is hard not to envy governments which have the capacity to carry through such measures, however marginally they might enhance the survivability of their societies in the event of nuclear war.

The Western position, on the other hand, appears both paradoxical and, quite literally, indefensible, so long as our operational strategy quite explicitly envisages the initiation of a nuclear exchange. The use of theatre nuclear weapons within Western Europe, on any scale, will involve agonizing self-inflicted wounds for which our societies are ill-prepared; while their extension to Eastern European territory will invite retaliation against such legitimate military targets as the ports of Hamburg, Antwerp or Portsmouth, for which we have made no preparations at all. The planned emplacement of nuclear weapons in Western Europe capable of matching in range, throw-weight and accuracy those which the Russians have targeted on to that area may be effective in deterring the Soviet Union from initiating such an exchange. But it will not solve the problem so long as the Russians are in a position to secure an operational victory without recourse to nuclear weapons at all. Deterrence works both ways.

VII

It cannot be denied that the strategic calculus I have outlined in the above pages has disquieting implications for the defence of the West. We appear to be depending on the technological dimension of strategy to the detriment of its operational requirements, while we ignore its societal implications altogether – something which our potential adversaries, very wisely, show no indication of doing. But the prospect of nuclear war is so appalling that we no less than our adversaries are likely, if war comes, to rely on 'conventional' operational skills and the logistical capability to support them for as long as possible, no less than we have in the past.

Hostilities in Europe would almost certainly begin with the engagement of armed forces seeking to obtain or to frustrate an operational decision. But as in the past – as in 1862, or in 1914, or in 1940–1 – social factors will determine whether the outcome of these initial operations is accepted as decisive; or whether the resolution of the belligerent societies must be further tested by logistical attrition; or whether governments will feel sufficiently confident in the stability and cohesion of their own peoples, and the instability of their adversaries, to initiate a nuclear exchange. All of this gives us overwhelming reason for praying that the great nuclear powers can continue successfully to avoid war. It gives us none for deluding ourselves as to the strategic problems such a war would present to those who would have to conduct it.

Two Controversial Pieces

SURVIVING A PROTEST

IN January 1980 I succumbed to what Evelyn Waugh once so accurately described as 'the senile itch to write to *The Times*'. The temptation had been provided by a spasmodic correspondence about three issues that were being considered in isolation and ought, in my view, to be looked at together. These were: Civil Defence, the installation of 'cruise-missiles' in the United Kingdom, and the continued possession by this country of a 'Strategic Nuclear Deterrent'.

In that letter (which was printed on 30 January), I suggested that the installation of cruise-missiles in this country might lead to their sites being targeted by the Russians for pre-emptive attack with weapons whose destructiveness, though appalling, would yet be on too local and limited a scale to warrant the retaliatory use of our own strike-force – since this would provoke a massive 'city-busting' counter-stroke by the Russians in return. If we were to accept cruise-missiles, I suggested, we should also do what we could to protect our civil population; not only as a precaution against such attacks but because without such evident protection the use of these weapons would be incredible. 'Limited' Soviet nuclear strikes might also be launched with the object of creating conditions of such 'political turbulence' in this country that the retaliatory use of our nuclear weapons would be incredible.

The letter was intended to express scepticism about the utility of both cruise-missiles and our strategic deterrent, and was generally so read. But evidently I said too much and not enough. In the first place I took for granted the general awareness that the presence of nuclear-equipped aircraft in this country, together with a number of vital NATO command headquarters and communication systems, has made these islands a target for Soviet attack for the past 30 years. Cruise-missiles are only a greatly improved version of the manned systems with which we have lived for an entire generation, and their capacity for rapid dispersal makes them very much less vulnerable to pre-emption than the manned aircraft they replace, though this might not deter the Russians from making the attempt to destroy them in place. What is new, however – and this I should also have pointed out – is the Soviet capacity for selective and accurate targeting: in itself a reflection of and riposte to the development of Western technology. This development, a transformation almost as revolutionary as that brought about by nuclear weapons themselves, has equipped both sides with a far greater capacity to destroy each other's weapons instead of simply eliminating their populations. In these circumstances, protection of populations is possible in a way that twenty-five years ago it was not. And if it is possible then it ought in my view to be done.

I report this in a fairly neutral way, but since neutrality on such issues can be deceptive I should obviously make clear my conviction that this is a most sinister and undesirable development. It may have to be accepted as a fact of life, but it makes the prospect of nuclear war none the less nightmarish for making it appear marginally more possible. Rashly I took it for granted that this was too obvious to need to be stated. Quite how rash I had been I did not realize for three months – until April, in fact, when the historian and polemicist E. P. Thompson published under the auspices of the Campaign for Nuclear Disarmament a pamphlet entitled *Protest and Survive*, devoted entirely to an onslaught on my letter and to the truly monstrous motives that Mr Thompson attributed to me in writing it.

According to Mr Thompson my intention was 'to hurry the British people across a threshold of mental expectation, so that they may be prepared, not for "deterrence", but for actual nuclear war'. My arguments, he said, were

designed [my italics] . . . to carry us across a threshold from the *unthinkable* (the theory of deterrence, founded upon the assumption that it *must* work) to the *thinkable* (the theory that nuclear war may happen, and may be imminent, and, with cunning tactics and proper preparations, might end in 'victory').

More than this, the arguments are of an order which permit the mind to progress from the unthinkable to the thinkable *without thinking* – without confronting the arguments, their consequences or probable conclusions, and indeed without knowing that any threshold has been crossed . . .

Professor Howard himself has certainly thought the problems through. His letter was a direct political intervention. He called upon the British authorities to rush us all, unthinkingly, across this thought-gap. His language . . . reveals a direct intention to act in political ways upon the mind of the people, in order to enforce a posture, not of defence, but of menace.

The object which I, together with the 'high strategists of NATO' had in mind, according to Mr Thompson, was to create a 'war psychosis', in which the idea of a threat from without would be reinforced by a threat from within;

and it is necessary to inflame these new expectations by raising voluntary defence corps, auxiliary services, digging ever deeper bunkers for the personnel of the State, distributing leaflets, holding lectures in halls and churches, laying down two weeks' supplies of emergency rations, promoting in the private sector the manufacture of Whitelaw Shelters and radiation-proof 'Imperm' blinds and patent anti-Fall-Out pastilles . . . And it is also necessary to supplement all this by beating up an internal civil-war or class-war psychosis by unmasking traitors, by threatening journalists under the Official Secrets Act, by tampering with juries and tapping telephones, and generally by closing up people's minds and mouths.

All this I read with understandably mixed feelings. First there was the alarm felt by anyone who suddenly finds himself matched against the polemical equivalent of Björn Borg on the Centre Court. Once this ebbed it was replaced by gratification that I was now assured of immortality. Like Mr Robert Montgomery, whose execrable verse will never be forgotten so long as men still read Macaulay's *Essays*, so will I be preserved for posterity as the dim Professor plucked from deserved obscurity to be transfixed with a single contemptuous shaft by the formidable Thompson; whose works, like those of his exemplars Paine and Cobbett, will certainly be printed as masterpieces of polemical prose long after my own works (including this one) have been deservedly forgotten. But stronger than either emotion was my blank astonishment that a brief letter in which I was trying to think through some problems that perplexed and still desperately perplex me should have been seen as a cunningly designed move in a deep-laid conspiracy to fasten the shackles of despotism yet more firmly upon the free-born 'People of England', to whom Mr Thompson's pamphlet was addressed.

These reflections were interrupted by phone calls from enthusiastic entrepreneurs anxious to arrange a 'confrontation' between Mr Thompson and myself, on television, in Oxford Town Hall, or anywhere else. But I did not see what the confrontation was going to be about. I was, and remain, deeply sceptical about the utility of cruise-missiles, though I cannot see why they are *morally* more objectionable than less discriminating weapons. I regard civil defence – as do the Swedes, the Swiss, and the Russians themselves – as no more than a sensible precaution in a highly dangerous world. I asked the CND for the opportunity to make all this clear in print. But the request was brusquely refused. So I asked Mr Thompson to come and explain his ideas more fully in the relatively calm atmosphere of an Oxford seminar, which he very kindly did. When I pointed out to him my own lack of enthusiasm for cruise-missiles he made a most generous apology for having treated me unjustly; an apology which he later printed in the correspondence columns of the *Guardian*. There the matter rests happily between us. But since Mr Thompson also invited me to give my own objection to cruise-missiles 'a more public airing' I accepted the hospitality of the columns of *Encounter* [in November 1980] in order to take the question a little further.

I quite realize that in his philippic against me Mr Thompson felt no more personal animus than a sniper feels against an unwary enemy soldier who wanders into his sights. So far as he was concerned I was one more representative of the Governmental forces, the Establishment, the Thing, that hydra-headed monster of power which was seeking, as it had always sought, to defraud the people of their rights and liberties and had now discovered in the creation of a 'war psychosis' a new way to do it. *Why* I should have wanted to do this – *why* I should have composed with such malevolent skill a letter designed to carry the entire British people across so critical a mental threshold – remains unexplained. But Mr Thompson is in no doubt that the Establishment is out to get him and those who think like him.

At the next international crisis (real or fictitious) [he went on to warn us] there will be a co-ordinated, univocal, 'civil defence' bombardment . . . with extreme precautions to prevent any dissenting voices from having more than the most marginal presence.

I am afraid that this is simply paranoia; and it is as pointless to ask a paranoid of the Left why 'they' want to take away his liberties as it is to ask a paranoid of the Right why the Russians should want to conquer the world. If indeed I were a paranoid of the Right I would no doubt treat Mr Thompson's pamphlet exactly as he treated my letter. The terrifying statistics he deploys about the damage caused by even the most limited of nuclear strikes; the heart-rending account he gives of the suffering caused at Hiroshima (without mentioning the other significant fact that it was precisely the *absence* of any Japanese deterrent retaliatory capacity that made the infliction of such suffering possible); the effort he deploys in dissuading us from equipping ourselves with weapons whose capacity to inflict comparable damage on an adversary could deter such attacks on us; his urgent efforts to persuade the peoples of Western Europe to abandon nuclear weapons whether or not the Russians do the same: whose interests, I would ask, does this serve? Is not Mr Thompson an avowed Marxist? Is he not deliberately attempting simultaneously to disarm and to terrify 'the People of England' (Mr Thompson's own phrase, incidentally: the Scots and the Welsh can look after themselves) into acquiescing in the ever-increasing extension of Soviet power? Is his pamphlet not in fact a direct political intervention, designed to hurry the British People, as I prefer to call them, unthinking across the threshold from a posture of defence to one of surrender?

Fortunately I am not a paranoid of the Right, and I do not regard Mr Thompson in the same sinister light as he clearly regards me. On the contrary, I believe him to be in exactly the same position as myself: desperately worried about the state of the world, casting about for some means to improve it, and lamenting that this proper concern prevents him from getting on with serious historical studies. But our search for a solution will not get very far if we believe that we are wrestling, not with an intractable but not insoluble problem of international politics, but with Forces of Evil that are out to get us. For these Forces are not located in Whitehall, or in Moscow, or in the Pentagon, or even in Oxford. If they are to be found anywhere it is in our own minds, and it is thence that they must be exorcized if we are to see the problems of the world clearly enough to be able to prescribe solutions that will make the situation better rather than worse. So while accepting Mr Thompson's apology I would only beg him in future to stop being silly; to cease attributing malignancy to those with whom he disagrees; and to try to discuss these matters in the adult fashion that their deep seriousness demands.

E. P. Thompson has come to strategic studies late in the day, so it is not surprising that his understanding of the rationale of cruise-missiles is rather confused. He sees them as a device foisted upon Europeans by 'the hard men in the Pentagon', who wish to fight a limited nuclear war in Europe that would leave the United States intact. *Why* they should want to fight such a war, or indeed any war, remains unexplained. It is therefore necessary to take a few moments to consider how the proposal to deploy cruise-missiles actually originated, and to see how it is supposed to fit into the concept of 'deterrence'.

The basic 'model' of nuclear deterrence is simple. Nuclear weapons enable the powers that possess them to threaten an adversary with the prospect of destruction on a nightmare scale. Since no assured means of defence against them has been devised, their use, or threatened use, has to be deterred by a comparable capability on the other side. This is supposed to create a 'Balance of Terror' which effectively abolishes nuclear weapons as an instrument of policy. Like a gothic arch, the conflicting pressures create a zone of stability within which international political activity can be carried on as if they did not exist.

This simple doctrine, devised in the 1950s, was out-of-date almost before it was proclaimed. In the first place, it assumed (as the French were quick to point out) that every state that aspired to independence should possess its own nuclear capability. If one does not accept such logic, a non-nuclear power threatened by a nuclear adversary needs the protection of a nuclear ally. But how can that ally be relied upon if it is itself vulnerable to nuclear attack? In the second place, it assumed that the nuclear delivery capability was itself invulnerable or could be made so. But as missile technology developed during the 1960s and '70s, this assumption became questionable in its turn. The maintenance of a 'credible deterrent', i.e. one not vulnerable to a pre-emptive strike, has thus become increasingly difficult *technically*; and this, in its turn, has complicated the *political* difficulty of providing a credible nuclear guarantee to an ally. This is the problem which the "hard men in the Pentagon" have been trying to solve for the past twenty-odd years.

Even in the days of massive US nuclear superiority over the Soviet Union, Western Europe provided a hostage the problem of whose defence baffled the strategists. Given that Soviet superiority in 'conventional' weapons could not be matched by the West Europeans, how could American nuclear superiority be harnessed to the defence of their continent once the Russians had developed the capacity to deter its use by a substantial retaliatory capability of their own? In the 1950s the US Army in Europe had introduced the idea that 'battlefield' nuclear weapons might be used to replace 'conventional' forces in a tactical role. But a few exercises revealed that civilian casualties would be on so horrendous a scale that the remedy would be a great deal worse than the disease; especially since the Russians could respond in kind. Technological refinements such as 'the Neutron Bomb' only touched the fringes of the problem, and both Lord Mountbatten and Lord Zuckerman fought a gallant battle in and out of office against the doctrine that nuclear weapons, on however limited a scale, could be considered an 'acceptable' means of conducting war. It was their remarks on this totally different problem, incidentally, that E. P. Thompson tore out of context to buttress his own case.

Nevertheless if our conventional defences are inadequate and 'tactical' nuclear weapons are unusable, how is the problem of 'deterrence' to be solved? Are other forms of 'limited nuclear war' any more acceptable? This problem was first discussed by Robert McNamara and his associates in the Pentagon in the early 1960s; and the package of ideas known as 'the McNamara Doctrine' included the possibility of targeting Soviet military installations ('counterforce') rather than civilian objectives ('counter-city', or 'counter-value') in such a way as to give the Russians the greatest possible inducement, when they themselves retaliated, to avoid American civilian targets as well. It might then be possible (hoped McNamara) to preserve the credibility of nuclear deterrence without invoking total and immediate holocaust.

But there were two problems about the McNamara Doctrine. The first was the difficulty of making any real distinction between 'counterforce' and 'countervalue' targets that would be unmistakable during a political crisis. Under any conditions the 'collateral damage' caused by a nuclear attack on military objectives would cause huge civilian casualties on a scale that could not be conceived of as 'acceptable'. In the second place, was not this 'counterforce' strategy indistinguishable from a pre-emptive strategy designed to disarm the Russians and leave their cities as hostages? How could it be reconciled with the doctrine, simultaneously being proclaimed by Mr McNamara, of 'Mutually Assured Destruction'? Mr McNamara and his successor James Schlesinger tried to explain that the military objectives they had in mind to attack would not be Soviet missile-sites but 'Other Military Targets'. But any conviction their words may have carried was lost when the Americans initiated the deployment of 'MIRVs': the multiple, independently-targeted warheads that increased the American strike capability by a factor of upward of three. If any single innovation destabilized the balance of terror, it was this.

That the Russians would respond to the American challenge in kind was inevitable. Hence McNamara's initiation of Strategic Arms Limitation Talks to try to "put a cap" on a weapons race that would be at once destabilizing and ruinously expensive. Inexorably, as the Russians drew first level and then ahead of the Americans in the number of their launchers (the Americans, however, retaining a comfortable lead in warheads), Soviet fears of an American pre-emptive strike were replaced by American fears of a Soviet pre-emptive strike; fears stoked up by such bodies as 'The Committee on the Present Danger', whose perception of the Soviet Union bears a close family resemblance to Mr Thompson's image of the Pentagon. In the eyes of these pessimists a situation will soon arise, if it has not done so already, in which the Russians would be able by a single pre-emptive strike to 'take out' every single American land-based missile. The enormous retaliatory power of the American sea-based missiles would be paralysed by the threat of further attack on American cities. So the President would have no alternative save meekly to 'surrender'. These arguments have recently been used to justify a further massive increase in US defence expenditure and force deployments, to which the Soviet Union will no doubt feel compelled to reply in kind.

Even if one believes these fears to be absurdly exaggerated, the growing uncertainty about the central balance has inevitably reacted on the problem of European defence. It is a problem that 'the hard men in the Pentagon' no doubt sincerely wish would go away. Life would be a great deal simpler for them if they had only the protection of their own continent to worry about, and one wonders whether E. P. Thompson thinks they *enjoy* having to find the means to defend peoples who should have the wit and resources to do the job for themselves. Right-wing forces in the United States have been busy informing the Soviet Union that Russian nuclear superiority will soon be so great that no American nuclear guarantee to Western Europe is worth the paper it is written on. So given the continued and undeniable imbalance of conventional forces, what deterrent is there left against a Soviet attack on Western Europe – an attack that could be nuclear, or conventional, or both?

This is where the much misunderstood 'theatre nuclear balance' comes in (a question quite different from the problem of 'tactical nuclear war' to which Lord Zuckerman was addressing himself). The Soviet Union developed, early in the 1960s, 'Intermediate Range Ballistic Missiles' targeted on Western Europe, the SS4s and SS5s. They caused much concern to Western strategists even in those halcyon days of American nuclear superiority; and a whole succession of schemes was devised, including the famous 'Multilateral Nuclear Force', to neutralize them. But they were immobile, inaccurate, and highly vulnerable to pre-emption by US strategic weapons. They have now been replaced by an improved model, the SS20s, which are not only mobile and equipped with multiple warheads but reportedly highly accurate. Taken together with the so-called 'Backfire' bomber, these present the Russians with the option, by attacking purely military targets – command headquarters, airfields and communication centres, in the UK as well as on the European Continent – of rendering Western Europe defenceless before the United States could do anything about it: leaving it to the Americans to decide whether they wished to respond by strikes against the Soviet Union that would bring inevitable devastation upon their own heads.

This is the Problem that confronts 'the hard men in the

Pentagon'; and for E. P. Thompson to accuse them of planning to fight a 'limited war' in Europe is to stand reason, logic, and history on its head. Their object is precisely to *prevent* such a war and to assuage the fears of Western Europeans that, confronted by a threat that did not extend to their own continent, the Americans would be effectively deterred from intervening. It is primarily to reassure the Europeans, to prevent them from seeking safety in either neutralism or in a further development of their own nuclear weapons, that the Pentagon has come up with the proposal to install in Western Europe missiles with a range and accuracy comparable to that of the SS20s: the Pershing II missiles and now-famous ground-launched cruise-missiles, the GLCMs.

The rationale for this seems a little confused. According to some these are 'bargaining chips' and will not be installed if the Russians can be persuaded to eliminate their SS20s and Backfires in a further round of SALT talks. According to others, including our own British Secretary for Defence, their installation has now been irreversibly decided. I am myself as sceptical about the whole programme as I was about the MLF proposal some 16 years ago. In the first place these missiles will remain under American control, and any damage they inflict on the Soviet Union (and however precise their targeting, the extent of that damage will be appalling) will be seen as having been inflicted by Americans. The probability of retaliation against the United States would be no less than if the missiles had been based on American soil. Why, then, should their use be any more credible, in the eyes of the Europeans or the Russians, than that of weapons based on American soil? What additional guarantee do they offer?

The Americans have already assigned to NATO a force of Poseidons, submarine-based missiles, to reinforce the 'theatre nuclear balance'. Two arguments have been advanced to indicate why they no longer serve this purpose. First, they are not visibly linked to Europe; and second, their accuracy is less than that of ground-based launchers, so they could not be used in a precise counterforce role. The first of these arguments is double-edged, to put it mildly. However much people may demand security, their reaction when weapons are actually installed in their backyards is always predictably ambiguous, as the Americans themselves found when they tried to install Anti-Ballistic Missiles to protect their cities. The old Polaris sales-jingle expresses a profound political truth:

> Put the missile out to sea,
> Where the real-estate is free,
> And it's far away from me . . .

Not even E. P. Thompson has ever raised any objection to the Poseidons. And as for their inaccuracy, why should this matter? These are presumably second-strike, retaliatory weapons, intended not for a surprise attack on SS20 sites (which are mobile anyway) but as a deterrent whose known capacity for inflicting punitive damage will dissuade the Kremlin from initiating the use of its own weapons at all. What indeed would be the value of such improved accuracy, the Russians are bound to ask, except for a pre-emptive attack? So far from stabilizing the 'theatre balance', in fact, the GLCMs could introduce a new element of instability. On this point E. P. Thompson and I are in entire agreement; and I would wish him well in his campaign if he were to dissociate himself from its unilateral and neutralist overtones and provide convincing evidence of a comparable effort on the part of the Soviet peoples to dismantle the no less provocative and destabilizing SS20s.

Why should 'the hard men in the Pentagon' have taken this initiative at all?

The answer is, I believe, because they are not nearly hard enough. In fact they are as soft as butter, anxious to make provision for every remote eventuality, however implausible, that their overactive imaginations can visualize. Lord Salisbury, contemplating the British military in the 19th century preparing to defend India against an attack from Russia whose nearest railhead was still 1,000 miles away, commented that if they had their way they would garrison the moon against an attack from Mars. If the men in the Pentagon were as hard as they are painted they would have sent the 'Committee on the Present Danger' packing long ago with the comment that, if they really believed that the Russians would risk a surprise attack against American land-based missiles on the assumption that it would be 100 per cent successful and that there would be no retaliation from the enormous and intact submarine force, then they would believe anything. In the same way they would have dismissed the fears of their European allies. If we truly believe that the United States would watch the military and political elimination of an area where they have stationed hundred of thousands of troops with all their families, hundreds of their best aircraft and tanks, masses of military equipment including tactical nuclear weapons, to say nothing of a huge investment of capital and God knows how many American citizens resident or in constant transit – if all this is not enough, what difference will cruise-missiles make? If they were as hard as E. P. Thompson apparently believes, they would long ago have told us to stop whining about 'decoupling' and begging them for reassurance, and instead get on with the job of providing for ourselves that level of *conventional* defence that our combined wealth, manpower and technical expertise would make possible if we set our minds to it – and if, I would add in parenthesis so far as Britain is concerned, we did not divert funds into procuring the most expensive available 'independent deterrent', the strategic rationale for which remains to me utterly obscure.

From this you will see why I consider both GLCMs and Trident to be a waste of money. The existing degree of American commitment to Europe – far more indeed than we have any right to expect from an ally in peacetime – combined with the formidable force of Poseidons at SACEUR's disposal should be ample to dissuade the Soviets from launching a nuclear strike against us. If it is not, nothing will be. Whether it would deter a quick *conventional* attack, however, is another matter. If the Russians ever came to think that they could reach the Rhine in 24 hours and the Channel in 48 before the question of using nuclear weapons arose at all, then peace might really be in the balance. This is the problem to which the West Europeans should be addressing themselves – not fussing about American nuclear guarantees.

E. P. Thompson's own solution to the problem of European security is apparently to create, by popular pressure, a Non-Nuclear Zone from Poland to the Atlantic. He claims considerable support in Eastern Europe, which is hardly surprising. The East Europeans have no nuclear weapons, nor are the Russians likely to allow them to acquire any. Mr Thompson will find much official enthusiasm for his cause in, for example, Prague. The Soviet Union itself, he admits, presents a more difficult problem, but it might, he believes, be shamed into following suit 'by Rumania or Poland . . . distancing themselves from Soviet strategies'. That is all he has to say about the Russians, and even he might admit, on reflection, that it leaves something to be desired.

Mr Thompson's implication is, however, that if we in Western Europe have no nuclear weapons, the Russians will not threaten us with theirs; and that, in the event of a nuclear war, we should remain an oasis of peace and calm – an oasis so secure that we need not even take the precautions for the defence of our civilian population adopted long ago by those professional neutrals, the Swedes and the Swiss. Indeed even to entertain the idea of taking such precautions would apparently, in Mr Thompson's view, invite attack.

E. P. Thompson leaves a lot of questions unanswered. Does he want the Americans to withdraw the Poseidons they have assigned to NATO? Is he happy about the level of conventional defence? Should Britain remain in the alliance at all, and if so on what terms? If we leave, should we take as our model France, Sweden, or Switzerland (all of them, incidentally, very heavily armed States)? Does he believe that the West as a whole should unilaterally abandon nuclear weapons, or that we should press on with negotiations for multilateral disarmament? And if we do so, can he suggest how we solve some of the major problems of balancing force reductions and verification that have baffled statesmen for the past 20 years?

I hope I have made it clear that there is much in what E. P. Thompson says with which I agree, so I would be genuinely interested to know his views on these questions. During the past two decades the arms race has acquired a momentum, fuelled by scientific ingenuity, by bureaucratic inertia, by inter-service rivalries in the USA and by the worst-case analysis of the military planners on both sides, that has made a mockery of arms-control negotiations. We badly need new initiatives and new ideas. The introduction of Ground-Launched Cruise Missiles is unnecessary, expensive, and most unlikely to stabilize a balance which is in my view far more stable than either E. P. Thompson or 'the hard men in the Pentagon' believe. But in principle there is nothing about the GLCMs that is particularly sinister or particularly new. They will not increase the danger in which this country already stands as a member of the Alliance. (And in so far as I ever suggested that it would I was wrong, I apologize and I withdraw.) The argument of E. P. Thompson and his colleagues that GLCMs are in some sense more *immoral* than an earlier generation of nuclear weapons because they are more accurate and can be targeted against military rather than civilian objectives is one that I must admit myself quite unable to follow; as is the associated suggestion that, unlike their predecessors, they are intended not for *deterrence* but for *use*. All weapons, especially nuclear weapons, are intended for *deterrence*. Their purpose is to persuade an adversary that he can gain nothing by using force – even defensive force – as an instrument of his policy. But if they are not known to be usable, how can they deter? Much as I deplore their introduction, I can see that the object they are intended to serve, so far from fighting a 'limited nuclear war' in Europe (something which, like Lord Zuckerman, I have regarded for twenty-five years as being wholly impossible), is to make it clear to the Russians that they have no prospect of getting away with anything of the kind.

On fundamental matters I am afraid that E. P. Thompson and I are unlikely ever to agree, because obviously we argue from such very different premises. Mr Thompson belongs to the tradition of Tom Paine and Jeremy Bentham. He clearly believes that wars are caused by the forces of the Establishment for their own short-sighted and self-interested purposes, and that if only the People would rise in its majesty and shout STOP! then wars would cease in all the world. Peoples must therefore unite against Establishments. My own view, on the other hand, is that international conflict is an ineluctable product of diversity of interests, perceptions, and cultures; that armed conflict is immanent in any international system; but that war can and must be averted by patience, empathy, prudence and the hard, tedious, detailed work of inconspicuous statesmanship – qualities which are notably absent from populist movements whose universal characteristic is a desire for the instant and total satisfaction of their demands. The appalling consequences of failure in the nuclear age make the exercise of these prudential qualities more vital than ever before. Romantic gestures will do nothing to help.

This difference between us is probably too deeply rooted in personality-traits and experience to be resolved, so there is little point in continuing the argument. I would not claim a unique degree of insight denied to so distinguished a historian as E. P. Thompson. What I do claim, however, is that my views accord a great deal more closely with those of the Marxist-Leninists who direct the destinies of the Soviet Union than do his; and this is a matter of some relevance.

E. P. Thompson belongs to the golden years of the Second International, but the world moved on long ago into the leaden era of the Third. The present rulers of the USSR are avowed disciples of Lenin, who was an avowed disciple of Clausewitz. They are as frank in preaching and practising the use of military force as a legitimate instrument of socialist or communist policy as they are prudent in using it when the results are unlikely to be effective. In their very extensive writings on military strategy one searches in vain for a distinction between 'deterrence' and 'war-fighting'; that threshold by which E. P. Thompson sets such store. They do not even recognize a qualitative distinction between nuclear and conventional weapons. And their prudence extends, as E. P. Thompson somehow failed to remind his readers, to measures of civil defence far more sweeping than those which he took me to task for suggesting that we should adopt over here.

For the Soviet leadership, Western Europe presents a twofold threat. Politically, the attractiveness of our pluralistic system and the (comparatively) successful economy that goes with it is a standing challenge to her dominance over Eastern Europe, if not to her own internal regime. Militarily, we provide a base for American weapons targeted on her homeland. The elimination of these, as Mr Thompson advocates, would certainly ease the military difficulties of the Soviet Union. But unless the Europeans replaced them with comparable systems of their own (and neither the French nor the British weapons are comparable) the Soviet Union would then possess a crushing military superiority, both nuclear and conventional, over her rich, weak and divided neighbours. And can Mr Thompson seriously contend that this would not gradually develop into a political dominance?

I do not myself believe in any simple 'lessons of history', and I have learned to mistrust historical analogy as a lazy substitute for analytic thought. But there are certain recurrent patterns of power and of imperial expansion in the past that have been too persistent to be ignored. I know of few occasions when small, wealthy and militarily weak states, involved in political rivalry with large and powerful neighbours on their frontiers, have retained their autonomy for very long. The fears of a nuclear holocaust that E. P. Thompson and his associates have been so sedulous in stoking up, fears which if they had their way would be entirely one-sided, would in the event of a confrontation provide an overwhelming incentive for us to see things the Russian way: to abstain from causing them internal or external embarrassment; to provide them with trade on highly advantageous conditions; to accept (as does Eastern Europe) their hegemonial leadership; and, not least, to eliminate those elements in our political systems that they found disturbing, as they have eliminated those in Eastern Europe. Foremost among such elements would be such courageous, old-fashioned, stubbornly independent radicals as E. P. Thompson himself, and that would be a great pity. Our task is in fact to preserve the independence of a political system in which it is possible for E. P. Thompson – unlike his opposite numbers in the Soviet Union – to Protest and still Survive.

ON FIGHTING A NUCLEAR WAR

THIRTY-FIVE years have passed since Bernard Brodie, in the first book that he or indeed anyone else had written about nuclear war, set down these words:

The first and most vital step in any American security program for the age of atomic bombs is to take measures to guarantee to ourselves in case of attack the possibility of retaliation in kind. The writer in making this statement is not for the moment concerned about who will *win* the next war in which atomic bombs have been used. Thus far the chief purpose of our military establishment has been to win wars. From now on its chief purpose must be to avert them. It can have almost no other useful purpose.[1]

For most of those thirty-five years, the truth of this revolutionary doctrine was accepted in the Western world as self-evident, and our whole military posture became based on the concept of deterrence that Brodie had defined so presciently and so soon. The fear of nuclear war *as such* was

1. Bernard Brodie (ed.), *The Absolute Weapon* (Harcourt Brace, New York, 1946), p. 76.

considered sufficient deterrent against the initiation of large-scale violence on the scale of the Second World War, and the policy of the United States, its allies, and perhaps also its adversaries was to create a strategic framework that made it not only certain that a nuclear attack would provoke a nuclear response, but likely that an attack with conventional weapons would do so as well. It was agreed almost without a dissenting voice that nuclear wars were 'unwinnable'. A nuclear exchange on any scale would cause damage of a kind that would make a mockery of the whole concept of 'victory'.

When Brodie died, that consensus was beginning to disintegrate. In the last article he published, on 'The Development of Nuclear Strategy', he reprinted the passage and defended it. While accepting the changes that had occurred both in weapons technology and in the structure of the military balance over the past thirty years, he saw no reason to alter his view. It was necessary to develop and to deploy nuclear weapons in order to deter their use by others. Such weapons, he believed, might perhaps be utilizable on a limited scale in the European theatre. But as instruments of policy, as strategic tools in a general war, they could have no utility. Nuclear war was unfightable, unwinnable.

Was he wrong? Let me offer my own answer to that question.

Bernard Brodie's belief that a nuclear war could not be 'won' did not of course mean that he did not hold strong views about the optimal deployment and targeting of nuclear weapons, a matter on which his opinion was greatly valued by successive Chiefs of the Air Staff. The maintenance of a credible capacity for nuclear retaliation, and its structuring so as to create maximum political and psychological effect, was a problem with which he concerned himself deeply throughout his career. But if deterrence failed and these weapons had in fact to be used, what then? What should the political objective of the war be, and how would nuclear devastation help to attain it? How and with whom was a peace to be negotiated? Above all, in what shape would the United States be, after suffering substantial nuclear devastation herself, to negotiate any peace?

Brodie could have asked further questions, and no doubt did. What would be the relations between the Soviet Union and the United States after such a war? What would their position be in an international community that could hardly have emerged intact from a nuclear battle on so global a scale? In what way could the post-nuclear world environment be seen as an improvement on the pre-war situation and one which it was worth enduring – and inflicting – such unimaginable suffering in order to attain? It is not surprising that, in his 1978 article, Brodie should have defined 'the main war goal upon the beginning of a strategic nuclear exchange' as being 'to terminate it as quickly as possible and with the least amount of damage possible – on both sides'.

This phrase was taken up a year later by one of Brodie's keenest critics, Mr Colin Gray, who countered: 'Of course the best prospect of all for minimizing (prompt) damage lies in surrendering pre-emptively. If Bernard Brodie's advice were accepted, the West would be totally at the mercy of a Soviet Union, which viewed war in a rather more traditional perspective.'[1] By the time that article appeared, Bernard Brodie had died, but I can well imagine his sardonic response: 'Would the Soviet Union or anyone else view *anything* in a "traditional perspective" *after* a nuclear exchange?'

Colin Gray's question does however go to the heart of the problem that has led many people in the United States to reject the conventional wisdom of Brodie's position as no longer relevant in a new and harsher age. Today, there is widespread doubt that a posture of nuclear deterrence, however structured, will be enough to prevent a Soviet Union that accepts nuclear war as an instrument of policy and has built up a formidable nuclear arsenal from thinking the unthinkable, from not only initiating but fighting through a nuclear conflict in the expectation of victory, whether the United States wishes to do so or not. And if such a conflict is forced upon the United States, how can she

1. Colin Gray, 'Nuclear Strategy and the Case for a Theory of Victory', *International Security*, Vol. 4, No. 1 (Summer 1979), pp. 54–87.

conduct it effectively unless she also has a positive objective to guide her strategy, other than the mass annihilation of Soviet civilians? Should she not also regard nuclear war 'in a rather more traditional perspective'?

The controversy over this question will be familiar to every student of foreign policy and military affairs. But it is worthwhile to at least briefly review it, in an effort to clarify current perceptions on the matter.

Let me make it clear from the outset that on the fundamental issue of nuclear war-fighting, I side with Bernard Brodie rather than with his critics. As I understand it, the criticism of the deterrent posture arises from two linked sources. The first is the development of missile technology; the growing accuracy of guidance systems, the miniaturization of warheads, the increasing capability of target-acquisition processes, the whole astounding panoply of scientific development in which the United States has, to the best of my knowledge, taken the lead, with the Soviet Union, at great cost to its economy, keeping up as best it can. Incidentally, I find it curious that a scientific community that was so anguished over its moral responsibility for the development of the first crude nuclear bombs should have ceased to trouble itself over its continuing involvement with weapons-systems whose lethality and effectiveness make the weapons that destroyed Hiroshima and Nagasaki look like clumsy toys. Be that as it may, it is the continuous inventiveness of the scientific community, and I am afraid primarily the Western scientific community, that has made the pursuit of a stable nuclear balance, of mutually assured *deterrence* (which seems to me the correct explication of that much abused acronym MAD) seem to be the chase for an *ignis fatuus*, a will o' the wisp.

The second ground for criticizing the original concept of deterrence is the widespread belief that the Soviet Union does not share it, and never has shared it. The absence from Soviet textbooks of any distinction between a 'deterrent' and a 'war-fighting' capability; the reiterated statements that nuclear weapons cannot be exempted from the Clausewitzian imperative that military forces have no rationale save as instruments of State policy; the confident Marxist-Leninist predictions of socialism ultimately prevailing over the capitalist adversary whatever weapons-systems or policies he might adopt: does this not make it clear that American attempts to indoctrinate the Soviet Union in strategic concepts quite alien to their ideology and culture have failed? And this perception of the Soviet Union as a society prepared to coolly contemplate the prospect of fighting a nuclear war as an instrument of policy is enhanced by a worst-case analysis of its capacity to do so; its first-strike capacity against US land-based ICBMs; its much discussed civil defence programme to reduce its own casualties to an 'acceptable' level; and an historical experience of suffering which, according to some authorities, enables its leaders to contemplate without flinching the prospect of frightful damage and casualties running into scores of millions if it enables them to achieve their global objectives.

In dealing with those who hold this view of the Soviet Union I am conscious, only too often, that I am arguing with people whose attitude, like that of committed pacifists, is rooted in a visceral conviction beyond the reach of any discourse that I can command. It was a realization that was borne in on me by their deployment of two arguments in particular. The first was that since the Soviet Union had suffered some twenty million dead in the Second World War, they might equally contemplate further comparable losses in pursuit of a political objective sufficiently grandiose to warrant such a sacrifice. Now the United States has never suffered such losses and I hope that it never will. But it is a matter of historical record to what shifts and manoeuvres Stalin was reduced in his attempt to *avoid* having to fight that war; and speaking as a representative of a people who sustained nearly a million war dead between 1914 and 1918, I suggest that the record also shows that readiness to risk heavy losses in a further war does not necessarily increase in direct ratio with the sacrifices endured in the last.

The second argument that I encountered with even greater astonishment was that which maintained that Soviet civil defence measures provided an alarming indication of

Soviet intentions to launch a first strike. These arguments were all the more curious in that they were advanced almost simultaneously, and often from the same sources, as the very well-reasoned advocacy of a United States civil defence programme of an almost identical kind; a programme adopted by President Kennedy's Administration and abandoned only in face of the kind of popular and Congressional resistance with which the Soviet leadership does not have to contend. The difference between the development of civil defence in the two countries thus tells one rather more about their respective political structures than about their strategic intentions. Until recently indeed it would not have occurred to anyone outside a tiny group of strategic analysts in the United States that civil-defence preparations were anything except prudent and proper precautions for a remote but horrible finite possibility. Unfortunately their view is now more widely spread; and those of us in Europe who have been urging the advisability of taking even minimal precautions for civil defence now find ourselves accused by true believers on the left, as the Russians are accused by true believers on the right, of planning to precipitate the very catastrophe against which we seek to insure.

The debate about Soviet intentions has been conducted by people so far more expert than myself that I shall not seek to add to it beyond underlining and reinforcing Bernard Brodie's gently understated comment on those who see the build-up of Soviet forces over the past two decades as incontrovertible proof of their aggressive intentions:

Where the Committee on the Present Danger in one of its brochures speaks of 'the brutal momentum of the massive Soviet strategic arms build-up – a build-up without precedent in history', it is speaking of something which no student of the American strategic arms build-up in the sixties could possibly consider unprecedented.[1]

In fact one of the oldest 'lessons of history' is that the armaments of an adversary always seem 'brutal' and

1. Bernard Brodie, 'Development of Nuclear Strategy,' *International Security*, Vol. 2, No. 4 (Spring 1978), pp. 65–83.

threatening, adjectives that appear tendentious and absurd when applied to one's own.

The sad conclusion that I draw from this debate is that no amount of argument or evidence to the contrary will convince a large number of sincere, well-informed, highly intelligent and now very influential people that the Soviet Union is not an implacably aggressive power quite prepared to use nuclear weapons as an instrument of its policy. My own firmly-held belief, however, is that the leadership of the Soviet Union, and any successors they may have within the immediately foreseeable future, are cautious and rather apprehensive men, increasingly worried about their almost insoluble internal problems, increasingly aware of their isolation in a world in which the growth of Marxian socialism does little to enhance their political power, deeply torn between gratification at the problems which beset the capitalist world economy and alarm at the difficulties which those problems are creating within their own empire; above all, conscious of the inadequacy of the simplistic doctrines of Marxism-Leninism, on which they were nurtured, to explain a world far more complex and diverse than either Marx or Lenin ever conceived. Their *staatspolitik*, that complex web of interests, perceptions and ideals which Clausewitz believed should determine the use of military power, thus gives them no clearer guidance as to how to use their armed forces than ours gives to us.

The evidence for this view of Soviet intentions seems to me at least as conclusive as that for the beliefs of, for example, the Committee on the Present Danger, who will no doubt consider me to be as visceral, emotive and irrational in my beliefs as I have found all too many of their publications. I would only say, in defence of my own views, first that they take rather more account of the complexities of the historic, political, and economic problems of the Soviet Union than do theirs; and secondly, for what it is worth, that they correspond more closely with those held by most of the Europeans among whom I move than do those of the Committee on the Present Danger. Naturally in Europe as elsewhere there is a diversity of views, and there can be few more enthusiastic supporters of Mr Paul Nitze than my own Prime Minister. Nonetheless, I have found in Europe a far more relaxed attitude towards the Russians than I have ever encountered in the United States; because, paradoxically, we are not more frightened of them than are Americans, but rather less. I think we find it easier to see them as real people, with real, and alarming, problems of their own: people of whom we must be constantly wary and whose military power and propensity to use it when they perceive they can safely do so is certainly formidable; but with whom it is possible to do business, in every sense of the word, and certainly not as people who have any interest in, or intention of, deliberately unleashing a nuclear war as an instrument of policy.

And here again I should like to underline, if possible with even greater emphasis, what Bernard Brodie had to say about the Soviet dedication to Clausewitz's theory of the relationship of war to policy, if only as an act of personal homage to both Brodie and Clausewitz. Clausewitz was a subtle, profound and versatile thinker, and his teaching about the relationship between war and policy was only one of the many insights he provided into the whole phenomenon of war. 'War', he wrote, 'is only a branch of political activity; it is in no sense autonomous . . . [It] cannot be divorced from political life – and whenever this occurs in our thinking about war, the many links that connect the two elements are destroyed, and we are left with something that is pointless and devoid of sense.'[1]

In so far as the Russians believe this and hammer it into the heads of successive generations of soldiers and politicians, we should admire and imitate them. When they castigate us for ignoring it and for discussing nuclear war, as we almost invariably do, *in vacuo*, they are absolutely right, and we should be grateful for their criticism. When I read the flood of scenarios in strategic journals about first-strike capabilities, counterforce or countervailing strategies, flexible response, escalation dominance and the rest of the

1. Carl von Klausewitz, *On War* (Princeton University Press, 1976), Book VIII, Chapter 6B, 'War is an Instrument of Policy'.

postulates of nuclear theology, I ask myself in bewilderment: this war they are describing, *what is it about?* The defence of Western Europe? Access to the Gulf? The protection of Japan? If so, why is this goal not mentioned, and why is the strategy not related to the progress of the conflict in these regions? But if it is not related to this kind of specific object, what are we talking about? Has not the bulk of American thinking been exactly what Clausewitz described – something that, because it is divorced from any political context, is 'pointless and devoid of sense'?

I do not deny that Soviet theoreticians attempt to fit nuclear weapons into their Clausewitzean framework, and maintain that, should nuclear war occur, nuclear weapons should be used in order to forward the overall goals of policy and ensure a victory for the armed forces of the Soviet Union. But one only has to state the opposite of this doctrine to accept that it is in theory unexceptionable, and that it would be difficult for them to say anything else. The ideological and bureaucratic framework within which this Soviet teaching has evolved has been convincingly described in recent articles by such experts as Ambassador Raymond Garthoff and Mr Benjamin Lambeth,[1] and I find convincing the formulation propounded by the latter:

[The Russians] approach their strategic planning with the thoroughly traditional conviction that despite the revolutionary advances in destructive power brought about by modern weapons and delivery systems, the threat of nuclear war persists as a fundamental feature of the international system and obliges the Soviet Union to take every practical measure to prepare for its eventuality . . . They appear persuaded that in the nuclear age no less than before, the most reliable way to prevent war is to maintain the appropriate wherewithal to fight and win it should it occur.

Logical as this doctrine may appear, and no doubt necessary for the maintenance both of ideological consis-

1. Raymond L. Garthoff, 'Mutual Deterrence and Strategic Arms Limitation in Soviet Policy', *International Security*, Vol. 3, No. 1 (Summer 1978), pp. 112–147; and Benjamin Lambeth, 'The Political Potential of Soviet Equivalence', *International Security*, Vol. 4, No. 2 (Fall 1979), pp. 22–39.

tency and of military morale in the Soviet Union, the West's response, it seems to me, should *not* be to imitate it but to make it clear to the Russians, within their own Clausewitzean framework, that it simply will not work: that there is no way in which the use of strategic nuclear weapons could be a rational instrument of State policy, for them or for anyone else.

This view commands a satisfyingly wide consensus – or did until recently. Mr Paul Nitze himself, in his famous plea for a maximalist US defence posture, emphasized that the object of the measures he proposed 'would not be to give the United States a war-fighting capability: it would be to deny to the Soviet Union the possibility of a successful war-fighting capability', and another leading thinker of the maximalist school, Mr Colin Gray, also accepts that 'one of the essential tasks of the American defence community is to help ensure that in moments of acute crisis the Soviet general staff cannot brief the Politburo with a plausible theory of military victory'.[2] But Mr Gray believes that another task of the defence community is to brief the White House with a plausible theory of military victory, and that is surely a very different matter.

Mr Gray is a Clausewitzean and believes that US strategy should be geared to a positive political object. 'Washington', he suggests, 'should identify war aims that in the last resort would contemplate the destruction of Soviet political authority and the emergence of a post-war world order compatible with Western values.'[3] For this it would be necessary to destroy, not the peoples of the Soviet Union in genocidal attacks on cities, but the apparatus of the Soviet State. The principal assets of the latter he identifies as 'the political control structure of the highly centralized Communist Party of the Soviet Union and government bureau-

1. Paul Nitze, 'Deterring our Deterrent', *Foreign Policy*, Number 25 (Winter 1976–7).

2. Colin Gray, 'Nuclear Strategy: the Case for a Theory of Victory', *International Security*, Vol. 4, No. 1 (Summer 1979), pp. 54–87.

3. Colin Gray and Keith Payne, 'Victory is Possible', *Foreign Policy*, Number 39 (Summer 1980).

cracy; the transmission belts of communication from the centre to the regions; the instruments of central official coercion (the KGB and armed forces); and the reputation of the Soviet state in the eyes of its citizens . . . The entire Soviet political and economic system', he writes, 'is critically dependent upon central direction from Moscow. If the brain of the Soviet system were destroyed, degraded, or at minimum isolated . . . what happens to the cohesion, or pace of recovery, of the whole?"[1]

Now about this scenario there are several things to be said, and I am only sorry that Bernard Brodie is not still around to say them. The first problem is one that Mr Gray quite frankly admits himself. 'Is it sensible', he asks, 'to destroy the government of the enemy, thus eliminating the option of negotiating an end to the war?'[2] The answer is no, it is not; unless we believe that out of the midst of this holocaust an alternative organized government would somehow emerge, capable, in spite of the destruction of all internal communications networks, of taking over the affairs of State. The alternative is, presumably, the conquest, occupation, and the re-education of the Soviet peoples in 'Western values' – an interesting but ambitious project which might be said to require further study.

Secondly, it is quite unrealistic to assume that such strikes against centres of government and communications could be carried out without massive casualties, numbering scores of millions, among the peoples we would be attempting to 'liberate'. And if historical experience is any guide at all, such sufferings, inflicted by an alien power, serve only to strengthen social cohesion and make support for the regime, however unpopular it might be, a question literally of physical survival. We now know that the strategic bombardment of Germany only intensified the control exercised by the Nazi regime over that unhappy nation. The sufferings inflicted on the Russian peoples during the Second World War – those twenty million casualties which, we are asked to believe, only whetted their appetite for starting a Third – not

1. Gray, 'Nuclear Strategy', *loc. cit.*
2. Gray, 'Victory is Possible', *loc. cit.*

only strengthened Stalin's tyranny; it went far to legitimize it. The prospect of any regime in the least compatible with what Mr Gray calls 'Western values' emerging from a blood-bath on a yet more horrific scale is, to put it mildly, pretty remote.

Finally, what would be going on here while the strategic strike forces of the United States were conducting their carefully calibrated and controlled nuclear war? I shall leave out of account the problems of command and control, of maintaining fine-tuning and selective targeting under the kind of nuclear retaliation that is to be expected during such an attack. This is the famous 'C^{3}I factor' (Command, Control, Communication, Intelligence) addressed in President Carter's Directive No. 59 of August 1980, and some of the United States' finest technologists are no doubt working on the problem. Even if they do come up with plausible solutions, however, nobody can possibly tell whether in practice they will work; and for strategic planners to prepare to fight a nuclear war on the firm assumption that they would work would be criminally irresponsible. Nor do I address the question, more interesting to the allies than perhaps it is to the superpowers, of what would be happening in Western Europe during such an exchange. Dr Kissinger, in a much reported speech delivered in Brussels in September 1979, informed his audience that 'the secret dream of every European was . . . if there had to be a nuclear war, to have it conducted over their heads by the strategic forces of the United States and the Soviet Union'.[1] In fact I have yet to meet an intelligent European who thinks that anything of the kind would be possible, or that Western Europe would under any circumstances be omitted from the Soviet targeting plan. Few of us believe that there would be much left of our highly urbanized, economically tightly integrated and desperately vulnerable societies after even the most controlled and limited strategic nuclear exchange.

But it is the implications for the United States itself that I want to consider. Mr Gray and his colleagues admit that

1. *Survival*, November–December 1979, p. 266.

there is a problem here, but they assert that 'strategists can claim that an intelligent United States offensive strategy, wedded to homeland defences, should reduce US casualties to approximately 20 million, which should render US strategic threats more credible'.[1] Well, perhaps they can claim it, the same way that Glendower could claim, in Shakespeare's *Henry IV*, that he could 'call spirits from out the vasty deep'; they should be asked in return though, 'but will they come when you do call for them?' How valid is such a claim – especially since a Soviet leadership in its death-throes would have no possible incentive, even if it had the C³I capability, to limit the damage to 20 million or to any other figure?

But even if it *is* valid, and granted that 20 million is a preferable figure to 180 million, it is not clear to me that Mr Gray has thought through all the implications of his suggestion. Those twenty million *immediate* casualties – and we leave out those dying later from residual radiation – are only the visible tip of an iceberg of destruction and suffering of literally incalculable size. Most readers will be familiar with the very careful and sober report by the Congressional Office of Technology Assessment on 'The Effects of Nuclear War',[2] which came to the conclusion that

The effects of nuclear war that cannot be calculated are at least as important as those for which calculations are attempted. Moreover even these limited calculations are subject to very large uncertainties . . . This is particularly true for indirect effects such as deaths resulting from injuries and the unavailability of medical care, or for economic damage resulting from disruption and disorganization rather than direct destruction.

As for a small or 'limited' attack, the impact of this, points out the Report, would be 'enormous . . . [and] the uncertainties are such that no government could predict with any confidence what the results . . . would be, even if

1. Gray and Payne, *loc. cit.*
2. U.S. Congress, Office of Technology Assessment, 'The Effects of Nuclear War', 1979.

there was no further escalation'. Certainly the situation in which the survivors of a nuclear attack would find themselves would be unprecedented.

Natural resources would be destroyed; surviving equipment would be designed to use materials and skills that might no longer exist; and indeed some regions might be almost uninhabitable. Furthermore, pre-war patterns of behavior would surely change, though in unpredictable ways.

As for the outcome of the conflict in which these sufferings were incurred, I can only quote from a memorandum that Bernard Brodie wrote for Rand Corporation over twenty years ago but which has lost none of its relevance.[1]

Whether the survivors be many or few, in the midst of a land scarred and ruined beyond all present comprehension, they should not be expected to show much concern for the further pursuit of political-military objectives.

Under such circumstances, the prime concern of everyone, American, Russian, European – to say nothing of the rest of the world, which is always left out of these scenarios – would be simply to survive, and in an unimaginably hostile environment. As to what would become of 'Western values' in such a world, your guess is as good as mine. It is my own belief that the political, cultural and ideological distinctions that separate the West from the Soviet Union today would be seen, in comparison with the literally inconceivable contrasts between *any* pre-atomic and *any* post-atomic society, as almost insignificant. Indeed I am afraid that the United States would probably emerge from a nuclear war with a regime which, in its inescapable authoritarianism, looked much more like that which governs the Soviet Union today than that of the Soviet Union would in any way resemble the government of the United States; and this would almost certainly be the case in Western Europe.

Admittedly, this is all guesswork. But what is absolutely clear is that to engage in nuclear war, to attempt to use

1. 'Implications of Nuclear Weapons on Total War'. Rand Memorandum, July 1957, p. 1118.

strategic nuclear weapons for 'war-fighting' would be to enter the realm of the unknown and the unknowable, and what little we do know about it is appalling. Those who believe otherwise, whether they do so, like the Soviet writers, because of the constraints imposed by their ideology and cultural traditions, or, as do some Americans, out of technological *hubris*, are likely to be proved equally and dreadfully wrong; as wrong as those European strategists who in 1914 promised their political masters decisive victory before Christmas.

I take issue with Mr Colin Gray in particular not because I do not admire his work, but simply because he has had the courage to make explicit certain views that are now circulating widely in some circles in the United States and which, unless publicly and firmly countered, might become influential, with catastrophic consequences. I also believe that if a thinker as intelligent as Mr Gray is unable to provide nuclear strategy with a positive political object, no one else is likely to succeed any better. But this does not mean that Clausewitz's theory has to be abandoned, and that nuclear weapons can serve no political purpose. Clausewitz accepted that strategy might have a *negative* object and pointed out that, historically, this had more often than not been the case. This negative object he defined as being to make clear to the other side 'the improbability of victory ... [and] its unacceptable cost';' in a word, deterrence; or, to reiterate Mr Gray's own admirable words, to 'ensure that in moments of acute crisis the Soviet general staff cannot brief the Politburo with a plausible theory of military victory'.

This takes us back to where we began, to Bernard Brodie's warning that: 'The first and most vital step in any American security program ... is to take measures to guarantee to ourselves in case of attack the possibility of retaliation in kind.' In principle nothing has changed since then, even though in practice the problem has become enormously more difficult. In particular, Bernard's phrase 'in kind' has acquired a significance that he could not possibly have

---

1. Clausewitz, *op. cit.*, Book I, Chapter 2, 'Purpose and Means in War'.

anticipated. With the diversification of nuclear delivery systems, deterrence becomes an ever more complex business; and prudent account has to be taken of the contingency that deterrence might fail, so as to provide feasible alternatives between holocaust and surrender. But the object of such 'intra-war deterrence' would still be, as Mr Brodie put it, 'to terminate the strategic exchange as quickly as possible and with the least amount of damage possible – on both sides', in the interests not just of the United States but of mankind as a whole. Can one doubt that in 1914 rational European statesmen would have cut their losses and made peace at the end of the year if they had not been driven on by popular pressures and delusive expectations of victory? Or that if they had done so, the world would be a rather better place than it is today?

What about Bernard Brodie's other pronouncement, that 'thus far the chief purpose of our military establishment has been to win wars. From now on its chief purpose must be to avert them'; does this remain valid? Well yes, it does; but with respect to Bernard's shade, there is nothing new about this. It has always been the role of military establishments in peacetime to dissuade their opponents from using force as an instrument of policy – even, if needs be, of *defensive* policy – by making it clear that any such action on their part would be counter-productive; either because they would *lose* in such a war, or because they could gain victory only at an unacceptably high cost. That still seems to me to be true. And it also seems to me to be true that such a deterrent posture lacks conviction if one does not have the evident capacity to fight such a war – in particular, to defend the territory which our opponent may wish to occupy.

This is where a 'war-fighting capability' comes in; a capability, not to fight through a war to an impossible, mutually destructive 'victory' – and let us remember Clausewitz's epigram 'in strategy there is no such thing as victory' – but to set on victory for our opponent a price that he cannot possibly afford to pay. And for this we must have the evident will and readiness to defend ourselves and one another: something that can only be made clear by the presence or availability of armed forces capable of fighting for territory; adequately armed, adequately trained, adequately supported and, in our market economies, adequately *paid*.

This is the war-fighting capability that acts as the true deterrent to aggression, and the only one that is convertible into political influence. There is as little reason to suppose that Soviet nuclear superiority will give them political advantages in the 1980s as that American nuclear superiority lent weight to the foreign policy of the United States in the 1960s. The neighbours of the Soviet Union are primarily impressed by the war-fighting capacity of her *conventional* forces, and the rest of the world by her growing capacity to project that force beyond her frontiers. Within Europe, the 'theatre nuclear balance' concerns only a tiny group of specialists. The presence and fighting capability of the United States Army and Air Forces are seen as the real, and highly effective, deterrent against Soviet attack. I have expressed elsewhere my regret that the British Government should have decided to spend five billion pounds out of our very restricted defence budget on a strategic nuclear strike force, which can only be at the expense of the conventional forces we can contribute to the Alliance. And however much the present administration of the United States may feel it necessary to spend on new strategic nuclear weapons systems to match or overmatch those of the Soviet Union, the effect on America's influence within the international community is likely to be negligible if it is not matched by a comparable and evident capability to defend American interests on the oceans and on the ground with forces capable of *fighting*.

For the best part of a century the peoples of industrial societies have been applying technological expertise and industrial power, initially to assist but increasingly to replace the traditional military skills and virtues on which they formerly relied for the protection of their political integrity. As a result they have been able to attain their objects in war only at the cost of enormous and increasingly disproportionate destruction. With the advent of nuclear weapons, the disproportion becomes insensate. It is politically so much easier, so much less of a social strain, to produce nuclear missiles rather than trained, effective military manpower and to believe that a valid trade-off has somehow been made between the two. It has not. And the more deeply we become committed to this belief, on both sides of the Atlantic, the greater will be the danger that we are trying to avoid: on the one hand, the impossibility of defending the specific areas and interests that are seriously threatened by a potential adversary, and, on the other, the possibility that, in a lethal mixture of *hubris* and despair, we might one day feel ourselves compelled to initiate a nuclear war. Such a war might or might not achieve its object; but I doubt whether the survivors on either side would very greatly care.

War in the Making and Unmaking of Europe

IT is not fashionable today to suggest that War ever has, or ever could serve, any constructive purpose. To put forward any such view is to risk being branded as a militarist, if not a Fascist. The Heraclitean doctrine that conflict is the creator of all things went out with the Great War, popular as it had been even in Britain before 1914. The thesis of the great German economic historian, Werner Sombart, that war had furthered the cause of human progress by facilitating the process of capital accumulation, expounded in his study *Krieg und Kapitalismus*, evoked a passionate refutation from the American economic historian J. U. Nef, who argued in his book *War and Human Progress* that we would have developed much faster if mankind had been able to avoid war. Not everyone would maintain that the development of capitalist society was necessarily a good thing; but a very convincing thesis could be argued that the cause even of socialism has been most powerfully, if indirectly, furthered by the great wars of the twentieth century. But whether one likes it or not, war has played for better or worse a fundamental part in the whole process of historical change; and whether one regards it as being for better or for worse depends on the kind of alternative possibilities, inherently unverifiable, that one cares to substitute for the historical record.

Whether Europe would have been a better place without the wars which make up such a large part of her history is, as a question, rather beside the point. The question is whether, without war, Europe would have come into existence as a recognizable entity at all. During the half-millennium from the fifth until the tenth centuries, what we have come to know as 'Europe' was emerging from a process of almost uninterrupted conflict. And it was during this process that people became gradually aware of a common culture connecting them, legitimizing or creating their values, which they were defending against alien cultures and which it was their wish, even their duty, to extend. They did not call this common culture 'Europe'. They called it 'Christendom'; and it was this concept that provided purpose and unity. It was the Holiness that was the important thing about the Holy Roman Empire. It was the charisma provided by the Church that enabled Charlemagne and his successors to exercise a primacy, however partial, however short-lived, over the other martial families warring for local dominance.

And the importance of Christendom, at least in secular terms, was that it was a warrior society. Ecclesiastical organization and doctrine was subordinated to the needs of a warrior ruling class (and those gentle souls who are today shocked by the appearance of the Christian Church keeping itself up to date by donning the uniform of the freedom fighter tend to forget the many long centuries during which the Church sanctified and often inspired the activities of equally ruthless military orders on the Marches of Europe). Christendom was linked, from Ireland to Poland, by an overlapping pattern of ecclesiastical and military organization, so that a priest or a knight could travel the length and breadth of the continent and feel himself a member of a single community with a common language and a common code of conduct. It was a very eclectic community indeed. Forged out of the tumultous conflicts of tribes moving successively out of Asia and settling in the West because they could go no further, it met, battled with, and ultimately absorbed successive threats to its stability, notably the Norsemen from Scandinavia and the Magyars from the East. A third, the Mongols disappeared as suddenly as they came. But the strongest of these outside pressures remained unabated throughout the Middle Ages, localized but still formidable from the sixteenth until the eighteenth centuries, apparently moribund in the nineteenth century but to revive, amazingly, towards the end of the twentieth: the Moslems, the adherents of a religion even more passionate and no less bellicose than Christianity. It was this external threat that defined both the frontiers and the role of Christendom, created a sense of unity and purpose, played a central part in cultural perceptions, provided an adversary against whom in moments of real crisis all Christians felt the need, even as late as the end of the seventeenth century, to unite. It was perhaps the Siege of Vienna in 1684 that witnessed the last appearance of Christendom as a self-conscious society. Thirty years later, at the Treaty of Utrecht, the European world consisted simply of 'Powers'; potentates who, whatever magnificent titles they might bear at the hands of the Holy Roman Empire, thought of themselves and comported themselves as absolute monarchs – absolute from any obligations, that is, to any authority other than their own. Into this entirely secular society of States even the old adversary, the Ottoman Empire, was, two centuries later, to be absorbed.

War thus contributed to the creation of European society in two ways. In the first place it defined its boundaries. In the South, Europe was that region successfully defended against, or reclaimed from, the Moslem world. It included Spain, where the *reconquista* could not be regarded as complete until the final expulsion of the Moors at the end of the fifteenth century. Eventually it included the Balkan peninsula, which was finally re-absorbed into Europe only at the beginning of the twentieth, as a result of the Balkan Wars. In the East, the frontiers of Europe, or rather of Christendom, were extended, crushing pagan Slavs and Wends, until they made contact with that other branch of the Christian family, almost as remote and fabled as that of Prester John in Africa, which traced its descent from Rome via Byzantium. In the sixteenth century the Turkish invasion tore South-East Europe away from Christendom; from the Battle of Mohacs until the Peace of Carlowitz the lands of the Crown of St Stephen were European *irredenta* under Turkish control, and fighting the Turks along these Marches of Europe, under the increasingly skilful leadership of the Habsburgs, became a way of life which moulded Balkan society until our own era. It is easy to forget that for the best part of a thousand years Europe saw itself as a society under siege; a thousand years during which its distinctive social, economic and political structure became established.

This structure was largely established by, and for the convenience of, the military elites who bore the burden of the fighting, and who developed a life style built round the activity of fighting. When they were not fighting the barbarians or the Moslems they were fighting one another, and the political and legal structure of Europe gradually emerged out of their continual contests over honour and inheritance. One of the most significant stages in the development of this order lay in the distinction, gradually made between the ninth and the twelfth centuries, as to who did and who did not have the right to make war. Those who rightly deplore the institutionalization of war, the legitima-tion of violence in the hands of political authorities, seldom consider the alternative; the use of violence as an instrument of daily intercourse in the hands of anyone strong enough to use it. The robber baron was a very familiar figure in medieval Europe, as was the unemployed knight living off the country in the intervals of more respectable forms of employment. The slow consolidation of power in the hands of a limited number of princes, the elimination of 'private war' and the fixing of a great conceptual barrier – in which the Church played a major part – between authorities who had a right to make war and those who did not, was an essential step towards the creation of an orderly society. Only in such an order could there occur those developments in trade, manufacture and cultivation that brought into being a civilization which would one day condemn as backward and barbaric the military ancestors who had made its activities possible.

It was between the beginning of the sixteenth and the end of the eighteenth centuries that we discern that great transformation in the political consciousness of Europe whereby princes ceased to be regarded as the owners of properties and became instead the heads, possibly indeed the servants, of states. The age of Charles V gave way to that of Frederick the Great. The State was a distinctively

European concept; and those who, from Rousseau onwards, have deplored its existence and seen in it the root of all slavery and all war have seldom considered what the alternative was; a welter of overlapping jurisdictions, conflicting claims on the loyalty and the purse of the common man enforced by whoever had the immediate power to do so. The State created a common focus of loyalty and of authority, an authority with obligations as well as rights; and once such a focus had been established, the possibility was open for those subject to that authority to take possession of it, and govern themselves. Government has to be established before self-government becomes possible; states before there can be nation-states.

Students of political theory trace the origins of the State to Greek theory and practice, and to the influence of Roman Law, and they are of course right to do so. But if one examines the manner in which European states actually emerged between the sixteenth and the eighteenth centuries, one does not find it to be the result of scholarly perusal, by Princes and their advisers, of the texts of Aristotle, or Justinian, or Marsiglio of Padua. Where such ideas were useful to the establishment of the power of the Prince – and the ideas of the Roman lawyers were very useful indeed – they were of course adopted; but the search, the requirement, for power came first; and that power was necessitated above all by conflict. The experience of the Thirty Years War made it very clear what happened to princes, and indeed to communities, who did not have the capacity to defend their territories. Such defence called for troops, regularly and adequately paid, and for expensive fortifications. That required an effective fiscal system. But since the best conceivable fiscal system is of little value in an impoverished and starving community, a further requirement was a flourishing trading, agricultural and industrial society whose increment could be regularly creamed off by the Prince and his officials. The interesting question, whether the wealth, and in consequence the civilization, of Europe would have increased more rapidly or less if it had not been deliberately fostered by State or State-sponsored authorities who consciously regarded wealth as their most effective weapon in their continual mutual conflicts, is one that I must leave to authorities of the eminence of Nef and Sombart to debate. One can only record that between about 1650 and about 1750 the increase in wealth, especially through trade, the growth of military and especially naval strength, and the consolidation of State power internally and externally were generally considered throughout Europe as interdependent and essential. Rousseau and his successors were conceptually correct in arguing that, but for states, there would be no wars – so long as one accepts the tautological definition of 'war' as armed conflict between states. But it is at least arguable that without states there would have been no wealth either. It was of course the dream of the *philosophes* that when the producers of wealth assumed control of the State they would no longer have their increment creamed off to fight wars. But we know only too well what happened when, a century or so later, they actually did.

The European states system, adolescent since the Peace of Westphalia in 1648, came of age with the treaty of Utrecht in 1713 – or, rather, the whole complex of Treaties embracing Utrecht, Rastadt and, a few years later, Passarowitz and Nystad. Traditional criteria of property-rights or religious allegiance, if they survived at all, did so only as the thinnest of veneers on a structure of naked power, consciously held together by a concept of 'balance'. And power meant military power. Other forms of power were recognized and admired; the mercantile wealth of England, for example, or the diplomatic and cultural prestige of Venice; but unless this could be transformed if necessary into military or naval power, as the wealth of England under pressure could be but the prestige of Venice could not, it did not qualify its possessor for membership of a club whose sole criterion for admission, and rating once admitted, was military effectiveness. Military performance during the quarter-century of fighting which preceded the settlements, and that alone, determined the place of states in the new order. France and the House of Austria had maintained their primacy. Spain, rejuvenated by

Bourbon blood, struggled gamely to keep up her subscription, but by mid-century had accepted subordinate rank, as had Sweden, the Netherlands and that old enemy the Ottoman Empire, which was now reduced by the armies of Prinz Eugen almost to the status of a comic pantomime demon. Prussia had, through her military contributions and nothing else, made herself a considerable power in the German sub-system, and by the same means was shortly to become a formidable one on a continental scale. England, a peripheral, virtually a negligible quantity throughout the seventeenth century, now sat, thanks to the achievements of Marl-borough's armies, at the top table; and so did a new and still unknown figure: Russia.

Was Russia a European Power? Is she a European Power now? It is a question that has puzzled everyone, not least the Russians themselves, ever since Peter the Great fought his way into the European club at the beginning of the eighteenth century. In terms of the simple criteria that then applied there was no doubt about it. The Russians had a large and effective army. They also had a fleet. No question in the Baltic or in Eastern Europe could be settled without taking them into account; and their participation in the Baltic and German sub-systems made them part of the European balance as a whole, a possible adversary or a useful ally to be courted and consulted. But she was a Power, as Peter the Great realized, only because and to the extent that she was able to participate in the life of Europe at a very much deeper level. He, indeed, was perhaps the first man to see the relationship between what we would now call 'development' and state power; who realized that his society could only compete in the world, become an actor rather than the victim of more powerful neighbours, if it were radically transformed economically and socially. To com-pete with 'the West', the West had to be copied. Russian ships could dominate the Baltic (thus making it safe for Russian trade, which in its turn would pay for the ships) only if Western ship-building techniques were learned from the English and the Dutch and the French. Russian armies could hold their own against their Polish, Swedish and

German neighbours only if they learned their trade from those neighbours. So foreigners had to be invited to Russia and given privileged treatment, not just, as in the past, to trade, but to teach the natives the secrets of their manufactories and their technological skills. To become part of the European system rather than the victim of it, to acquire the military and naval strength and skill to be accepted as a partner, it was necessary to absorb European culture, of which European technology and military power was only one element. The same lesson was to be learned a little later by the Turks; by the Chinese and Japanese; and gradually, reluctantly, by the entire world.

There was a second way in which Russia was to be a prototype for the developing world. The process of 'Europeanization', or 'development', set up enormous strains within her society. The great cultural division which found expression in the conflict between 'westernizers' and 'Pan-Slavs', between the civilization of St Petersburg and that of Moscow, was not only to determine the subsequent course of Russian history, it was to provide a pattern for those far broader problems which we see in all developing societies in our own day; not least the most remarkable phenomenon of our own times, to which I have already alluded; the revival of a militantly anti-Western Moslem civilization. The cry so often on the lips of Third-World leaders today, "We want your technology but not your culture", expresses the sentiments of many Russians for the past three hundred years, long before they were absorbed into the doctrine and practice of Lenin, Stalin and their successors.

Nevertheless, a westernized elite developed in Russia that looked to Europe for its models, to Paris or London or Rome or Berlin; a Europeanized aristocracy, and as time went on a gentry and a bourgeoisie as well, often more conscious of their cultural affinity with similar groups in the West than with their compatriots; some of them unhappy about this and trying dramatically to make amends by their political activities; but always an upper crust on the surface of their society, eventually to be broken up and destroyed in the gigantic upsurge of the Revolution. But in this respect the

Russian experience did not simply foreshadow the experience of the Third World, with its unhappy and insecure Europeanized elites. It embodied in exaggerated form a problem which affected Europe itself, and indeed to some extent still does.

For within the states of Europe, to a greater or lesser extent, the common values which we have been discussing, the perceptions of mutual interest and social bonds, were also confined to elites. These elites, especially during the nineteenth century, began to penetrate more deeply into their native societies, to draw in a wider spectrum of social classes. The thinly spread network of knights and clerics who held Christendom together in the Middle Ages expanded to include merchants, lawyers, bureaucrats, men of letters and an increasingly numerous leisured class with the means and the time to travel, learn languages and become conscious of the culture which bound them together. But they remained within their own communities a small minority, even if a minority which still retained unchallenged social control. The great mass of the inhabitants of Europe would not have thought of themselves as being 'European'. In France, until an astonishingly late date, they did not even consider themselves to be Frenchmen. Their *pays* was strictly regional, confined to the province, the district, the village, even, in which they lived. Foreigners began over the hill. And what was true of France must have been true of the rest of Europe. Language may have provided a precarious bond, though given the wide range of dialect it would be dangerous to generalize even about this. But until the end of the nineteenth century, perhaps indeed very much later, it would be reasonable to conjecture that the inhabitants of different regions of Europe would have regarded themselves as having very little in common, and a great deal to divide them. And not the least of the divisive factors would have been, ironically, that which had once provided a tenuous bond of unity; the Christian religion, which from the sixteenth century had fulfilled the grim promise of its founder, to bring not peace, but a sword.

The first process which drew men out from their regional *pays* and compelled them to be conscious of belonging to a wider community was, surely, compulsory military service. Such compulsion to service in a purely local militia for the defence of one's own immediate locality was as old as European society itself. But had young men ever been drawn *away* from that community by the hundreds of thousands, and embodied in an organization serving a new, vast entity of whose existence they had previously been unaware (if indeed it existed at all) before 1789 – or, to be more accurate, 1794? By the *Loi Jourdan* and subsequent conscription ordinances, the men of Normandy, Languedoc, Picardy, Franche-Comté, Auvergne, Limousin, Provence, were hauled away and turned into *Frenchmen*. It was a process so disagreeable that one province, Brittany, fought a bitter civil war to avoid it. Even in the mid-nineteenth century one of the chief problems the French Army had with its recruits was dealing with the almost pathological phenomenon of *nostalgie*: home sickness. And not only were they turned into Frenchmen, losing their patois and learning to speak, read, and sometimes even write a common language: they were sent *abroad*. With the inhabitants of the countries which they invaded at the behest of Napoleon – peoples whom it would still be premature to call Spaniards or Italians or Germans or Russians, peoples who, if they thought of themselves as anything, would have done so as Castilians or Basques or Catalans, or Florentines or Savoyards or Neapolitans, or Saxons or Hessians or Bavarians, but doubtfully even that – with these peoples the individual soldier in the Napoleonic armies may have been inclined to feel the sympathy of one peasant for another. But he came among them as one of an alien group, the more tightly integrated as a result of that alienness. Hostility was, as sociologists would put it, 'structured into the situation'. Torn away from their own communities, they created new ones in their military units, whose colours and eagles, emblazoned with national symbolism, took the place of their village steeples as a symbol of home. As for the peoples whom they came among, their reaction is well known. If these invaders, whose requisitions made it impossible to regard them as anything but enemies, were Frenchmen, and seemed to owe much of their power to their consciousness of the fact, what were they themselves? Were they not themselves members of a comparable Nation? And if they were not, would it not be their fate to be subordinated, perhaps absorbed, by those who were?

The Napoleonic Wars thus played a part both in the making and the unmaking of Europe. On the one hand they brought virtually the whole of Europe, however briefly and incompletely, under the control of a single political authority; and in the few years at his disposal, Napoleon did an amazing amount towards the creation of a single European administrative, judicial and even economic system. Much of what we in England regard as being so distinctively 'European' dates from that time: the system of calculation of distance and measures, the police, the legal system, the whole structure of the *Code Napoléon*. And the fact that Britain was *not* conquered emphasized, even if it did not entirely create, the sense of separateness which the British felt from their continental neighbours; a sense which went deeper than the xenophobia which characterized all the communities in Europe vis-à-vis one another. This sense of difference was compounded by the economic growth which was beginning to make Britain a distinctly richer society than her neighbours, and by the development of those overseas connections which during the nineteenth century were, briefly, to turn Britain away from Europe altogether. But the Napoleonic Wars had given the inhabitants of Continental Europe a common traumatic experience which the British had not shared. The Second World War, as we shall see, was to do the same. In 1815 the rueful definition which became current after 1945 might have already been applied: 'A European is someone whose country has been occupied by foreigners.'

But at the same time, those wars brought about the far stronger and no less enduring development of centrifugal nationalism which the statesmen at Vienna in 1814 saw, far more than the threat of a revived France, as the real danger to the balanced European system of states which had come of age a hundred years earlier at Utrecht and which they now worked so self-consciously to restore. What Metternich and his colleagues feared was the threat it posed, not so much to the international system as such, but to the political structures of which it was composed and the social framework which supported them. It is doubtful whether even they realized how intensely *divisive* the force of nationalism would become, and what effect this would have upon the structure of European society. For the French experience was, inevitably, infectious. Even before the events of 1870, armies were being seen as the embodiment, sometimes the sole embodiment, of the nation. *'In dein Lager ist Österreich'*, in thy camp is Austria, the Viennese poet Grillpartzer apostrophized Marshal Radetsky. In the second half of the century this experience became intensive and universal, as conscription became intensive and universal. Peasant boys were hauled from remote mountain villages, from the Urals to the Pyrenees, made to pledge allegiance to a flag, taught to sing patriotic songs glorifying their national past and put through a process of training designed at least as much to mould their minds and personalities as to teach them how to handle their weapons. And their minds and personalities were not moulded as Europeans. They were moulded as Germans, Russians, Frenchmen, Italians, Britons or Austrians (though this last took some doing) and prepared for the probable eventuality of having to fight Britons, Germans, Austrians, Frenchmen or Russians; and to look forward to the prospect with a certain degree of relish. State power, in the intensely competive atmosphere of the late nineteenth century, was seen more than ever as military power; but military power now involved the effective indoctrination of the entire population in a religion of nationalism.

This may not explain why war came in 1914, but it does explain why it took the form it did; why it could not be simply another brief, even if bloody conflict to readjust the balance of the European system. And the part which that war played in the unmaking of Europe need hardly be stressed. National hatreds became fanatical; all concepts of cultural community across national borders became stigmatized as at best unpatriotic, at worst treasonable. Our own royal family, a branch of the international cousinage which had played so honourable a part in holding Europe together, had to forswear its humdrum, decent German lineage and create a new name and identity for itself acceptable to the readers of the Northcliffe press. The world of easy international literature and learning, wherein anyone who considered himself reasonably cultivated could enjoy the literature and learning of at least two foreign languages, withered away. The Europeanized elites, if they were to survive at all, had to assume a new role as the leaders of embattled Peoples in Arms.

Secondly the structure of the State system itself disintegrated. By the Revolution to which we have already referred, Russia was lost to Europe; lost as completely as if she had been overrun by a new Mongol or Hunnish invasion. The elites who had since the time of Peter the Great connected the Russian Empire to the European system with gradually strengthening links were shrugged off in a vast peasant revolt. Little less catastrophic was the destruction of the Habsburg Empire, which had, since the days of Prince Eugen, played so leading a part in reclaiming South-East Europe from the Ottomans and embodying it into the European cultural and political and economic structure; valiantly attempting, even if with indifferent success, to reconcile the differences of German and Magyar and Slav in a non-national but still viable European state.

The successor states in Eastern Europe remained floating in a kind of limbo between two worlds, one dead, one powerless to be born. For unlike all previous peace settlements, unlike, in particular, Utrecht and Vienna, the Versailles settlement of Europe did not reflect the realities in the change in the balance of power in such a way that national prestige reflected national capabilities. Utrecht and Vienna had confirmed the fact, proved by a quarter-century of war, that although France was the strongest power in the system, she could not establish a hegemonial supremacy over a combination of her neighbours; and that if she wished to expand her influence she had to do so within the generally accepted rules of the game, by diplomacy, influence, alliances. But twentieth-century Germany was a very different matter. Between 1870 and 1914 Germans had chafed within the constraints of a system which, they felt, did not accord them the position in the world to which their enormous potential, military, economic and cultural, now entitled them. Bismarck's efforts to keep the ambitions of Imperial Germany within bounds broke down under his successors for one very simple reason: those ambitions were justified by the realities of the situation. The international system of 1814, even as modified by the Treaty of Frankfurt of 1871, no longer mirrored the true balance of power. Germany was no longer one equal power among five in Europe. She was not even *primus inter pares*. She was incomparably stronger; strong enough, as events showed, to impose a true hegemony.

We must now enter the fascinating if academically disreputable world of 'what might have been', or, to give it its trade name, 'counter-factual hypothesis'. There can be little doubt that Germany, together with an Austrian ally who was little more than a satellite, could have defeated France and Russia alone by 1917. It is also highly probable that she could, if there had been no question of American intervention, have defeated Britain as well. Not only does it seem most unlikely that the Royal Navy could have mastered the German U-boat campaign without the help of the US Navy; but if there had been no prospect of American intervention on the Western Front, Ludendorff could have consolidated his conquests in the East at leisure and chosen his own moment for launching a shattering offensive against his exhausted adversaries in the West. It may be going too far to say that without American help the Allies would have lost the Great War, but it is hard to deny that without American help they could not possibly have won it. The New World had to be called in to redress the balance of the Old and the Versailles settlement reflected the true distribution of power only so long as the United States remained within the system. Without that counter-weight, the European system would have reverted to a natural German hegemony, tested almost to destruction under the strains of war. The Versailles settlement was therefore not so much unjust as unrealistic. To plunge deeper into the realm of counter-factual hypothesis, if Hitler had not had such boundless ambitions and had not been in such a hurry to achieve them, the sheer industrial and economic power of Germany, even suffering under the burdens of defeat, even under the direction of the most moderate and reasonable of statesmen, would have brought her the unquestioned hegemony of Europe within at most another decade. And if Germany's neighbours, seeing this possibility and disliking it, had tried to prevent it by war, then the events of 1939–41 give some indication of what the result would have been.

This hypothesis is, for obvious reasons, seldom discussed, either in Germany or anywhere else. I think it has been rather obscured for two reasons. First, the Imperial Germany of 1914, although it aspired to *Weltmacht*, the status of a World Power, did not *explicitly* aspire to the hegemony of Europe, that *Herrschaft*, which it did in fact lie within her capacity to exert. Perhaps those who thought in such terms had their sights so firmly set on the rival World Power, England, that they took Europe very much for granted. Second, although Hitler certainly aspired to the hegemony of Europe, it was for him only a preliminary step towards the establishment of a far greater *Reich*, one whose frontiers stretched illimitably to the East. Europe, for Hitler, was no more than a necessary base to be consolidated before further expansion. It was not until the last years of the war that he began a belated and unconvincing campaign for European unity against the incoming hordes from the barbarous East.

Hitler's War, like Napoleon's wars, both made and unmade Europe; but it made it only indirectly and unmade it perhaps for ever. As in the days of Napoleon, Europeans were united by a common experience of suffering; the *corvées* of labour, the alien occupation, the air raids, the gruesome escalation of resistance and repression, the mounting hopes of liberation, the shadow of the concentration camps, the only-half-guessed-at horrors of the Final Solution. Even the German people themselves, during the last years of *Totalkrieg* when what has aptly been called 'The SS State' took charge of Germany, were living under a reign of terror almost worse than a foreign occupation. The effect of these years on the generation which experienced them is something that even now we are hardly able to grasp. It was a nightmare of which people prefer not to speak. But it was an experience that set the peoples of Continental Europe even more apart from those of the British Isles, who had suffered nothing remotely comparable; and it created a deep cultural abyss between them and the peoples of the United States, who had suffered nothing at all. The peoples of the Soviet Union had, however, suffered incomparably more. Hitler's armies had forcibly brought several scores of millions of them back within the frontiers of Europe, and Himmler's police and extermination squads extended to them the new European cultural pattern. One has only to visit Eastern Europe comparatively briefly to appreciate the extent to which Soviet power there rests not only on the presence of Soviet armies, but on the recollection of these shared experiences, which propaganda keeps continually green.

As for the unmaking of Europe, Hitler's War provided the detonator which activated the immense latent potential of the two Continent-states whose capacity to exercise world power on a scale dwarfing any European nation had been foreseen by de Tocqueville and by Seeley long before the nineteenth century ended. Their intervention, and eventual victory, resulted in the destruction of the Europe which had developed since the Dark Ages; the Europe which had stretched, in de Gaulle's words, from the Atlantic to the Urals. They divided it in half and integrated the two halves into new and antagonistic political and cultural systems. These powers had derived their cultures from Europe; the United States entirely, the Soviet Union to a very considerable degree. One must not underestimate the extent to which a new Europeanized elite has grown up in the Soviet Union, like a new skin grown to replace the old; an elite the more self-conscious as the Soviet leaders try to distance themselves from the People's Republic of China. Nor on the other hand must we exaggerate the power exercised in the United States by those friendly, rich, Eurocentric Americans who are the pillars of the Atlantic Community and without whose generosity our cathedrals and colleges and cultural life would long ago have lapsed into irremediable decay. But neither group exercises unquestioned dominance within their immense and complex societies, most of whose members regard Europe as something very alien and very far away. Europe is no longer of central importance in the thoughts and calculations of the leaders of these super-powers; for both it is a problem, and one which they wish would go away.

How far is 'Europe' now anything more than a historical memory and a geographical expression? Certainly we cannot consider the European Economic Community, with its frontiers so drawn as to exclude Dresden and Leipzig, Warsaw and Prague, Budapest and Belgrade, Leningrad and Stockholm and even Vienna, as being in any sense 'Europe'. Or, rather, it bears the same relation to Europe as the Holy Roman Empire did to the real Roman Empire; an attempt, in a very small part of the original territory, to recreate a myth for political purposes; and it merits exactly the same measure of rather wry sympathy and support as did the Holy Roman Empire itself. It is a useful piece of mechanism so long as it is not taken too seriously or required to support a political burden beyond its very limited capabilities. But not even the Holy Roman Empire depended, as does the Community, on the protection and good will of a vastly superior military power. In its present and, I am tempted to say, any foreseeable form, the European Community has significance only as part, though an immensely important one, of a world economic network whose centres of decision lie as much in New York and Tokyo as in Frankfurt or London, and as part of a military system where there is one centre of decision only, and that is in Washington. I do not believe that Western Europe ever could create for itself an independent centre of military power, and I emphatically do not believe that it should.

Could the old Europe be recreated, or rather could a new Europe be created within the original boundaries? For this nostalgic vision I must admit to having even less sympathy. What *were* the original boundaries? Did they or did they not include Russia? To exclude her would be arbitrary: her western, especially her Baltic provinces are culturally akin to their neighbours to the West, and Moscow is now an entirely European city, and Leningrad always has been. But if Europe extends to the Urals, the Soviet Union extends now far beyond – a geographical fact which escaped de Gaulle's attention; and a Europe extending from the Atlantic to Vladivostok cannot be what Europeanists have in mind. If, on the other hand, one does exclude the Soviet Union and conceives that by some miracle the other states of Eastern Europe could be 'liberated', the pattern re-emerges that two wars were fought to avoid: a Europe entirely dominated by a reunited Germany. Both halves of Germany separately have established themselves as major economic powers. In comparison with their united strength, the rest of Europe would be dwarfed almost as completely as it is today by the United States. Whatever we may feel in Britain about the possibility of such power passing into the hands of so intelligent, learned and industrious a people, the prospect is still not one which appeals to Frenchmen, Dutchmen, Danes, Poles, or, not least important, Russians.

In my view, therefore, the old Europe, the Europe made and unmade by military conflict and military power, belongs to the past, and I cannot contemplate a 'New Europe' with either conviction or relish. The name still has a certain nostalgic magic, which can and perhaps should be used for specific purposes of policy. But if it is true that those who do not understand the past are compelled to repeat it, it is no less true that the more we understand about the past, the less desire we have to recreate it. There is not really very much in the history of Europe that merits our regrets.

The British Way in Warfare

A REAPPRAISAL

AN INVITATION to deliver a lecture in honour of our senior historian of the Elizabethan Age[1] is likely to arouse, in one whose speciality lies in the military affairs of the recent past, not so much gratitude as alarm and despondency. This is not his territory, and in venturing on to it he is bound to make a fool of himself. Yet the Age of Elizabeth is not so remote from the military events of the twentieth century as might at first sight appear. Perceptions of the Elizabethan period have exercised a very considerable influence indeed over British strategic thought during the past hundred years. The works of naval and military historians from Colomb and Mahan in the nineteenth century through Julian Corbett to Herbert Richmond and Liddell Hart in the twentieth are studded with references, quotations and analogies drawn from the Age of Elizabeth. How often does one come across those two sonorous quotations: Francis Bacon's 'He that commands the sea is at great liberty and may take as much or as little of the war as he will'; and Walter Raleigh's 'Whosoever commands the sea commands trade; whosoever commands the trade of the world commands the riches of the world, and consequently the world itself'?

On the other hand, even if they have not quoted him directly, how often have British statesmen echoed the advice which Lord Burghley gave to the Queen, that she should commit herself to the support of the Netherlands against the armies of Spain in 1584:

Although her Majesty should thereby enter into a war presently, yet were she better able to do it now, while she may make the same out of her realm, having the help of the people of Holland and

1. Sir John Neale, in whose honour this lecture was given at University College London in 1974.

169

before the King of Spain should have consummated his conquests in these countries . . . and shall be so strong by sea and so free from all other actions and quarrels . . . as that her Majesty shall no wise be able with her own power, nor with the aid of any other, neither by sea nor land, to withstand his attempts, but shall be forced to give place to his insatiable malice.[1]

Such was the burden of advice given by Sir Eyre Crowe and his colleagues in the Foreign Office about the Germany of the Second Reich, and by their successors under Vansittart about Hitler: the need to take pre-emptive action before a concentration of military and naval strength developed on the Continent such as no British government, 'neither with its own power, nor with the aid of any other, neither by sea nor land' (nor, one must add, in the air), would be able to withstand. Perhaps the attitudes of these men were shaped by historical experience to an extent of which they were not always fully conscious. Certainly those experiences of the past seemed to have, for their immediate problems, an undeniable and perhaps a comforting relevance. The generation that fought the Second World War was buoyed up by the sense that this kind of thing had occurred fairly often before, and it was fortunate in having as its national leader a historian who never failed to remind them of it.

But the generation that fought the First World War had no such comforting folk memories to look back on. The British experience of 1914–18 seemed horribly unique in our history. Some – probably the majority of historians – would now argue that this was the result of social, economic and technological developments in the nature of warfare, which no statesman could control and to which the military leaders of all belligerent nations were equally and understandably slow to adjust. But others saw it as the direct consequence of mistaken policies, political and strategic, for which specific statesmen and soldiers could be blamed; and in particular as

1. Conyers Read, *Sir Francis Walsingham* (Oxford, 1925), Vol. III, pp. 82–3. It is a quotation familiar to professional historians if not to the general public, appearing not only in Motley's *The United Netherlands* but in A. L. Rowse, *The Expansion of Elizabethan England* (London, 1955), pp. 241–2.

the result of an aberration from traditional strategies which ever since the sixteenth century had brought Britain victory over her enemies at acceptable cost.

The leading spokesman of this latter school was the late Sir Basil Liddell Hart. It was he who coined the phrase 'The British Way in Warfare' in a book published in 1932 and written with the express purpose of showing 'that there has been a distinctively British practice of war, based on experience and proved by three centuries of success'. From that practice a theory should have been developed naturally; but its growth had, in his view, been 'stunted by shallow thought and deformed by slavish imitation of Continental fashions. The consequences of that malformation are to be found in the years 1914–18 and have been felt ever since.'[1]

This distinctive British practice, wrote Liddell Hart, was based on 'mobility and surprise'. When Britain began to expand in the sixteenth century 'we succeeded in overtaking and overcoming our rivals because we alone steered clear of the delusive attraction of Continental victories'. Instead, we invested in profitable if piratical maritime trading enterprises, and in the struggles against Spain 'sea mobility was pitted against land strength'.[2] Cromwell also employed an 'indirect strategy' against Spain by raiding her treasure fleets. In the wars against Louis XIV it was basically the pressure of British sea power which crippled the French economy. Sea power in the War of the Austrian Succession nullified the French victories by land. In the Seven Years War Chatham 'vigorously carried out a grand strategy that became the purest example of our traditional form'; for while direct military effort on the Continent was largely replaced by subsidies to Allies, 'under cover of direct sea pressure on France, indirect military action was applied to the overseas roots of French power'. Finally in the Napoleonic struggles 'we eschewed the main theatre of war and employed our land-based forces for sea-based operations against the enemy's vulner-

1. B. H. Liddell Hart, *The British Way in Warfare* (London, 1932), p. 7.
2. *Ibid.*, pp. 25–6.

able extremities'. As a result it was possible to bring the conflict to an end 'without a British Army setting foot in the main theatre of war'.[1]

Liddell Hart's views reflected the sufferings of his generation, and they commanded widespread and influential support in military as well as maritime circles. A few years earlier the Chief of the Imperial General Staff had publicly expressed his regret that 'for years past British soldiers have been nourished on the ideas of Continental strategists generally expressed in terms untuned to British ears';[2] and the Liddell Hart files contain many letters from other eminent contemporaries endorsing his views.[3] The extent to which this revulsion against Continental warfare affected the attitudes and policies of the British governments in the 1930s is becoming increasingly clear as scholars work over the cabinet records for those years. But it would be doing Liddell Hart an injustice, both as a historian and as a controversialist, to suggest that this analysis of British strategy was anything more than a piece of brilliant political pamphleteering, sharply argued, selectively illustrated, and concerned rather to influence British public opinion and government policy than to illuminate the complexities of the past in any serious or scholarly way.

Liddell Hart must in fact be regarded as the last and perhaps the most formidable in the long series of protagonists of that 'maritime school' of strategy whose greatest exemplar was Dean Swift, who had advanced arguments

1. *Ibid.*, pp. 35–7.
2. Field-Marshal Lord Milne in his foreword to Sir Frederick Maurice: *British Strategy: A Study of the Application of the Principles of War* (London, 1929), p. xv.
3. See Jay Luvaas, *The Education of an Army: British Military Thought 1815–1940* (London, 1965), p. 424. Luvaas considers that 'in his efforts to prevent Britain from returning to the unlimited policy in land commitments that had dictated British strategy in the First World War and from building up a large conventional army on the Continent, Liddell Hart probably did not influence British policy so much as he articulated the experience of those who could not get the 1914–18 experience out of their systems'.

very similar to Liddell Hart's in his pamphlet *The Conduct of the Allies* two centuries earlier. If there was indeed a 'British Way in Warfare' it was the outcome of a continuous dialectic between this maritime school and their 'Continental' opponents; a dialectic which can indeed be traced back to the Elizabethan Age. Then the issue was debated between those who supported Sir John Hawkins, with his ambitious plans for a maritime blockade of Spain and his urgent recommendations 'that we have as little to do in foreign countries as may be (but of mere necessity) for that breedeth great charge and no profit at all'; and those who believed with Sir Francis Knollys and the bulk of the Queen's councillors that 'the avoiding of Her Majesty's danger doth consist in the preventing of the conquest of the Low Countries betimes'.[1] Britain's geographical position as an island separated from, yet part of, the European land mass has made this dialectic central not only to her strategy but to her political economy and indeed her culture, throughout her historical experience. We have not escaped from it yet.

The idea that there was a specifically 'British' or 'maritime' school of strategy distinct from the 'German' or 'Continental' school based on the teaching of Clausewitz, originated with the naval historian Sir Julian Corbett[2] in the first decade of this century. In his capacity as Lecturer at the Royal Naval College, Greenwich, and historical adviser to the Admiralty, Corbett became as closely involved in the great strategic controversies which preceded the First World War as Liddell Hart was to be before the Second, but his pronouncements were more cautious and his analysis more subtle than that of his successor. Corbett was at least as

1. J. A. Williamson, *Sir John Hawkins, the Time and the Man* (Oxford, 1927), p. 451. Charles Wilson, *Queen Elizabeth and the Revolt of the Netherlands* (London, 1970), p. 59.

2. Corbett published *Drake and the Tudor Navy* in 1898; *The Successors of Drake* in 1900; *England in the Seven Years War* in 1907; and *The Trafalgar Campaign* in 1910. *Some Principles of Maritime Strategy* appeared in 1911, and there he drew the distinction referred to in the text. (References are to the 2nd edn of 1919.)

much a critic of the maritime school as he was a spokesman for it. Indeed, some fifteen years of unremitting study of Britain's maritime wars, from the Elizabethan to the Napoleonic Age, had convinced him that 'maritime strategy' was not an alternative to 'Continental strategy' but an extension of it. For Corbett Clausewitz was not, as he was for Liddell Hart, a false prophet; rather he was a great if incomplete thinker whose teaching should be, not rejected, but extended to include the maritime dimension which he had ignored. The task for British strategists he saw as being to harmonize the use of naval and military power. Corbett rejected the current simplistic doctrine about 'command of the sea' which his contemporaries had derived from Mahan: 'unaided', he wrote, 'naval pressure can only work by a process of exhaustion. Its effects must always be slow, and so galling to both our commercial community and to neutrals that the tendency is always to accept terms of peace that are far from conclusive. For a firm decision, a quicker and more drastic form of pressure is required.' The paramount concern of maritime strategy was therefore to determine the mutual relations of the army and navy in a single war plan. 'It will not suffice to say the primary object of the army is to destroy the enemy's army, or that of the fleet to destroy the enemy's fleet. The delicate interactions of land and sea factors produce conditions too intricate for such blunt solutions.'[1]

These conclusions were surely unexceptionable: by indicating that, for a maritime power, strategic calculations were a far more complex matter than they were for those land-based states which Clausewitz had in mind when he wrote *On War*, Corbett performed a real service to strategic thought. But he pressed on to a far more questionable argument. 'Maritime strategy', he suggested, made possible the application of limited power even to the achievement of the unlimited objective of total victory. Control of the sea, he argued, enabled Britain to select a theatre of operations where a limited effort could effectively aid the

1. *Some Principles of Maritime Strategy* (2nd edn, London, 1919), pp. 11–12.

larger operations of Continental allies without being subordinate to them. The exercise of such limited effort, argued Corbett, implied no lack of warlike spirit, but 'a sagacious instinct for the kind of war that best accords with the conditions of our existence'.[1] Thus where Liddell Hart saw the essence of the British Way in Warfare as lying in mobility and surprise – the qualities which he was later to describe as 'The Direct Approach' – for Corbett it was the application of limited force to the attainment of an unlimited object. (Both, incidentally, assumed the existence of Continental allies less fortunately placed.) This limited force could be exercised either by operations for the conquest of overseas territory, or by operations 'more or less upon the European seaboard designed, not for permanent conquest, but as a method of disturbing our enemy's plans and strengthening the hands of our allies and our own position'.[2]

For Corbett, as for Liddell Hart, British strategy at its purest and most successful was to be found in the conduct of the Seven Years War by the elder Pitt. Then Pitt selected as his main objective the conquest of North America; but he realized that this would be possible only if France was kept occupied on the Continent and prevented from making land conquests for which Britain would have to exchange her American gains when it came to making peace. This could be done only by Britain's Continental ally, the King of Prussia; but the King of Prussia was hard pressed by three mighty enemies and calling for help. The nature of the help Pitt proposed to send was expounded to the King by the British Ambassador in the following terms:

His [Britannic] Majesty is determined that the fleet intended for the Channel service shall at once be made subservient to the views of defending the British dominions and of protecting trade, and yet at the same time to cover a number of land forces considerable enough to alarm the coasts of France and to oblige that Power to withdraw a great part of the troops intended to annoy the King [of Prussia] and

1. *Ibid.*, p. 66.
2. *Ibid.*, p. 51.

his allies in Germany, in order to protect their own coasts from invasion.[1]

This was indeed a splendid illustration of the versatility of sea power at its apogee. One force could simultaneously protect Britain from invasion, cover her own offensive and wage trade war. But the impending threat which it posed to the coasts of France, though it certainly caused alarms and diversions, did not oblige the French to withdraw 'a great part' of their troops from the German front; any more than in the Second World War Allied operations in the Mediterranean achieved their object of forcing major diversions from the Russian front. Corbett himself agrees that the success of Britain and her allies in the Seven Years War was due less to the skill of Pitt's strategic calculations than to two strokes of providential luck: the fact that Ferdinand VI of Spain lived until 1759, keeping Spain neutral and leaving France to fight her maritime wars single-handed; and the fact that Elizabeth of Russia died in 1762, thus relieving Frederick the Great from an intolerable burden. Had the Tsarina survived for even one more year and kept her army in the field, it would have then been impossible for Frederick to have carried on; and then, argued Corbett, 'Hanover, Holland and the Netherlands would have been at the mercy of France and the treaty of peace could scarcely have been on a better basis for us than the *status quo ante bellum*'.[2] British maritime power and her colonial conquests would in fact have been as effectively nullified as they had been by Marshal de Saxe's victories in Flanders nearly twenty years before.

Yet this insight into the limited effectiveness of Pitt's strategy did not prevent Corbett from putting it forward, in 1907, as a model to be followed in any forthcoming war against Germany. In that year he acted as adviser to the Admiralty Committee, charged with drawing up alternative proposals to put up against the General Staff's plans for direct military help to the French Army. The proposals of this Committee proved to be almost a carbon copy of the

1. Corbett, *England in the Seven Years War* (London, 1909), Vol. I, p. 190.
2. *Ibid.*, Vol. II, pp. 373–6.

strategy applied by the elder Pitt – the strategy in whose study Corbett must at that time have been immersed, since his study of *England in the Seven Years War* was published in the same year. British sea power was to be used to blockade German trade; German ports should be bombarded; a series of raids on the German coast would 'keep the whole littoral in a perpetual state of unrest and alarm'. In addition a German island should be occupied, to compel the German fleet to come out and fight. None of this, the Committee admitted, could prevent German forces from overruning the Low Countries but 'the political effect, when it comes to negotiations for peace, would be of vast importance'.[1]

It is hard to believe that so scrupulous a scholar as Corbett really thought that twentieth-century problems could be quite so simply treated by the application of eighteenth-century recipes. The reference to peace negotiations pinpoints only one major difficulty. In the era of colonial competition it had always been possible to gain what modern statesmen would call 'leverage' on France by overseas conquests, to obtain restitution of which she had to relinquish her own conquests in the Low Countries. But no such hostages could be seized from Germany. Once she had overrun Belgium and Holland, what inducements would be

1. For the Committee Report see P. K. Kemp, ed., *The Papers of Admiral Sir John Fisher* (Navy Records Society, London, 1960), Vol. II. Also by M. P. A. Hankey, *The Supreme Command* (London, 1961), Vol. I, p. 39. In particular the proposal to seize an island to compel the German fleet to come out to fight was taken straight from the Seven Years War. In 1758 Wolfe had advised, 'The Ministry of England do not see that to possess the Isle of Aix . . . is one of the most brilliant and most useful strokes that this nation can possibly strike. It stops up at once the harbours of Rochefort and Rochelle, obstructs and ruins the whole trade of the Bay of Biscay, inevitably brings on a sea fight which we ought by all means to aim at, and is the finest that can be made with a small force.' Corbett's comment is significant: 'By seizing an island vital to the French position they must either suffer the consequences, both during the war and at the balancing of account when it came to making peace, or else they must take the offensive with their fleet and expose it to destruction . . . As a strategic device it is so obvious, so powerful, and so exactly suited to our peculiar resources, that the only wonder is it has so seldom been put into force.' *England in the Seven Years War*, Vol. I, pp. 269–70.

available to get her out again? Further, how could diversions of the kind Corbett proposed help an ally who might be decisively crushed in a few major battles before they could begin to take effect? And most problematic of all, would such diversions be even practicable now that the development of railways had given land powers a degree of flexibility rivalling, if not surpassing, that of sea power? At this last question Corbett did no more than glance uneasily: 'It is generally held that modern developments in military organization and transport will enable a great continental power to ignore such threats. Napoleon ignored them in the past, but only to verify the truth that in war to ignore a threat is to create an opportunity.'[1]

But this was playing with words. What was 'generally held' was, not that a Continental power could ignore such threats, but that it could crush them. The rough handling which the Admiralty proposals of 1907 received at the hands of General Staff logistical experts may help to explain the more cautious claims which Corbett made for limited interventions when, five years later, he published his *Principles of Maritime Strategy*. There he suggested only that Napoleonic precedents indicated that the mere threat of such diversions enabled small British forces to pin down enemy forces of far greater strength than their own. When intervention came, he suggested that it should take one of two forms: a stroke to disorganize enemy plans after it was too late for him to adjust them; or one to deprive him of the fruits of his victory by the introduction of 'a small, fresh force from the sea'.[2] For the first, Corbett possibly had in mind the attack on Antwerp, in the left rear of the anticipated German line of advance, which was favoured by certain circles in the Army. The second idea was evidently based not only on the precedent of the Peninsular War but on the experience of the war of 1870 – which had shown that even after the defeat of a regular army in decisive battle, resistance could still be prolonged within the country as a whole, and that it might not be too late to bring help. But to adopt such a course would be to

1. *Some Principles of Maritime Strategy*, p. 59.
2. *Ibid.*, p. 60.

reject a strategy directed at securing an early and decisive victory in favour of one which might at best mitigate a defeat. After all, the British forces under Sir John Moore and later Sir Arthur Wellesley had not been sent to the Peninsula in *preference* to joining a strong allied army in North-West Europe. They went there because there was no such army for them to join, and there was really nowhere else for them to go.

This brings us to an aspect of strategy of the elder Pitt which both Corbett and Liddell Hart ignored. With the exception of the purely maritime wars against the Dutch, the Seven Years War was the first occasion in modern British history when we did *not* have an ally directly across the Channel or the North Sea. In 1756, of our traditional allies in that area, one, the House of Austria, was now unfriendly, and the other, the Netherlands, had relapsed into exhausted and timorous neutrality for the first time in two centuries. If the Low Countries had been a theatre of war as in the days of Elizabeth or of Marlborough, is it really conceivable that Pitt would have regarded his cumbrous policy of raids and diversions as a serious *alternative* to fighting there – or that his Continental allies would have accepted it as such? These diversions might indeed have been a supplement; much as Marlborough planned the Toulon expedition of 1707 to enable his Mediterranean allies to draw French strength away from the principal theatres of war. But they could hardly be seen as a substitute for operations in the theatre where British forces could be most easily and cheaply deployed.[1]

Again, in the Napoleonic Wars the British fought in the Low Countries whenever they had allies there to fight for. It was only when Napoleon had consolidated his hold on the area after the War of the Second Coalition that the younger

1. W. S. Churchill, *Marlborough* (London, 2 vol. reprint 1947), Vol. II, pp. 216–7, 250–6. Churchill describes the object of the Toulon expedition as being to create 'the root of an immense rodent growth in the bowels of France, leading to a fatal collapse either on the northern or on the southern front and perhaps on both'. Like virtually all such amphibious expeditions, tactical failure ruined an imaginative strategic plan.

Pitt and his successors turned to a strategy of raids, diversions and secondary fronts as a matter, not of preference, but of necessity. Wellington fought in the Peninsula as the Eighth Army fought in the Western Desert, because it was the only place where he *could* fight. As soon as the Low Countries offered themselves again in 1815 as a theatre of operations, British forces were sent there without a moment's hesitation. Nobody, so far as I can discover, suggested that the amphibious flexibility provided by British sea power should be used to send Wellington to stage a diversion at Brest instead.

From this argument two conclusions would seem to follow. First, a commitment of support to a Continental ally in the nearest available theatre, on the largest scale that contemporary resources could afford, so far from being alien to traditional British strategy, was absolutely central to it. The flexibility provided by sea power certainly made possible other activities as well: colonial conquest, trade war, help to allies in Central Europe, minor amphibious operations; but these were ancillary to the great decisions by land, and they continued to be so throughout the two world wars. Secondly, when we did have recourse to a purely maritime strategy, it was always as a result, not of free choice or atavistic wisdom, but of *force majeure*. It was a strategy of necessity rather than of choice, of survival rather than of victory. It enabled us to escape from the shipwrecks which overtook our less fortunately-placed Continental neighbours; it gave us a breathing space in which to try to attract other allies; it enabled us to run away – which, as a method of 'taking as much or as little of the war as one will', is never to be despised; but it never enabled us to *win*.

But what about trade war and Continental blockade? Did this ever present a serious alternative to Continental intervention? The effectiveness of this weapon changed with circumstances. There was perhaps never a period when such a strategy would have paid better dividends than during Elizabeth's wars with Spain, if only it could have been made to work. But it never actually did. The efforts of the Spanish monarchy to reduce the Netherland rebels to obedience demanded the effective functioning of an economy almost wholly dependent on the regular arrival of silver fleets from America. If those fleets could be intercepted, Spanish power, exercised as it was through armies which were mercenary in the most exact and exacting sense of the world, would wither at its roots.[1] 'The hurt that our State should seek to do to him', wrote the Earl of Essex of the King of Spain, 'is to intercept his treasures, whereby we shall cut his sinews and make war on him with his money.'[2] There was little dissent from this view. Expedition after expedition was fitted out for this lucrative endeavour; none of them achieved their object. An older school of naval historians has blamed this persistent failure on the parsimony and incomprehension of the Queen herself,[3] and specialists have disputed the point for nearly eighty years. But it was a historian with the experience of another war behind him, Professor Bruce Wernham, who probably saw the answer: such a strategy, under sixteenth-century conditions, was simply too difficult. 'Far sighted men', he wrote in *Before the Armada*,[4] 'are often blind to the obstacles at their feet, and just as the 1914–1918 war produced ideas about the use of air power that could only be realized with the aircraft and technical equipment of 1944–45, so the Elizabethan war produced ideas about the use of sea power that needed the fleets of Nelson's day for their effective execution.' One need only study the tragic accounts of missed opportunities, administrative incompetence, confusion in command and sheer inability to cope with such natural hazards as storm and sickness which make up four-fifths of Elizabethan naval history to appreciate how little the forces of that time were fitted to deal with the Clausewitzian element of friction in war on the ambitious scale which they attempted. Ironically,

1. See Geoffrey Parker, *The Army of Flanders and the Spanish Road 1567–1659* (Cambridge, 1972), *passim*, especially pp. 152–3.

2. Quoted in Herbert Richmond, *Statesmen and Sea Power* (Oxford, 1946), p. 9.

3. See e.g. the introduction by M. Oppenheim to Vol. I of *The Naval Tracts of Sir William Monson* (Navy Records Society, London, 1902), p. 12.

4. R. B. Wernham, *Before the Armada: the Growth of English Foreign Policy 1485–1588* (London, 1966), p. 385.

England was least capable of conducting a maritime strategy at the time when it might have been at its most effective.

With the seventeenth century we come to that period, lasting for nearly two hundred years, when 'war' and 'trade' became virtually interchangeable terms; when the capture of colonies and the trade which went with them became not so much a method of warfare as its object.[1] It is thus pointless to ask whether, at this time, interruption of trade was an effective means of conducting war; it was what the war was all about. As General Monck put it with military directness in demanding a renewal of war against the Dutch in 1662: 'What matters this or that reason? What we want is more of the trade the Dutch now have.'[2] Trade meant wealth, wealth enabled one to wage war, war made possible yet more trade: who could resist the lure of this logic? What could be more enjoyable and lucrative than to smash the Dutch fishing monopolies, to snap up French sugar islands, to break into the protected economy of the Spanish Indies? What a waste of time and effort was all that marching and counter-marching in France and Flanders! War could, and should, be made to pay. 'It is more in the true interests of these Kingdoms in general', wrote a pamphleteer in 1745, 'that we should continue in a state of war [with France and Spain], so that war is carried on only by sea, than in a state of peace . . . our commerce in general will flourish more under a vigorous and well-managed naval war than under any peace which should allow an open intercourse with those two nations.'[3]

So that war is carried on only by sea: the great dream of the English mercantilists. But if the war *was* carried on only by sea, British statesmen at the end of the day had to hand back

1. See Edmond Silberner: *La guerre dans la pensée économique du XVI au XVIII siècle* (Paris, 1939); G. L. Beer, *The Old Colonial System* (New York, 1912), Vol. I; Jacob Viner, 'Power versus Plenty as Objectives of Foreign Policy in the 17th and 18th Centuries', *World Politics*, Vol. I, p. 1.

2. Charles Wilson, *Profit and Power: A Study of England and the Dutch Wars* (London, 1957), p. 107. Dr Maurice Ashley, the biographer of Monck, has however cast some doubt on the authenticity of this quotation.

3. Richard Pares, *War and Trade in the West Indies* (London, 1936), p. 62.

all the overseas conquests made possible by maritime power to a France whose land power enabled her to overrun the Low Countries, not to mention Hanover. And though later strategic writers may have regarded these conquests in the light of 'leverage' at the peace conference, contemporary Englishmen did not look on them in that light at all: these were lucrative prizes which they wanted to keep: prizes for the possession of which they had gone to war in the first place. Further, although trade war could paralyse sixteenth-century Spain and destroy seventeenth-century Holland, its effect on eighteenth-century France was no more than an embarrassment: as Richard Pares put it, 'it only touched the circumference of her national life'.[1] France was worn down not by the economic pressures of blockade, by the interruption of her trade with the West Indies, but by the crushing expense of continual war against Continental adversaries. And if by diplomacy or conquest she was able to dispose of those adversaries and unite the Continent, then not only was Britain's maritime supremacy at risk (as it was in the American War of Independence), but all vent could be denied to the commercial products which that supremacy enabled her to monopolize. In Napoleon's Continental system the worst fears of British statesmen throughout the eighteenth century came true; a situation which, with Continental ports barred to British goods, trade meant not

1. *Ibid.*, p. 393; The impact of blockade on France was mainly regional; particularly on the entrepôts of the West Indian and Levant trades, Bordeaux and Marseilles. The sugar and coffee trade in Bordeaux during the Seven Years War fell to 27 per cent of its pre-war level. But even in Bordeaux the overall volume of trade was only slightly affected by the war: wine exports actually increased, and the total trade done with, for example, Holland, fell only to 80 per cent of its pre-war value. F. G. Pariset, ed., *Bordeaux au XVIIIe siècle* (Bordeaux, 1968), pp. 288–9. In any case the main factor affecting the French economy was not overseas trade but the fluctuation in the price of cereals. When blockade coincided with grain shortage, as it did in the 1740s, the result was serious; but its effect during the good harvest years at the end of the Seven Years War does not appear to have been significant. E. Labrousse and others, *Histoire Economique de la France* (Paris, 1970), Vol. II, pp. 502, 556. I am indebted to Dr Rohan Butler for these references.

wealth but glut, slump, unemployment, starvation and revolutionary threat.[1]

Undeniably, once the British armies had been bundled out of the Continent and their allies had all been subjugated by Napoleon's land victories, the blockade of the Napoleonic Empire was certainly the most effective and probably the only course open to the British government, short of making the best peace they could. Again, it was a strategy of necessity, not one of choice. But if Napoleon had been able to consolidate his hold on the Continent, for how long could that blockade have been maintained? If French resources, wrote an alarmed observer in 1811,

... which have hitherto been directed, with such fatal energy, to extending her conquests on shore, may hereafter be applied to naval affairs, it seems to me very doubtful whether we could possibly preserve, for any great number of years, such a preponderance by sea against France alone in her present extended state as to blockade the fleets of that one nation in all its ports; [and once France commanded all the resources of the Continent] there must be from the nature of things in course of time a superiority in number of ships and men on the part of our enemies which may be carried by them to such an overwhelming pitch, as no valour nor skill on our part will be able to withstand.[2]

Napoleon's armies, in fact, still had to be painfully, expensively and bloodily defeated in battle; and Britain owed her seat at the peace table mainly to the fact that some of those battles had been won by British troops under the Duke of Wellington.[3]

By the twentieth century, blockade directed against highly industrialized nations dependent on overseas trade not only for wealth but for sheer survival had become a more

1. Richard Pares, 'American versus Continental Warfare 1739–63', *English Historical Review*, Vol. XLI (1936), pp. 429–65.

2. C. W. Pasley, *Essay on the Military Policy and Institutions of the British Empire* (London, 2nd edn, 1811), pp. 2–3.

3. Corbett himself found it necessary to rub this in: 'We know what Nelson did at Trafalgar, and forget that its real importance was what it afterwards enabled Wellington to do. We speak glibly of sea power and forget that its true value lies in its influence on the operations of armies.' *The Successors of Drake* (London, 1900), p. 410.

powerful instrument than ever before. In the First World War the Royal Navy was indeed able to apply direct pressure to the sources of German national life with terrible results. But for a powerful land power the remedy still lay to hand. If Germany could gain mastery of the ports of Western Europe, British sea power became precarious. If, in addition, she could seize the resources of Eastern Europe from the Vistula to the Volga, that power could be made almost irrelevant.[1] The effectiveness of Britain's maritime power still depended on the fighting capacity of Britain's Continental allies, East and West. The moment of truth for Britain's strategic planners in the First World War came, not in August 1914, when the decision was taken to send a small force across the Channel to help our Allies on a strictly limited basis, but a year later, when those Allies appeared to be within measurable distance of total collapse. Then Kitchener entered into an open-ended commitment to his French colleagues, much as Elizabeth had had reluctantly to accept a similar commitment when the United Provinces had appeared to be on the verge of collapse in 1584. And it is not to be forgotten that the Elizabethan commitment was, over the next twenty years to drain the resources of the Tudor monarchy and thereby to create for the next generation financial, political and social problems not incommensurate with those bequeathed to posterity by the First World War.

Kitchener's decision was subsequently to be bitterly attacked by, among others, Colonel Maurice Hankey, a staunch advocate of the maritime school. Kitchener, wrote Hankey after the war, 'understood sea-power but little, and started off on the basis of a continental army ... The collapse of the French and the failure of the Russian steam-

1. There were many influential figures in German society, from the Kaiser down, who saw the First World War merely as a 'First Punic War', the second being reserved for the destruction of the British Empire. Hans W. Gatzke, *Germany's Drive to the West* (Baltimore, 1966), pp. 11–12. For Hitler's long-term designs on England, see Andreas Hillgruber, *Hitlers Strategie: Politik und Kriegführung 1940–41* (Frankfurt a/M 1965), pp. 564–78.

roller played into his hands.' But what else was there for Kitchener to do? What options could the flexibility of British sea power still offer? The amphibious diversion which Hankey himself had helped to project, the attack on the Dardanelles, a brilliant, almost a flawless strategic concept, had met the fate of virtually every British amphibious operation since the Age of Elizabeth: Lisbon in 1589, Cadiz in 1595, Cadiz again in 1626, Brest in 1696, Toulon in 1707, Lorient in 1746, Rochefort in 1757, Walcheren in 1809; all brilliant in conception, all lamentable in execution. The surprise and mobility which Liddell Hart had seen as the essence of British maritime strategy, so far from ensuring success, had resulted over the centuries in an almost unbroken record of expensive and humiliating failures from which Wolfe's seizure of Quebec stands out as one of the very few exceptions. The comments of Clausewitz on such operations as these are sad but apt. 'It would be a mistake to believe that surprise is a key element of success in war. In theory it is very promising: in practice it generally gets stuck because of the friction engendered by the whole apparatus.'[1] Not until the massive industrial supremacy of the United States was cast into the balance, making possible an overwhelming local superiority by land, sea and air, did amphibious operations come into their own as a major tool of strategy.

If France and Russia had collapsed, as in 1915 appeared all too probable, the flexibility of British sea power could have done as little against a German-dominated Europe as it was able to in 1940–2: without air power, indeed, considerably less. Under such circumstances Corbett's ideas about 'the application of the limited method to the unlimited form' of war, and Liddell Hart's later elaborations on the same theme, seem like anachronistic survivals from some earlier and happier age. It was ultimately to take the unlimited application of force not only by Britain but by two powers with resources immensely greater than her own to attain the objective of the defeat of Hitler's Germany.

1. Karl von Clausewitz, *Vom Kriege* (Berlin, 1832), Book III ch. 9 (my translation).

But not all earlier ages were happier ones. That of Elizabeth quite certainly was not. Perhaps the greatest achievement of Sir John Neale and his successors has been to emancipate us from that school of historians who could see the Elizabethan period only through the golden mists of Britain's subsequent maritime expansion, commercial wealth, military glory and political power. They have reminded us that, then as now, England was a small country with almost insoluble internal problems and very slender resources – of which only a small portion could be spared for military purposes; enmeshed, as rather a minor actor, in a world of power politics in a new age of tantalizing possibilities and appalling dangers, in which all traditional landmarks were being eroded; an age where only the skilful, the resolute and the devious seemed likely to survive. Above all, it was a country in which there were no cheap or easy answers; either for statesmen or for strategists.

The Use and Abuse of Military History

FOR military historians with backgrounds as professional soldiers, the idea of military history having a 'use' is a perfectly natural one. They would hardly have taken to historical studies if they had not held it. But the historian who comes to military studies from academic life may have to overcome a certain inner scepticism about the use that can be made of his studies. This is partly for reasons which I will deal with later, connected with the general nature of academic history as it has developed during the past century. It is due also to a certain fear in academic circles, where military history is liable to be regarded as a handmaid of militarism, that its chief use may be propagandist and 'myth-making'. I should like to examine this fear at once, because it is not entirely without a basis of truth.

When I use the phrase 'myth-making', I mean the creation of an image of the past, through careful selection and interpretation, in order to create or sustain certain emotions or beliefs. Historians have been expected to do this almost since history began to be written at all, in order to encourage patriotic or religious feeling, or to create support for a dynasty or for a political regime. They usually have done so with no sense of professional dishonesty, and much splendid work they have produced in the process. The Tudor chroniclers who described the Middle Ages often did so in order better to set off the glories of their own times. The nationalist historians of nineteenth-century Germany such as Sybel and Treitschke, the maritime and nationalist historians of Victorian England, wrote with a definite didactic purpose, to awaken emotions of patriotism and loyalty. In totalitarian regimes it is difficult and sometimes impossible to write any other kind of history. Even in mature democracies, subject to very careful qualifications, the 'myth', this selective and heroic view of the past, has its uses. The regimental historian, for instance, has, consciously or unconsciously, to sustain the view that his regiment has usually been flawlessly brave and efficient, especially during its recent past. Without any sense of ill-doing he will emphasize the glorious episodes in its history and pass with a light hand over its murkier passages, knowing full well that his work is to serve a practical purpose in sustaining regimental morale in the future.

The purist will deny that any purpose, however utilitarian or noble, can justify suppression or selection of this sort, either in regimental histories or in popular military histories. It certainly has some short-term dangers, which are often overlooked, as well as the moral dangers inseparable from any tampering with the truth. The young soldier in action for the first time may find it impossible to bridge the gap between war as it has been painted and war as it really is – between the way in which he, his peers, his officers and his subordinates *should* behave, and the way in which they actually do. He may be dangerously unprepared for coward-ice and muddle and horror when he actually encounters them, unprepared even for the cumulative attrition of dirt and fatigue. But nevertheless the 'myth' can and often does sustain him, even when he knows, with half his mind, that it is untrue. So, like Plato, I believe that the myth does have a useful social function. I do not consider it to be an 'abuse' of military history at all, but something quite different, to be judged by different standards. It is 'nursery history', and I use the phrase without any disparaging implications. Break-ing children in properly to the facts of life is a highly skilled affair, and the realities of war are among the most disagree-able facts of life that we are ever called upon to face.

It is in fact the function of the 'historian proper' to discover and record what those complicated and disagree-able realities are. He has to find out, as Leopold von Ranke, the father of modern historiography, put it, 'what really happened'. And this must inevitably involve a critical examination of the 'myth', assessing and discarding its patriotic basis and probing deeply into the things it leaves unsaid. If these investigations reveal that our forces were in fact no braver than the enemy and no more competent than those of our allies, that strokes of apparently brilliant generalship were due to exceptional luck, or that the reputations of wartime commanders were sometimes grossly inflated, this is only to be expected, though the process of disillusionment is necessarily a disagreeable one and often extremely painful. For many of us, the 'myth' has become so much a part of our world that it is anguish to be deprived of it. I remember my own bitter disillusion on learning that the English victory over the Armada in 1588 was followed, not by a glorious peace, but (after sixteen years) by as dishonourable a compromise settlement as England ever made, and by twenty years during which we were little more than a satellite of the great Spanish Empire. After this it came as less of a shock, on studying the Napoleonic Wars from Continental sources, to learn how incidental was the part Britain played in the climactic campaigns of 1812, 1813 and 1814 which finally smashed the Napoleonic hegemony of Europe, great though our indirect contribution to that overthrow undoubtedly was. Such disillusion is a necessary part of growing up in and belonging to an adult society; and a good definition of the difference between a Western liberal society and a totalitarian one – whether it be Communist, Fascist or Catholic authoritarian – is that in the former the government treats its citizens as responsible adults and in the latter it cannot. It is some sign of this adult quality in our society that our government should have decided that its Official Histories of the Second World War were to be 'histories proper', and not contributions to a national myth. Inevitably the honest historian discovers, and must expose, things which are not compatible with the national myth; but to allow him to do so is necessary, not simply to conform to the values which the war was fought to defend, but to preserve military efficiency for the future.

This brings me back to the question – Does military history

have any *practical* value? Here again the academic historian must have his doubts, and those are twofold.

First, the historian should be conscious of the uniqueness of every historical event. 'History does not repeat itself,' goes the adage, 'historians repeat one another.' The professional historian is concerned rather with establishing differences than with discerning similarities, and he usually shudders at the easy analogies drawn by laymen between Napoleon and Hitler, or Hitler and Khrushchev, or Pitt the Younger and Churchill. He is concerned with events occurring and people living within a certain society, and his task is to explain them in terms of that society. Analogies with events or personalities from other epochs may be illuminating, but equally they mislead; for only certain features in situations at different epochs resemble one another, and what is valid in one situation may, because of entirely altered circumstances, be quite untenable the next time it seems to occur. The historian must be always on the alert not to read anachronistic thoughts or motives into the past; and it is here that military historians without academic training are most likely to go astray. Hans Delbrück, perhaps the greatest of modern military historians, shrewdly put his finger on the weaknesses both of the military man who turns to history and of the academic who turns to military affairs. The latter, he pointed out, 'labours under the danger of subscribing to an incorrect tradition because he cannot discern its technical impossibility'. The former 'transfers phenomena from contemporary practice to the past, without taking adequate account of the difference in circumstances'.

As an example of an incorrect tradition subscribed to by academics, we may cite the belief, held almost without question until Delbrück himself destroyed it, that the army with which Xerxes attacked the Greeks in 481 B.C. was two and a half million strong – a clear logistical impossibility. As to anachronistic thinking by soldiers turned historians, it would be invidious to cite by name the many studies, by enormously able soldiers, who attribute to commanders in medieval or sixteenth-century warfare thought-processes which they could have developed only after a long study of Jomini or Mahan, or an intensive course at Camberley or Greenwich, or both. The business of entering into the minds of other generations, of appreciating what Professor Geyl has called 'the general otherness of earlier ages', is difficult and demands long training and wide reading. But the historian who thinks he *has* acquired it may become over-reluctant to admit that different ages and their events can ever profitably be collated or compared, which is, perhaps, no less of an error.

The second ground for doubt of the utility of military history, in the mind of the academic historian, is his awareness that he is studying not what happened in the past, but what historians *say* happened in the past. Spenser Wilkinson pointed out in his inaugural lecture at Oxford that the first job of the military historian was 'the sifting of the evidence with a view to the establishment of the facts. The second . . . is the attempt to arrange the facts in their connection of cause and effect.' But it does not work out like that. The number of possibly relevant 'facts' is infinite. (Are we not hearing constantly fresh evidence about Napoleon's medical condition which explains his behaviour at Waterloo?) And the historian's mind is not a blank sheet of paper, however much he may try to clear it of prejudice and preconceptions. He has to start with certain preconceived ideas and he may not be conscious of all of them. He will be interested only in answering certain questions. He imposes his own order on the data before him. To quote Geyl again, he 'must use his material by choosing from it, ordering it, and interpreting it. In doing so he is bound to introduce an element of subjectivity. . . . Behind the facts, behind the goddess History, there is a historian.'

This need for selection is particularly great in the case of the military historian, especially when he deals with operations. The evidence is confused and usually contradictory. Eyewitnesses are in no psychological condition to give reliable accounts of their experiences. Loyalty and discretion may result in the suppression of discreditable evidence, especially if all ultimately turns out well. Military historians, more than any other, have to create order out of chaos; and the tidy accounts they give of battles, with generals imposing their will on the battlefield, with neat little blocks and arrows moving in a rational and orderly way, with the principles of war being meticulously illustrated, are an almost blasphemous travesty of the chaotic truth. Some attempt must be made to sort order out of chaos; that is what historians are for. But we would do well, says the sceptical academic, not to take this orderly account even for an approximation to what really happened, much less base any conclusions on it for the future.

All these are good grounds for caution in 'using' military history. They are good grounds for regarding the tidy, dogmatic generalizations of certain staff-college crammers as being a monstrous *abuse* of military history which has gone on far too long. But I do not consider them grounds for regarding military history as useless. Given all these academic caveats, war is none the less a distinct and repetitive form of human behaviour. Unlike politics, or administration, or economic activity, which are continuing and constantly developing processes, war is intermittent, clearly defined, with distinct criteria of success or failure. We cannot state dogmatically that Britain is better governed now, or that her economy is more flourishing, than it was in 1761. We can disagree as to whether certain historical events – the Reformation, or the Glorious Revolution, or the Great Reform Act – were triumphs or disasters. The historian of peace can only chronicle and analyse *change*. But the military historian knows what is victory and what defeat, what is success and what failure. When activities do thus constantly recur, and their success can be assessed by a straightforward standard, it does not seem over-optimistic to assume that we can make judgments about them and draw conclusions which will have an abiding value.

But the academic historian is only one critic of the view that military history may have a use. Yet more formidable is the attack of the practical serving soldier – the man conscious of the technical complexities of his profession and understandably impatient of the idea that the experience of Napoleon or 'Stonewall' Jackson can have any relevance to an age of tanks and missiles and machine guns. With his arguments I am far worse equipped to deal. But certain useful things can still be said.

There are two great difficulties with which the professional soldier, sailor or airman has to contend in equipping himself as a commander. First, his profession is almost unique in that he may have to exercise it only once in a lifetime, if indeed that often. It is as if a surgeon had to practise throughout his life on dummies for one real operation; or a barrister appeared only once or twice in court towards the close of his career; or a professional swimmer had to spend his life practising on dry land for an Olympic championship on which the fortunes of his entire nation depended. Second, the complex problem of running an army at all is liable to occupy his mind and skill so completely that it is very easy to forget what it is being run *for*. The difficulties encountered in the administration, discipline, maintenance and supply of an organization the size of a fair-sized town are enough to occupy the senior officer to the exclusion of any thinking about his real business: the conduct of war. It is not surprising that there has often been a high proportion of failures among senior commanders at the beginning of any war. These unfortunate men may either take too long to adjust themselves to reality, through a lack of hard preliminary thinking about what war would really be like, or they may have had their minds so far shaped by a lifetime of pure administration that they have ceased for all practical purposes to be soldiers. The advantage enjoyed by sailors in this respect is a very marked one; for nobody commanding a vessel at sea, whether battleship or dinghy, is ever wholly at peace.

If there are no wars in the present in which the professional soldier can learn his trade, he is almost compelled to study the wars of the past. For after all allowances have been made for historical differences, wars still resemble each other more than they resemble any other human activity. All are fought, as Clausewitz insisted, in a special element of danger and fear and confusion. In all, large bodies of men are trying to impose their will on one another by violence; and in all, events occur which are inconceivable in any other field of experience. Of course the differences brought about between one war and another by social or technological changes are immense, and an unintelligent study of military history which does not take adequate account of these changes may quite easily be more dangerous than no study at all. Like the statesman, the soldier has to steer between the danger of repeating the errors of the past because he is ignorant that they have been made, and the danger of remaining bound by theories deduced from past history although changes in conditions have rendered these theories obsolete. We can see, on the one hand, depressingly close analogies between the mistakes made by the British commanders in the Western Desert in their operations against Rommel in 1941 and 1942 and those made by the Austrian commanders against Bonaparte in Italy in 1796 and 1797: experienced, reliable generals commanding courageous and well-equipped troops, but slow in their reactions, obsessed with security and dispersing their units through fear of running risks. On the other hand, we find the French General Staff both in 1914 and 1939 diligently studying the lessons of 'the last time' and committing appalling strategic and tactical blunders in consequence: conducting operations in 1914 with an offensive ferocity which might have brought victory in 1870 but now resulted in massacre; and in 1939 preparing for the slow, thorough, yard-by-yard offensive which had been effective at the end of the First World War and now was totally outdated. The lessons of history are never clear. Clio is like the Delphic oracle: it is only in retrospect, and usually too late, that we can understand what she was trying to say.

Three general rules of study must therefore be borne in mind by the officer who studies military history as a guide in his profession and who wishes to avoid its pitfalls.

First, he must study in *width*. He must observe the way in which warfare has developed over a long historical period. Only by seeing what does change can one deduce what does not; and as much can be learned from the great 'discontinuities' of military history as from the apparent similarities of the techniques employed by the great captains through the ages. Observe how in 1806 a Prussian army soaked in the traditions of the greatest captain of the eighteenth century, Frederick the Great, was nonetheless destroyed; and how the same thing happened in 1870 to a French army brought up in the Napoleonic mould. Consider whether in the conditions of warfare of 1914–18 the careful studies of Napoleon's or Moltke's methods, and the attempts to apply them on both sides, were not hopelessly irrelevant; and whether indeed the lessons which Mahan drew from his studies of eighteenth-century naval warfare did not lead our own Admiralty to cling to the doctrine of the capital fleet for so long that, in the age of the submarine and the aircraft carrier, this country was twice brought within measurable distance of defeat. Knowledge of principles of war must be tempered by a sense of change, and applied with a flexibility of mind which only wide reading can give.

Next, he must study in *depth*. He should take a single campaign and explore it thoroughly, not simply from official histories but from memoirs, letters, diaries, even imaginative literature, until the tidy outlines dissolve and he catches a glimpse of the confusion and horror of the real experience. He must get behind the order subsequently imposed by the historian and recreate by detailed study the omnipresence of chaos, revealing the part played not only by skill and planning and courage, but by sheer good luck. Only thus can he begin to discover, if he is lucky enough not to have experienced it at first hand, what war is really like – 'what really happened'.

And lastly, he must study in *context*. Campaigns and battles are not like games of chess or football matches, conducted in total detachment from their environment according to strictly defined rules. Wars are not tactical exercises writ large. They are, as Marxist military analysts quite rightly insist, conflicts of *societies*, and they can be fully understood only if one understands the nature of the society fighting them. The roots of victory and defeat often have to be sought far from the battlefield, in political, social and economic factors which explain why armies are constituted as they are, and why their leaders conduct them in the way they do. To explain the collapse of Prussia in 1806 and of France in 1870, we must look deep into their political and social as well as into their military history. Nor can we understand fully the outcome of the First World War without examining the social and political reasons why the Central Powers had so much less staying power than the Western Allies, so that Germany collapsed within a few months of her most sweeping triumphs. Without some such knowledge of the broader background to military operations one is likely to reach totally erroneous conclusions about their nature, and the reasons for their failure and success. Today, when the military element in the great power-struggles of the world is inhibited by mutual fears of the destructive power of the weapons available to both sides, such political and economic factors have an importance such as they have never possessed before; but even in the most apparently formal and limited conflicts of the past they have never been entirely absent.

Pursued in this manner, in width, in depth and in context, the study of military history should not only enable the civilian to understand the nature of war and its part in shaping society, but also directly improve the officer's competence in his profession. But it must never be forgotten that the true use of history, military or civil, is, as Jacob Burckhardt once said, not to make men clever for next time; it is to make them wise for ever.

Three People

LIDDELL HART

My own acquaintance with Basil Liddell Hart began in a way typical of the man. In about 1955 a letter arrived from him out of the blue expressing interest in a review I had written in the *New Statesman* and suggesting a meeting. An obscure young history lecturer at London University, I was given a splendid lunch at the Athenaeum, an invitation to stay at his country home, and involved in a correspondence which barely flagged for ten years, one letter of mine evoking about three from him. Even if there was no letter for him to answer he was undeterred. 'On going through my files,' he would write, 'I notice that you have not yet dealt with the point I raised in the second paragraph of my letter of July 17th of last year . . .' And when one visited him, to be entertained with excellent food and wine and endless whisky – everything the heart of man could desire except sleep – he would be lying in wait with a deceptively small piece of paper on which he had jotted down in his microscopic writing a few dozen topics on which he wanted information or discussion. One was hooked; willingly bound in an exacting, exhausting, delightful and immensely rewarding slavery. On 30 January 1970 we were granted by his death a forlorn and unwelcome release.

I write 'we' advisedly. Scores if not hundreds of students and disciples were bound to this implacable and loving master. With all he corresponded indefatigably: Israeli Colonels, French Generals, American Ph.D. students, British politicians, Japanese journalists, scholars of all lands. Their letters, together with those of Churchill, Eden, Wavell, Montgomery, Ironside, Gort, Hore-Belisha, T. E. Lawrence, Alfred Duff-Cooper and many others, are preserved in the enormous files which hourly threatened to engulf every house he inhabited; files themselves incapable of absorbing fast enough the documents which covered every inch of table space in his large study. At any given moment he was writing, probably, two books, both years past the publisher's deadline and three times the contracted length; several magazine articles; preparing a university lecture; reading half a dozen manuscripts, often by total strangers; as well as carrying on the huge correspondence I have described above. *And* he would sit up all night drinking whisky and lukewarm water arguing with his guests. *And* he would make himself available to any inquiring visitor who wanted to see him. *And* he seemed to have infinite time for the host of personal friends whom he grappled to himself, out of his huge acquaintanceship, with hoops of steel. He was a very remarkable man.

Liddell Hart in fact was a Sage, and almost the last. When did they begin, these independent thinkers supporting themselves by private means or journalism, establishing their bases in pleasant country houses, attracting scholars and disciples from all over the world, respected and a little feared by the Establishment they mocked? Voltaire was perhaps the archetype, but they proliferated in England in the first part of the twentieth century: the Webbs, Wells, Shaw, Russell, as well as Liddell Hart. There are not many left. Universities try to institutionalize them, if only as writers-on-campus; but a university provides a ready-made community with firm if flexible guidelines, while the true Sage must make his own. The Sage is a monarch, not a member of a republic. Above all the Sage, however deeply his roots may be sunk in the expertise of a single subject, billows uncontrollably outside it. Liddell Hart was no more simply a military thinker than Shaw was simply a playwright or Russell simply a philosopher. Like them, the passionate concern he devoted to his own subject gave him a passionate concern about everything else as well. And in Liddell Hart's case, the depth and intensity which he brought to it over fifty years have transformed the nature of military thought itself.

In reporting Liddell Hart's death, *The Times* surpassed itself. 'Between the wars,' it stated (and I quote the news item in its entirety) 'he published a training manual. The War Office deleted some of his theories, but one that survived, on rapid attack, was adopted by the German Army.' No other newspaper plumbed comparable depths of banality in describing the achievements of one of the major thinkers and historians of our time; but the general public impression was nonetheless that Liddell Hart's main contribution to military thought lay in his development of ideas about armoured warfare. Certainly his association with this development is well documented and its results during the first two years of the Second World War were spectacular. Inevitably its success gave him legitimate if melancholy satisfaction. But the concept of armoured warfare to which he contributed was in itself only part of a broader philosophy of war, and indeed of peace, which he worked at throughout his life, and which possesses a coherence and continuing relevance which merits an attempt to describe it in its entirety.

Inescapably, Liddell Hart's thought was shaped by the First World War. He was one of the generation of young men, cheerful, intelligent and patriotic, whose first experience of war was the Battle of the Somme. For scores of thousands it was to be their last. Of those who survived, perhaps the majority accepted that experience with all its horrors as inevitable and did not lose their faith in the military and social system which had made it possible. A minority, whose voice was becoming increasingly influential with each passing decade, turned blindly and bitterly against both. But a handful tried to think through clearly how such slaughter could have come about and how in future it could be avoided. War was hell, but mere wishing would not prevent its recurrence. Somebody had to consider how, if it did occur, it could be fought more cleanly, more decisively, above all more intelligently. There had been a time when one could speak without irony of an Art of War, when professionals had matched one another in skill and courage without destroying civilization in the process. Could such times never come again?

It was the hope of Liddell Hart – and one which he never entirely abandoned – that they could; and it was a hope which made him, as a young military correspondent in the 1920s, popular with the Services he had so recently left. His method was inductive. He began with the simplest form of infantry tactics, in experimenting with which he had already made a name for himself as a young officer training reinforcements. Infantry formations in the First World War were still determined by the basic weapons-system of the eighteenth and nineteenth centuries – the musket and the bayonet, which could be used effectively, either in the offence or in the defence, only by troops deployed in line. But the basic infantry weapon of the twentieth century was the machine-gun; so infantry should be redeployed in groups to serve it. The firing-line, Liddell Hart maintained, should be replaced by a 'combat-unit' of all arms, divided into sub-units each independently capable of manoeuvre and of exploiting the opening those manoeuvres created. But how to exploit them effectively? Perhaps, he suggested in a lecture in 1920, by 'the practical application of caterpillar track to all forms of transport in or near the battle zone'. And by 1922 he had developed a complete scenario whereby infantry and artillery, mounted in appropriate vehicles, could co-operate with tanks, with low-flying aircraft taking over the traditional role of artillery and with air transport being used for supply and reinforcements. It was a scheme which caught the keen eye of a certain Captain Heinz Guderian of the German Army.

From this new pattern of grand tactics, Liddell Hart went on to study possible developments in strategy. The deadlock of the Somme had been the result not simply of a faulty tactical doctrine but of a strategic doctrine which he traced back to Clausewitz's interpretations of Napoleonic warfare. This called for the greatest possible concentration of strength against the enemy's strongest point in order to overwhelm his forces in a decisive battle; a battle which would secure total victory. The nuances of Clausewitz's thought, he argued, had not been fully appreciated by his followers, and the result had been bloody war and bitter peace. The concept of 'concentration' must be abandoned in favour of one of manoeuvre. Rather than concentrating one's own forces, one should force the enemy to disperse by posing threats to alternate objectives, and surprise him by attacking at a place, or at a time, when he was unprepared. The strategy of frontal attack must be replaced by a strategy of indirect approach. The American Civil War had been won not by Grant's bloody battering on the Eastern Front but by Sherman's almost unknown campaigns in the West and South.

The trouble about this kind of strategic thinking was that it was related to a kind of war that, between 1918 and 1938, neither the British Army nor the British Government nor, above all, the British people had any intention of fighting again. For France, Germany and Russia the prospect of large-scale Continental war, if war ever did recur, was inescapable. The British hoped that they might escape it; indeed the view grew up, powerfully supported by Liddell Hart himself, that they could have escaped it in 1914 if only they had adhered to their traditional maritime strategy, 'The British Way in Warfare', and not got sucked into the Continental holocaust. The dichotomy between a 'Continental' and a 'maritime' strategy went far back into British history and had reappeared in bitter form during and after the First World War in the controversy between 'Westerners' and 'Easterners'. As a historian Liddell Hart espoused the latter. He associated himself closely with Lloyd George and gave professional advice on the writing of his *Memoirs*. And when in the early 1930s another war became a finite possibility, he turned from discussing how in the abstract war ought to be fought to prescribing in concrete terms how to prepare for the next.

The '30s were a terrible decade for those who had lived through the First World War. On the one hand the Great Powers seemed to be moving once again towards war with inexorable rapidity; on the other memories of the Western Front, somehow frozen during the 1920s under a hard carapace of pious reverence, were freshly unleashed and, together with horrified presentiments of the new possibilities of aerial bombardment, made the prospect of such a conflict appear utterly intolerable. Some sought refuge from the dilemma in the political formula of 'collective security', cheerfully disdaining the disagreeable task of thinking through the military implications of such an ambitious system of multilateral guarantees. With the aspirations of this group Liddell Hart had a deep instinctive sympathy, as he had with those of the pacifists themselves; but for the intellectual slovenliness which lay behind their reasoning he had no time at all. "If you want peace, *understand* war" was his motto. The problem which faced him was inescapable and must be resolved.

Of one thing he was certain: no solution lay along the lines of 1914–18. Britain should not again raise a large conscript army, put it on the Continent and use it in an offensive strategy in pursuit of total victory. Salvation lay rather in returning to traditional ways. Britain should leave major land-fighting to her Continental allies and concentrate on building up strength by sea and air. She should contribute the old weapon of blockade and the new one of air bombardment. Her Army should remain a small professional Imperial police force. If it contributed anything to a Continental conflict, it should be a few mechanized units which might just turn the scale; but it would probably be best to commit no land force to the Continent at all, and make it quite clear that in any future conflict Britain's liability should be strictly limited.

This was the view put forward in *The British Way in Warfare* (1932), in *Europe in Arms* (1937) and *The Defence of Britain* (1939), as well as in countless articles in *The Times* and elsewhere. Whether it influenced the decisions of the British Government during this period is hard to document, but certainly the policy of the Government coincided with it very closely indeed. In rearmament, priority was given to the Royal Air Force, the Royal Navy and the Air Defence of Great Britain. No measures were taken to enlarge the Army or to equip it to take part in large-scale land operations. No pressure came from within the Army itself for this to happen. Too many of its senior officers regarded it as a comfortable sanctuary from industrial society to welcome even the limited measures of streamlining and mechanization which were forced on them after 1937 by Leslie Hore-Belisha, with Liddell Hart himself as his unofficial but powerful adviser; and a whole military generation went to its graves cursing the two men who had tried to drag it, kicking and screaming, into the twentieth century. Fortunately a new generation was at hand – Alan Brooke, Bernard Paget, Bernard Montgomery, Harold Alexander, Ronald Adam, William Slim – of Liddell Hart's own contemporaries, who got the message in time.

But 'The British Way in Warfare' and the concept of limited liability were ideas of very doubtful relevance to twentieth-century Europe. They were based on study of an era before the French Revolution which was fundamentally different in two respects. First, limited war postulated a homogeneous political system in which all actors shared common values and were concerned only with limited improvements to their positions within the system. As Clausewitz had pointed out, it was the appearance of an actor who rejected the system which had led to the development of absolute war, not *vice versa*. The belief that any war against Nazi Germany could be limited was based on the same assumptions as the belief that she could be appeased: that 'peaceful co-existence' was indefinitely possible with a daemonic leader at the head of a nihilistic revolutionary movement. 'Limited liability' would have meant making peace with Hitler in 1940 once our original stake had been lost, as we had under comparable circumstances made peace with Napoleon in 1802, using our naval and air strength to secure the best possible terms.

In the second place 'The British Way in Warfare' had been successful against an adversary – France – who had overseas trade and possessions against which our naval strength could be effective and the loss of which was sufficiently serious to her economy to incline her to make peace. But even under these favourable conditions, once France succeeded in uniting or pacifying the whole of Western Europe and was able to concentrate on naval warfare, as she did in 1779, Britain's advantage disappeared. 'The British Way in Warfare', as sardonic Continentals have not been slow to observe, did not dispense with hard fighting on the Continent: it only meant that the British got their allies to do it for them. And if their allies were defeated, what then?

Nobody should have known better than Liddell Hart in 1939 that Britain's Allies were likely to be defeated. Probably nobody *did* know better. He had watched, with very mixed feelings, the development of Germany's armoured divisions. He had analysed the ponderous immobility of the French Army. Yet in *The Defence of Britain*, published a few weeks before the outbreak of the war, he wrote in reassuring terms about the growing strength of the defensive over the offensive, the developing effectiveness of anti-tank defences, of the ease with which armoured thrusts could be sealed off and dealt with by armoured counter-attacks – all in order to reinforce his argument that no British land force need be sent to the Continent. He wrote perhaps partly to reassure himself, partly to reassure others; but largely in a last-minute bid to avert what he saw as a disastrous return to the suicidal strategy of the First World War. For in the spring of 1939 the Government had at last decided to open staff talks with the French, to send an expeditionary force to the Continent, to double the strength of the Territorial Army, and to introduce Liddell Hart's *bête noire*, conscription. The total war which he regarded as the negation rather than the fulfilment of policy loomed ahead.

Total the war was indeed to be, though it did not involve Britain in another Battle of the Somme. Liddell Hart watched dourly from the sidelines. In the eyes of the British public, ironically, he was the apostle of the defensive whose teaching had been discredited by the events of 1940. It was a dismal period from which both his reputation and his self-confidence took long to recover. For the rest of his life he was to display an almost pathetic need for praise and appreciation, treasuring every scrap of evidence of his influence and every tribute to his abilities in a way that surprised his disciples, who took them for granted, and occasionally exasperated his dearest friends.

The course of the War afforded him little satisfaction. On the level of tactics and organization, indeed, his teaching was more than vindicated. The British infantry adopted the tactics he had devised for them twenty years earlier. The armoured forces of the belligerent powers operated in accordance with the principles he had laid down. In its tactical and strategic thinking the Allied High Command showed none of the sterile lack of imagination that had characterized its conduct of the First World War. But these operational improvements did not, as Liddell Hart had hoped, bring back the days of limited war and moderate peace. Britain herself avoided holocaust, but she did so only because she fought in alliance with two great powers who regarded their liabilities as unlimited, who raised forces on a gigantic scale and poured them out without stint. The Soviet Union was in no position to adopt a strategy of limited liability, and Churchill's Britain, rightly or wrongly, was in no mood to. The Second World War was fought brutally, often wastefully, but with a total commitment of effort; everything that Liddell Hart in his teachings had sought to avoid. It is difficult to see how it could have been otherwise. When the survival of peoples appears to be at stake, they are not nice in the methods they use.

Liddell Hart's eclipse was not undeserved. Nobody stressed more often the need for ruthlessly dispassionate analysis as a basis for both history and theory; but he himself sought to escape from the dilemma of his generation by what was, in the context of his times, little more than rationalization of nostalgic wishful thinking. There is a salutary lesson here for all academics who are rash enough to advise on policy. They need to subject themselves as well as their subject matter to searching examination in order to identify and make explicit the bias which is bound to affect their judgment. There is no such animal as a 'dispassionate' expert, and it is as well in these days of strategic studies and conflict-analysis to bear this in mind.

But once the smoke had cleared after the War, Liddell Hart's reputation, both as an analyst and as a historian, could be seen to rest on enduring foundations. As a policy adviser he may have shared the flawed assumptions of a tortured generation; but campaign after campaign in Europe had borne witness to his operational insight, and the most successful German military leaders, as well as the most honest British ones, paid generous tribute to his influence. The founders of the new Israeli Army, men who could afford to run no risks, soaked themselves in his writings, and their signed photographs joined those of the British, American and German generals which lined his study. As a historian his reputation rested on his still irreplaceable studies of the First World War and on his biography of General Sherman, which brought a new dimension to Civil War studies.

What, in conclusion, of his work as a military thinker since the war? About this, there are two things to be said. First, his warnings about the need for limitations on war have never been more relevant. In the 1930s they may have been premature: total victory was still possible and, alas, necessary. In the nuclear age Liddell Hart had only to repeat, this time with undeniable relevance, the lessons he had been preaching throughout his life: that force, if used at all, must be used with skill, and restraint, that the object of all war is a better peace, and that the nature of that peace will be determined not only by who wins but by the way in which the war has been fought. Secondly, Liddell Hart lived to see the work which he had carried on almost single-handed throughout his life assume the dimensions of an industry. Universities set up chairs of strategic studies; independent or government-sponsored institutes were formed; ministries concerned with defence or foreign policy set up special staffs of analysts; all taking implicitly or explicitly as their motto Liddell Hart's dictum 'If you want peace, understand war.'

All this may still not be enough to save governments from making ghastly mistakes. The men who work in these establishments and advise their rulers – like those who on moral grounds attack them – are no more immune from error and prejudice than was Liddell Hart himself. The problems with which they have to deal remain stubbornly resistant to neat intellectual or moral solutions. But at least they can bring to their task all the intellectual rigour and moral passion of which they are capable. And if they succeed half as well as did Liddell Hart, we can count ourselves lucky.

MONTGOMERY

The death of Field Marshal Viscount Montgomery of Alamein in March 1976 was the occasion of commemorations on a scale dwarfing those for any of his colleagues in the Second World War with the exception of Sir Winston Churchill. To a generation which did not know the war the reason may not be immediately clear. Montgomery was only one of the dozen or so senior British commanders of all three Services who led the country to victory, and the passing of others no less deserving has received at best only polite attention. Montgomery was by no means a well-loved figure. His successes were due as much to team-work on a vast scale as to his personal brilliance as a general, and they were won against adversaries who were greatly outnumbered in material and, usually, in men. Did he in fact have any remarkable qualities as a commander except the good luck to be on hand when, for the first time, the British Army was able to fight on equal or better terms with its adversaries – and except a flair for public relations which, in the eyes of his critics, amounted to a craving?

Certainly there is an element of unfairness in this concentration of hero-worship on the figure of Montgomery. There were indeed other military leaders to whom the nation owed at least as much if not a great deal more. But generals are in a special position. Their colleagues in the Navy and in the Air Force are inevitably more remote figures. With the passing of the great naval battle, with command of the sea being contested by innumerable minor actions and depending as much on scientific expertise as on seamanship, even the most formidable of admirals – even a Ramsay or a Cunningham – becomes an administrator exercising remote control. If one had to select a single man on whom the survival of the country depended in the darkest days of the War, one could do worse than to choose Admiral Sir Max Horton, who as Commander-in-Chief Western Approaches bore the brunt of the submarine attack at its height; but who outside the Navy (or now, indeed, inside) has ever heard of him? Within the Royal Air Force some particularly impressive Air Marshal – a Harris, a Slessor, a Cochrane – might stamp his personality on his own Command, but they did not become national figures. The Chiefs of Staff, those organisers of victory, never emerged from the shadows of Whitehall. But even in the Second World War generals still commanded armies and won or lost battles in the old style. Whether they won or lost them might ultimately depend on the success with which the Navy kept the sea lanes open, the Air Force swept its opponents from the skies and destroyed enemy material and communications, and the Army itself had been provided with adequate equipment. An infinity of causes contributed to the result. But over the results there presided, for better or worse, a single man. However much the cards may have been stacked in his favour, he could still lose his nerve and bungle the job. On the other hand, however inadequate his resources, his skill could still gain moderate successes or mitigate defeat. It was into his hands ultimately that the nation entrusted its resources and waited breathlessly on the result. With whatever advantages he might have begun, he still had to earn his success the hard way.

And Montgomery did have enormous advantages; advantages which his predecessors, starved as they were of material, might well envy. The British Army was the Cinderella of the three Services in the years before the War; it was a small force whose role was basically to police the Empire. Nobody contemplated the possibility that it would ever expand again as it had in the First World War. Not until

1939 was it allowed to equip itself to fight on a Continental scale at all; and it is not to be wondered at that when it did expand it did so clumsily and erratically, selecting both its equipment and its commanders by a process of grievous trial and error. In each encounter with the Germans during this period of growth it was decisively beaten – in Norway, in France, in Greece and in Cyrenaica. Its procurement policy was bad (both in tanks and anti-tank guns it was continually outclassed); its staff work was ponderous; its commanders proved all too often to be good regimental soldiers promoted far above their ceilings; its tactical doctrine was a hand-to-mouth affair; and, above all, the co-operation it received from the Air Force suffered from the continuing reluctance of that Service to dedicate itself to the close support of the land battle which the Luftwaffe provided for the German Army with such spectacular results. It was a tragic time in which much fine material was wasted, and reputations were ruined for lack of adequate instruments to deploy.

By 1942 this grim and prolonged prelude was coming to an end. This was the year which had always been foreseen in British rearmament programmes when arms production would reach full potential, and now American supply was beginning to supplement British as well. In the Western Desert the Matildas and Valentines of the first generation of British armour were replaced by Grants, and, even better, Shermans from the United States – a few vital months before the Germans deployed the improved Mark IVs which could counter them. The two-pounder anti-tank gun, a kind of souped-up pea-shooter, was giving way to the excellent six-pounders, which in their turn released field-artillery from the anti-tank role it had been compelled to adopt in favour of more offensive missions. In the hands of Air Chief Marshal Tedder – a man to whom Britain owes no less than it does to Montgomery – the Royal Air Force in the Eastern Mediterranean was transformed into an instrument of unique flexibility, combing the seas for enemy supply ships but on call for immediate support to front-line infantry.

Finally, the perfection of the techniques of signals intelligence were providing British commanders with an exact and
up-to-date knowledge of enemy problems and intentions
possibly unprecedented in the history of war. The British
and Commonwealth Forces who had been fighting for two
continuous years in the Western Desert, outclassed in
equipment, outmanoeuvred, out-generalled, knew what had
to be done if only they had the tools to do it with. By the
autumn of 1942 they had them, in overwhelming quantity:
over 1,000 tanks to the enemy's 500, 900 guns, 1,400 anti-
tank guns, nearly 200,000 men against the enemy's 100,000
(half of them Italian), and complete command of the air.

This superiority they enjoyed partly because by the late
summer of 1942 the Middle Eastern Theatre had assumed a
moral importance out of all proportion to its strategic
significance. This was the only theatre of war in which
British troops were fighting the Axis Powers. The number of
forces engaged was a small fraction of those contending in
the gigantic and decisive battles on the Eastern Front. But
the ebb and flow of battle across the Western Desert was
regarded throughout the world, like the thin thread of
mercury in a thermometer, as an indicator of British success
in the War as a whole. The performance of the Eighth Army
was a factor in the USA's decision on whether to support the
European theatre of operations at all, and perhaps also in the
perception of a desperately hard-pressed Soviet Union of the
seriousness with which her allies intended the defeat of
Germany. It was closely watched by those strategically
significant neutrals, Spain and Turkey; by Hitler's doubtful
satellites, Vichy France and Italy; and by the captive
populations of occupied France. No other factor was of
comparable importance to morale at home: the fall of the
tiny port of Tobruk in June 1942 was as shattering a blow to
the British nation as the fall of Singapore.

Churchill's tendency to dramatize and to personify often
distorted his judgement, but it did not lead him astray when
in August 1942 he paced his room muttering 'Rommel –
Rommel – Rommel – what matters except beating him?' It

was only with the greatest difficulty that he had persuaded the Americans to keep to their strategy of 'Europe First' in spite of the British refusal to launch an immediate cross-Channel attack, instead of turning away in disgust to the Pacific. The operation to which the Allies had now set their hand, in North Africa, depended for its success on the friendly neutrality of Spaniards and Frenchmen who had not hitherto been provided with a shred of evidence that Britain and her allies could ultimately master German power. A successful battle in the Western Desert was thus the keystone to the arch of Allied strategy, and the general who fought it was assured, overnight, of world-wide fame.

To make assurance doubly sure it was not enough to send to the Middle Eastern Theatre every gun, every tank and every aircraft that could be spared. The commanders had to be relieved of all other responsibilities – especially the responsibility which had so weighed on the mind of General Auchinleck (the Commander-in-Chief of that theatre in 1941–2) of safeguarding their rear against the menace of German forces descending through Persia and Iraq. A separate command was created to deal with that front, leaving the Commander-in-Chief Middle East free to concentrate entirely on the Western Desert. A new Commander-in-Chief arrived from England, the imperturbable and self-effacing General Alexander. All that was now needed was the Army Commander himself; and with the dearly loved and battle-experienced General Gott tragically removed from the running when the aircraft was shot down in which he was returning to take up his command, there appeared on this brilliantly lit scene, before the expectant audience, Lieutenant-General Bernard Law Montgomery.

It is easy to say, and many soldiers and writers have since said, that with all these advantages, with the cards stacked in his favour as they had never been for his predecessors, Montgomery could not miss. But not even his bitterest enemies have suggested that he was a mere nonentity created for and by the situation, a kind of pop star built up by skilful manipulators to meet a national need. He had star quality of his own – that nobody doubted who had had anything to do with him (least of all General Alan Brooke, the C.I.G.S. in whose Corps Montgomery had served as a divisional commander at Dunkirk). It was a quality which had set him apart from his colleagues in the peace-time army: a loneliness bred of an unhappy childhood; a dedication to his profession which he saw, not as 'soldiering' – that pleasant, clubbable occupation compounded equally of regimental duties, minor imperial skirmishes and field sports – but as preparation for war and for high command in war; a self-reliance and a self-mastery with which went a total imperviousness to the opinions of others. The alarm felt by those posted to serve under him was equalled only by that of those senior commanders who found him their subordinate. In defiance of any higher authority he serenely went his own way and made sure that all under his command went with him; and 'serenely' is the *mot juste*. R. W. Thompson, one of his bitterest critics, has written of his 'knack of creating oceans of serenity round himself'. Goronwy Rees (who served briefly on his staff) has left an unforgettable picture of the 'air of calm and peace' in which he moved – one 'almost incongruous in a soldier'. Incongruous, perhaps, but essential, and the more essential as one rises higher in command. This calm, this tranquillity, this clear-headed self-confidence unshaken by the most ferocious storms of war, is the foundation on which the morale of an entire Army comes to rest. Montgomery possessed it to an almost supernatural degree.

He was known then in the Army: known, admired, feared, not very well liked. He had served with distinction throughout the First World War, taken his profession with untypical seriousness during the inter-war years, commanded a division with outstanding efficiency in the Dunkirk campaign and then, as a corps commander in England, made himself notorious for the realism of his training, his dedication to physical fitness, the lack of ceremony with which he treated his chairborne staff, whose weekly runs became (depending on whether one was involved in them or not) a subject of amusement or dread. He himself neither drank nor smoked. He was a monastic figure, celibate since the tragic death of his wife, solitary, never at ease with his contemporaries or his seniors, relaxing only in the company of his disciples, of the admiring young. Goronwy Rees described his 'narrow foxy face, long-nosed, sharp, intelligent and tenacious, with very bright and clear blue eyes, and a small, light, spare body. The effect was not at all imposing, except for his eyes and an indefinable look on his face of extreme cleverness and sagacity, like a very alert Parson Jack Russell terrier . . .' This was the little man, utterly self-confident, totally self-contained, who took over the Eighth Army and led it in the most spectacular British victory of the Second World War.

It was in Montgomery's style to treat his predecessors in Africa with a negligence and an injustice for which he has been rightly criticized. It was not that he bore them malice or felt any jealously towards them; it was simply that before his coming there had, in his view, been Chaos and Old Night, and that with him there began a totally new order. Whether or not there had been contingency plans for the evacuation of the Delta, there would be none now. Whether or not Auchinleck had already fought a decisive battle in the Alamein position, Montgomery was going to fight one now. Whether or not there were already plans for a defensive stand at Alam el Halfa with a refused left flank, Montgomery intended to make some. Whether or not commanders had acquitted themselves with credit fighting in the desert, Montgomery had no time for them if they were not prepared wholeheartedly to accept him as the new Messiah and fit into the pattern which he was imposing on events.

What that pattern was to be, he left no one under his command in any possible doubt – and that 'no one' is inclusive. Montgomery knew that he was commanding *an Army*, and he made every member feel part of it. This his predecessors, with all their qualities, had not done. Until then the British Forces in the Western Desert had consisted of units with splendid names and records – 4th Indian, 9th Australian, 7th Armoured Divisions, 11th Hussars, 201st

Guards Brigade – with their own heroic leaders and their own distinctive styles. Divisional commanders, sometimes even brigade and regimental commanders, were tribal chiefs over whom corps and army commanders uneasily and ineffectively presided, and who did not hesitate to question their orders if they did not like them. Auchinleck, with his tremendous personality, could keep them in order, but that should not have been his job; he had other things to do with his time. And outside these glamorous fighting units there were the scores of thousands of men in the base depots and on the lines of communication, whose morale and efficiency was no less essential to victory in mechanised warfare than that of the forward troops who depended on them for sustenance. For these men, 'GHQ' was simply a sprawling office manned by faceless if uniformed bureaucrats who engendered an unending lava-flow of paper. The most they saw of a general was a scarlet flash of hat-band as a staff-car swept past in a swirl of dust.

But Montgomery knew, as few other British commanders knew, what a complex and fundamentally *unmilitary* organization the wartime British Army was. He had watched it growing while he was commanding at home; seen these young and not so young men leave their suburban homes and their jobs in factories or shops, be put through hurried courses of basic and professional training and fitted out with their hideous if serviceable battledress and their insanely unserviceable forage-caps, and realised that, dutifully as they might rise to the occasion if properly managed, these men were *not* soldiers. The self-sacrificing young subalterns, the tough, deferential, uncomplaining privates who had died like lemmings on the Western Front in an earlier war had not bred their kind to replace them. These men wanted to stay alive, wanted to get home, wanted to know what was happening and why. They wanted a leader with whom they could identify themselves and who could speak to them directly. They needed something of a demagogue: someone who knew that rhetoric was once one of the classical military arts.

Almost by accident Montgomery learned how to play this

role. He found that he *was* something of a demagogue – relaxed and happy with crowds, drawing from them and reflecting back their own emotions. Although unmistakably a General – that light, clipped voice, that erect bearing of command – he was not typical of his colleagues and he subtly emphasized his eccentricities. He learned how to handle that vital group which soldiers tend to regard as their natural enemies, the Press, and the Press rose to him. With their help he projected this charismatic image, not only throughout the Eight Army which basked in his reflected glory, but throughout the Army as a whole, and the nation, and ultimately the world.

But neither his own talent for publicity nor the readiness with which the Press exploited it would have been of much enduring value if the image which he projected had not been in itself an effective one, and if it was not nourished by persistent professional success. It was not the image of a romantic leader demanding heroic sacrifices, but of a professional giving reliable reassurances; one who did not promise more than he could perform, and who was thoroughly, almost insolently, on top of his job. There would inevitably be casualties, he indicated, but no more than strictly necessary to achieve the objective, and anything that foresight and ingenuity could do to minimise them would be done. The sonorous eloquence of Churchill had sustained the nation through three years when its survival had seemed in doubt; but it was the brisk direct note struck by Montgomery that made victory appear, for the first time, to be an entirely practical proposition.

That is why Montgomery's preparations for and conduct of the Battle of El Alamein had such resonance throughout the world and why comparison of his performance with that of his predecessors is a poor criterion of his actual achievement.

Much may legitimately be said in dispraise of him. First, if Auchinleck had not fought and won the First Battle of Alamein in July, there would never have been a Second in October; and Montgomery's refusal to recognize this, either at the time or later, was only too typical of that total absence of generosity that so deeply flawed his character. Secondly, the plan which he made for the battle did not in the event work. He underestimated the logistical difficulties of moving such large masses in such small space and the speed and stubbornness of the enemy reaction. But his real talents then showed in a manner for which, interestingly enough, he has never claimed credit; in his refusal to be perturbed at the collapse of his plans, his calm reorganization of his forces in the middle of the battle, and his capacity to remain totally in control of the chaotic situation and ultimately to impose his will on it. In this he showed those qualities of greatness as a commander which make it legitimate to suggest that even if he had not hugely outnumbered his enemy in tanks and guns, even if he had not enjoyed complete command of the air, even if Rommel's forces had not been paralysed for lack of fuel, and if Rommel himself had not been a sick and discouraged man, Montgomery would still have found some means to victory. As it was, he had the superiority and used it remorselessly. Alamein was a *bataille d'usure*, not a skilful manoeuvre. The casualties were grim enough – 13,500 dead, wounded and missing; but the victory was complete. Thirty thousand enemy prisoners were in British hands, and few of their formations remained intact.

Rommel was beaten, but he was not destroyed, and here is the third legitimate criticism that can be made of Montgomery. He excelled in the set-piece battle – the careful preparations, the ingenious deception, the thoroughness of the staff work, the huge accumulation of fire to cover movement. But once that had succeeded, the chapter was closed. He did not adjust himself rapidly to the needs of that most difficult and necessary of military operations, the pursuit. He was a Plumer rather than an Allenby. He would take no risks: too many had been taken by his predecessors, too many initial victories had been squandered by subsequent ill-judged dissipation of effort. Every move must be logistically sound; the quick striking head of his Army must not lose touch with the great cumbersome tail which had to heave itself out of the Delta and laboriously hump itself along the northern shore of Africa while Rommel got away

with the remnants of his army. The pundits rightly mark
Montgomery down for this. It would have been nice if
Rommel could have been put in the bag, and the destruction
of his elite forces would have made the subsequent capture of
Tunisia a great deal easier. But in terms of the overall
balance of the War it would have been a marginal advantage. The country lost little by Montgomery's caution, and to
his credit must be counted every British life that was thereby
saved.

It took the Eighth Army nearly twenty weeks to reach
Tunisia, a journey of 1,000 miles. There, at Medenine, they
fought a first successful defensive battle in prepared positions from which, as at Alam el Halfa, they refused to be
drawn; then a less happy battle at the Mareth Line, where
their initial attack was repulsed in some disorder, but where
Montgomery once again, as at El Alamein, calmly reorgan-
ised in the middle of the battle and started again, with
decisive results; and finally at the Wadi Akarit, a surprise
assault which went like clockwork – a battle of almost
Mozartian balance and precision, which was in many ways
Montgomery's finest achievement. It was also the end of the
run.

A few days later he hit the mountains, which he never
learned to master, and the Americans, whom he never
learned to understand. Pinned down in front of Enfidaville
the Eighth Army realized for the first time why the First
Army had taken so long to reach Tunis. Montgomery had to
ask for help; and it was the quiet General Alexander who
now stepped forward, gathered both forces together and
administered, with the deft elegance of a matador, the *coup de
grâce*.

Montgomery was not perturbed. He was the hero of the
hour and knew it. He was already in direct correspondence
with the Prime Minister. Returning to London in his
idiosyncratic uniform – the beret with two badges (one of
them nothing to do with him), the sweater protruding
beneath his beltless battledress blouse – he found himself a
national celebrity and traded on the fact. Whatever he did

now, they would not sack him. There now loomed ahead the invasion of Sicily, a highly complex operation involving the land, sea and air forces of three nations, of which Eisenhower was in overall command, with Alexander in charge of the land forces. Montgomery's position was simply that of commander of one of the two land armies involved. But when briefed about the overall plan, he responded with breathtaking insolence: 'I am prepared to carry the war into Sicily with the Eighth Army but must do so in my own way.' His own way involved the abandonment of a separate task for the American Third Army – the capture of Palermo while the Eighth Army drove north to Catania and Messina – and its reduction to the role of a flank guard to the British force. The plan was tactically sound enough, and General Eisenhower had the wisdom to acknowledge it. But after the landings – when the Eighth Army found it could make no progress in the plain of Catania and pushed the Americans off one of the few main roads in order to improve its chances – the Third Army under General Patton understandably revolted. Alexander belatedly freed them from their humiliating servitude, and Patton at once showed his genius by a great sweep round the island which not only captured Palermo but brought him into Messina several hours before the British. Certainly the British had had to contend with Hitler's toughest units in the mountainous foothills guarding the approaches to Etna; but it was not only the Americans who felt more than a twinge of *Schadenfreude* at Patton's well-deserved success.

Montgomery, in fact, was now entering the doldrums. He had not shone in Sicily, and there were no laurels to be won in Italy either. His elaborate preparations for crossing the Straits of Messina proved an absurd over-insurance when his troops landed on that undefended shore. He could do little to affect the issue at Salerno and did not show any great urgency in attempting to do so. Slogging up the east coast he was confronted with ridge after ridge of mountain through which there was no short cut; no alternative to a series of assaults in worsening weather which he could do no more than deliver with as much effectiveness and as few casualties as possible. Serving in a subordinate position, on a secondary front and in villainous terrain, this, after all the glorious tumult of the past year, must have been difficult indeed for Montgomery to endure.

But it was not to last for long. At the end of the year he departed to take command of Allied ground forces for the forthcoming Normandy landings, perhaps the most complex military enterprise in the history of the world. In some respects he was the obvious choice. He was now Britain's best-known soldier, and his appointment – once again, the decision of Alan Brooke – gave confidence, not only to the troops under his command but to the great mass of civilians who constituted the operational base, that this hazardous operation was going to be a success. And it was a well-deserved confidence. Montgomery had mastered the art which officers brought up in the small British Army had so little chance to learn – that of commanding large formations in the field. His command ultimately embraced some forty divisions, and his only complaint was that it was not larger still. The larger the responsibility, the more truly was he in his element.

But functioning on this scale he could not be his own master. The single vision that he wished to impose on events, the 'master plan' of which he so often spoke and wrote, had to be adjusted and complicated to fit in with that of colleagues, and in the process misunderstanding and conflicts arose in which he was not constitutionally inclined to compromise. So long as he remained in supreme command of all land forces all went well. As in Sicily he insisted that the over-ambitious proposals prepared before he took command should be reduced to provide that greater concentration of force which in his view was needed to guarantee success. As at Alamein he saw that no detail of preparation should be omitted, no resource of power or ingenuity should be spared to ensure initial success. The smoothness with which debarkation occurred on the British beaches, in contrast to the bloody shambles at the American, owed much to his anxious forethought. As at Alamein, the 'dog-fight' that followed the 'break-in' saw some clumsy handling of armour. The dusty traffic jams, the confusion and ultimate repulse of Tenth Armoured Division's advance through XXX Corps at Alamein was to be repeated in Normandy in the ill-fated operations 'Epsom' and 'Goodwood'. But once again the grinding attrition exhausted a weaker enemy whose communications were anyhow rendered almost impassable by air attack and sabotage, until there came the moment of collapse when the planned break-out could begin. Alamein was in many respects a dress-rehearsal for this, the climactic battle in the West in the Second World War; and this time the break-out was in the hands of General George Patton himself – a man supremely well qualified to conduct it.

With the end of the Battle of Normandy in August 1944 Montgomery reached the peak of his career and the pinnacle of success. The last year of the War was to be less happy for him. General Eisenhower moved across from England to assume a control of operations which Montgomery deeply resented. He could not accept that he was now just a member of a team and, with the huge increase of American forces under the command of General Bradley, no longer even a senior member. His reiterated, almost querulous, demands that there should be a single commander of ground forces, and that all resources should be concentrated on a single thrust, could be all too easily interpreted in terms of personal ambition rather than sound strategic thinking. In fact the two were not incompatible. Without a single command there could be no master plan, and without a master plan one had, as Montgomery constantly put it, a cat's (or alternatively, a dog's) breakfast. To see his clarity of vision, his inner conviction of success, sacrificed on the altar of inter-Allied politics, overridden by a Supreme Commander for whom he barely attempted to conceal his contempt, was bitter indeed.

But the master plan which Montgomery formulated for the defeat of Germany in the autumn of 1944 was a most untypical one. Gone was the concern for careful preparation, for a sound logistic base, and for overwhelming material superiority which had distinguished his earlier battles. What he now proposed was a daring thrust into the heart of Germany by the forces under his command – a distance of some 500 miles from the nearest supply bases, of which the principal one was still the Mulberry Harbour on the open beaches of Arromanches. The Arnhem disaster showed only too clearly what happened when troops over-extended themselves; and Montgomery made no particular provision in his plan for clearing the port of Antwerp. It was in fact a gigantic gamble on the state of German morale, and there was little evidence in the behaviour of German armies either before or later to indicate that it might have come off. The Ardennes counter-offensive in December was only the most spectacular demonstration of their capacity for rapid re-covery – and one which illustrated both Montgomery's ability to rise superbly to emergencies and his self-destruc-tive tendency to spoil his successes by the tactless arrogance with which he discussed them. Even more significant than this 'Battle of the Bulge' was the dour and bitter fighting in the Reichswald in the early months of 1945 when Hitler forced the Allies to pay, for every yard of German soil they occupied, a heavy price in blood. Only after that, when the last ounce of effort had been squeezed out of the Wehrmacht west of the Rhine, could the final triumph come. But until the very end Montgomery was discontented with this role and was demanding a greater share of resources and a change in Eisenhower's plans so that he could end the war with the apotheosis which would come with the capture of Berlin.

It was Montgomery's misfortune that the talents for military command with which he was so superbly equipped were not enough in themselves, in twentieth-century war-fare, to fit a man for the supreme heights of responsibility where politics and strategy become indistinguishable. Once he left the comparatively sheltered waters of an Army command for the open seas of higher strategy, the confusion of political cross-currents and contrary winds made his 'master plans' impossible. There one needed qualities of insight and tact which he had never learned to cultivate. To use a metaphor which he applied prolifically to others, he rose above his ceiling. Nevertheless the instinct of the British people of singling him out as the symbol of victory, a 'mascot' transcending profession and class, was a sound one. No British commander in the War showed a better grasp of the intricacies of his appallingly difficult profession, and none showed a better understanding of the men that he led.

KISSINGER

The presence of Henry Kissinger in the White House, let alone the State Department was in itself a matter for astonishment. In posts normally occupied either by members of the WASP establishment, or by representatives of one or other of the American political or regional groupings, or by Presidential cronies, this distinctively European figure with his ineradicable German accent seemed quite grotesquely out of place. America may be a melting-pot, but some melt faster than others, and Kissinger remained stubbornly unmelted. He once unwisely and inaccurately attributed the obsessive curiosity of the American public about his personality to the syndrome of the Lone Ranger, the mysterious stranger in the myth of the West. He flattered himself. It was due rather to simple amazement that someone who in terms of background and personality seemed so utterly unsuitable to wield power in Washington had ever succeeded in making it. It was the Yankee at the court of King Arthur in reverse; and the fact that the court was not Camelot but that of Richard Nixon, the embodiment of American philistinism, insularity and political chicanery at their worst, made it appear all the more bizarre.

The first volume of Kissinger's memoirs make it clear that he knew very well what he was doing there. He was the Merlin at this Round Table; the wise man drawing on deep wells of ancient magic to help this naïve, rumbustious, good-hearted people among whom his lot had been cast; rescuing them from the disasters into which their good intentions had already led them, setting them on a path that would avoid future catastrophe, and teaching them the skills by which their noble endeavours could be turned to good effect. He admired their 'boundless energy, pragmatic genius, unquenchable optimism', especially as embodied in Nelson Rockefeller, his first patron and pupil. 'For other nations', he observed, 'utopia is a blessed past never to be recovered; for Americans it is no farther than the intensity of their commitment.' Kissinger had arrived on the scene at a critical moment, when the golden age of American innocence was drawing to a close, and his protégés had lost their way in the dark wood of Vietnam. 'What remained to be determined', he considered, 'was whether we could learn from this knowledge, or consume our substance in rebelling against the reality of our maturity.'

Kissinger appreciated better than most the irony of the fact that it was Richard Nixon who brought him into the Government. He observed, and had little respect for, the processes by which the American people selected their President; how 'in contemporary America power increasingly gravitates to those with an almost obsessive desire to win it', so that the qualities required to grasp the nomination might have little in common with the qualities required to govern. He observed with truly olympian detachment the amazing antics of Nixon's courtiers, totally devoted to smoothing the path of their master. 'What they lacked in ideals and background', he drily observed, 'they made up in assiduity. Later it would become clear how little was the commitment to the future of such people without a past.'

As for Nixon himself, the Arthur who, if he had drawn the sword from the stone by his own unaided efforts, needed a great deal of help in wielding it, Kissinger's measured judgment was that he was 'not inconsiderable'. Many of his faults were positive advantages when it came to the exercise of power – or at least advantages where Kissinger was concerned. Nixon hated face-to-face negotiations – a curious feature in one who announced his intention of replacing an era of confrontation by one of negotiation. But as Kissinger not unjustly remarks, 'some of the débâcles in our diplomatic history have been perpetrated by Presidents who fancied themselves negotiators'.

And Kissinger believed, again not unjustly, that he himself was admirably equipped to do all the necessary negotiating. Nixon was secretive and suspicious to the point of paranoia. Nobody could call the jovial and extrovert Henry Kissinger paranoid, but his foreign-policy objectives and negotiating style called for a degree of confidentiality which, although normal enough among the European diplomats of the nineteenth century whom he had admired and studied, could be preserved in America in the late twentieth century only by unusual and irregular procedures. But, above all, Nixon could take decisions; and it was helpful that these were usually the decisions that Kissinger wanted him to take. 'He instinctively knew when the moment for decision had arrived: and he would then act resolutely, especially if he could insulate himself from too much controversy.' But Kissinger could not but observe how little pleasure Nixon derived from the wielding of the power that he had sacrificed so much to obtain. He acted, he writes, 'with a kind of joyless, desperate courage – torn between his insights and understanding of the international reality and his fatalistic insight that nothing he touched would ever be crowned with ultimate success'.

Kissinger's detachment was not only cultural; it was also in a sense professional. He was a historian before he was a statesman, not, like Clarendon or Guizot, a statesman turned historian; so he had an awareness, paralleled only perhaps by that of Churchill, that the events which he was helping to shape might one day be converted into history by himself – history which would possess a unique value for posterity. This led him at times into coy and rather rebarbitive self-consciousness, but it also made him commendably anxious to share his experiences in full, and particularly to leave behind him extensive pen-portraits of the great men of his time. The fullest are those of the adversaries with whom he negotiated, and these are distinguished by remarkable generosity. Dobrynin, Gromyko, Brezhnev, Le Duc Tho and Chou En-lai could not hope for fairer or more sympathetic assessments of their virtues and talents than they receive from Kissinger. His domestic adversaries, Melvin Laird, the Secretary for Defense, and the unfortunate William P. Rogers, the nominal Secretary of State, are treated, the one with admiration for a Machiavellian practitioner in Kissinger's own class, the other with the compassion which a persistent winner can afford to show a persistent loser. Dr Kissinger's ink is indeed quite unmixed with acid. Everyone he had to deal with were honourable men. Even his stubborn detractors in the media and academe he treats in sorrow rather than anger. Whether this is because Dr Kissinger does not want to make any unnecessary enemies at this stage of his career, or because he has absorbed at least the tedious blandness of American camaraderie in which everyone is a lovely person and all geese are swans, or because he is simply a warm-hearted and generous man, the reader must judge for himself. At all events, if he cannot think of anything agreeable to say about any of his colleagues, he prefers not to mention them at all. Certain members of the Kissinger entourage are very conspicuous by their absence from these pages.

As a historian, Kissinger also reflects at large on perennial issues of policy, especially foreign policy and the nature and limitations of power. Like others before him, he has found how limited is the range of options that confront even the most powerful decision-maker. Political leaders, he has discovered are 'locked in an endless battle in which the urgent constantly gains on the important. The political life of every political figure is a continual struggle to rescue an element of choice from the pressure of circumstance.' Statesmen, he maintains, 'cannot invent reality', nor, he indicates, can those not exposed to the pressures of power fully appreciate them. That is why even the most hostile of statesmen have problems and perceptions in common that cannot be shared with their peoples. Kissinger's perception of the problems of his adversaries was particularly acute, and that was why he negotiated with them with so large a measure of success.

For him neither the Russians nor the Chinese were ten feet tall, and only if one understood their fears could one understand, and so influence, their actions. 'The super-powers', he writes in a memorable paragraph,

often behave like two heavily armed blind men feeling their way around a room, each believing himself in mortal peril from the other whom he assumes to have perfect vision . . . Each tends to ascribe to the other side a consistency, foresight and coherence that its own experience belies. Of course, over time even two blind men can do enormous damage to each other, not to speak of the room.

Above all, Kissinger reflects on a problem that has occupied him, on and off, throughout his professional life: the difference in perception and morality between those who wield power and those who only comment on and judge them; between what Kant called 'the bureaucrats' and 'the philosophers'. It was a difference that for Americans the Vietnam war made anguished and almost unbridgeable and that has turned Kissinger into a figure whom many liberal American academics (and British journalists) cannot even now contemplate without becoming literally incoherent with rage.

Kissinger defines the difference calmly and dispassion-ately. 'The outsider', as he puts it,

thinks in terms of absolutes; for him right and wrong are defined in their conception. The political leader does not have this luxury. He can rarely reach his goal except in stages; any partial step is inherently morally imperfect and yet morality cannot be approxi-mated without it. The philosopher's test is the reasoning behind his maxims; the statesman's test is . . . the catastrophe he averts.

But because the catastrophe is averted and there is no means of proving whether this was due to the statesman's efforts or not, the dialogue between statesman and philosopher can never reach an agreed conclusion.

Kant asked (from within the benevolent despotism of eighteenth-century Prussia) that at least the philosopher's voice should be heard. There has been no problem about this in contemporary America. The difficulty has rather been the reverse; to persuade the philosophers to listen to the arguments of the bureaucrats. Kissinger complains of 'the lack of compassion, the overweening righteousness, the refusal to offer an alternative' which characterized his academic critics, and those who recall the combination of hysteria and dogmatism that swept through American universities in the early 1970s must admit that he does not overstate his case.

The dialogue became a confrontation in which rational discourse was notable by its absence; and when Kissinger complained of this to a group of university presidents, one of them replied with the terrifying words: 'We try to introduce fairness and reason to the debate – but only at risk to our own lives.' This ferocity was an aspect of American culture with which Kissinger did not succeed in identifying himself; and it was this, as he points out, that reinforced Nixon's bitter loneliness, drove him back on the small group of his sympathetic intimates, and came very close to unhinging him.

Kissinger's memoirs are of course an apologia; not in the currently understood sense of a defence against his critics but in the literal meaning of the word: a presentation of his beliefs. We may justifiably suspect that his policy did not have quite the coherence with which he has endowed it in retrospect, but it is clear that his actions were based on a set of coherent principles to an extent unusual among world statesmen. He had, after all, been thinking hard about foreign policy for fifteen years before he was required to practise it, which is more than can be said about most foreign ministers. He had formed clear views about the structure of the international system, which is more than can be said about most bureaucrats; and he had a combination of strength of will in maintaining his objectives and tactical skills in pursuing them which is a great deal more than can be said about most academics – at least, once they venture outside their own private jungles. One can thus accept his own statements as reliable evidence of his intentions, whether or not one agrees with his objectives or considers that he went the right way about implementing them.

Kissinger's intention, he explains, was 'to found American foreign policy on a sober perception of permanent national interest, rather than on fluctuating emotions that in the past had led us to excesses of both intervention and abdication'. He discerned in America 'an idealistic tradition that sees foreign policy as a contest between evil and good. There is a pragmatic tradition that seeks to solve "problems" as they arise. There is a legalistic tradition that treats international issues as juridical cases. There is no geopolitical tradition.' And this 'geopolitical tradition' involved seeing the world as consisting neither of warring ideologies nor of an integrated community susceptible to a rule of law, but of powers pursuing their own interests according to their best perception of them, the *froids monstres*, in de Gaulle's phrase, of the European tradition. Values and principles were certainly important; they

would inspire our efforts and set our direction. [But] . . . we would have to learn to reconcile ourselves to imperfect choices, partial fulfilment, the unsatisfying tasks of balance and maneuver, given confidence by our moral values but recognizing that they could be achieved only in stages and over a long period of time. It was a hard lesson to convey to a people who rarely read about the balance of power without seeing the adjective 'outdated' precede it.

Kissinger thus saw the international system in terms of structure rather than process. He had no time for those who believed that transnational flows and movements were eroding the traditional framework within which he sought to act. 'Non-state actors' were for him a trivial nuisance to be controlled through their patrons. The Third World had not yet gained entry to the club by developing states of sufficient significance to carry weight in the balance (though favoured Third World states like Iran might have their entrance fee paid for them). The world could be, and still had to be, manipulated by a concert of powers whose overriding interest in the stability of the system overrode their mutual suspicions. This involved a continuous process of communication between them, an appreciation of antagonistic interest and perceptions, an understanding of the interconnection

229

('linkage') of events throughout the world and a willingness to do deals over them. It was its failure to perceive these linkages that Kissinger held against the compartmentalized State Department and gave him something else in common with Nixon, who detested its members as a lot of toffee-nosed East-coast bastards. It provided the rationale for the creation of an alternative foreign policy (a *secret* in the French eighteenth-century sense) behind the backs of the State Department, manipulated from the White House through a system of personal 'channels' set up through individual contacts and all focusing on the person of Kissinger. Relations with the Soviet Union, with China, with the Federal German Republic, with Hanoi, with Israel and with Egypt were all handled in this clandestine manner.

This bizarre arrangement brought its own punishment. Kissinger had no friends among the public at large, and he developed none among the bureaucracy. The success of his byzantine manoeuvres depended entirely on the whim of his moody and unpredictable master. Fortunately Nixon shared or could be brought to share Kissinger's perception of the world. Even more fortunately, he did not see this rootless European, who possessed no independent power base, as in any sense a rival. So Nixon's support remained firm and Kissinger could pursue his clandestine and un-American policy undisturbed. One can only say that it won him more friends abroad than it did at home, and that it was eventually to prove his undoing.

The 'linkages' were immensely complex. In order to bring the war in Vietnam to an end it was necessary to isolate Hanoi. This involved creating an opening to China by exploiting her fears of the Soviet Union and her need for Western trade and expertise; and in Chou En-lai Kissinger found a subtle power-politician after his own heart. This made it possible to bring pressure to bear on the Soviet Union, as did the Russian desire for a settlement of the German question. The West German *Ostpolitik* initiative was initially viewed with hostility by Kissinger lest it upset his own plans, but thanks to another 'back-channel' he succeeded in integrating it into his system. The Russian search for détente provided 'leverage' (another favourite Kissinger word, reflecting his mechanistic view of world politics) in making them more cooperative over Cuba, India and the Middle East. The break-through in relations with Egypt (another 'back-channel' operation) made possible further pressures, not only on the Soviet Union but on Israel. The balls were juggled in the air with a finesse possible only if the performer does not have to work through bureaucratic channels and has no responsibility to public opinion. Not even the Russians enjoyed such freedom of action. The ponderous, elephantine mechanisms of American foreign policy were suddenly replaced by the precise and delicate manoeuvres of a prima ballerina. It could not, and did not, last indefinitely; but when the curtain was eventually rung down on the act because of the criminal malpractices of the managerial staff, the pattern of American foreign relations had been radically and perhaps permanently transformed.

Kissinger's successes were truly spectacular. He brought China back into the comity of nations. He reconciled Egypt to the West. He played a major part in helping the Germans to achieve a stable settlement without alarming their allies East and West. He established a dialogue with the Soviet Union on a new basis of understanding, and initiated the long and necessarily tedious procedures of the SALT talks. In southern Africa he initiated the process of healing the running sore of Rhodesia. Over Europe, curiously enough, he showed a remarkable unsureness of touch, and the few observations he makes about the European scene are both imperceptive and patronizing. The Third World he ignored, and perhaps in a longer historical perspective this will be seen as his gravest weakness. But his failure was greatest where it was most necessary that he should succeed – in bringing the war in Vietnam to a rapid and honourable conclusion. And for this his enemies, be they American academics or British radical journalists, have never forgiven him. They have reacted to these memoirs either with patronizing sneers or with personal abuse; while his successes in almost every other field they either deny or dismiss as irrelevant.

In this respect Kissinger does not make matters easy for himself. He concludes this volume with the signing of the Agreement of January 1972 with Hanoi (which we can now see as only one more stage in the humiliation of America and its abandonment of its allies) as if it were a truly major triumph of diplomacy. He had certainly worked hard enough for it, and it was no doubt the best that could be done under the circumstances; but the spirit of self-congratulation which inspires the concluding pages sounds disagreeably sanctimonious and false. In fact, whatever his tactical success (and he deserves all congratulations for it), it was only an episode in a strategic defeat. He did not obtain peace with honour in Vietnam. Could he have done so, or could anyone else?

As a believer in power politics who understood the finite nature of American interests, Kissinger was as anxious to end the war in Vietnam as anyone else – certainly no less than were the members of the liberal establishment whose naïve enthusiasm had led America into that morass and who could now hardly wait even to make their apologies before getting out. But Kissinger realized that moral values could not be ignored in power politics. 'We could not', as he puts it, 'simply walk away from an enterprise involving two administrations, five allied countries and thirty-one thousand dead as if we were switching a television channel.' Nor, he might have added, could America abandon many hundreds of thousands of Vietnamese who had staked not only their careers but their lives on the promise of American support, and still expect to live happily with a clear conscience ever after. The world was too small a place, and the betrayal of Vietnam was not likely to make it a more peaceful one. 'Linkages' were unavoidable.

We could not revitalize the Atlantic Alliance if its governments were assailed by doubt about American staying-power. We would not be able to move the Soviet Union towards the imperative of mutual restraint against the background of capitulation in a major war. We might not achieve our opening to China if our value as a counter-weight seemed nullified by a collapse that showed us irrelevant to Asian security. Our success in Middle East diplomacy would depend on our convincing our ally of our reliability and its adversaries that we were impervious to threats of military pressure or blackmail.

It may have been that Kissinger was too fearful. America's European allies, in particular, who had watched American involvement in Vietnam with pessimistic apprehension from the very beginning, were only too anxious to see her get out again as fast as possible. But even they did not demand that she should do so at any price. Prestige remains coin of the realm of international politics, and although America had certainly gained none by her lack of wisdom in getting sucked into Vietnam, she would certainly not improve matters if she now simply turned tail and ran.

But this was what Hanoi demanded; and this was a difficulty that Kissinger's liberal opponents were not then, and are not now, prepared to understand. Liberals are always reluctant to admit that there is ever really an enemy. They prefer to believe that the other side basically sees the world in the same way as they do themselves and that all conflict arises from misunderstanding – or from grievances for which one's own side is always to blame. It was so with the British liberal attitude to Hitler in the 1930s, as it was with the American liberal attitude to Hanoi in the 1960s: these, it was believed, were simply misunderstood nationalists whose misbehaviour, if indeed it had occurred at all, was an entirely justifiable reaction to the intolerable manner in which they had been treated in the past. Honourable men brought up in a secure and tolerant society find it almost impossible to conceive of the existence of hard, bitter fanatics who are not interested in settlement but only in fighting – and fighting for nothing less than total victory as a preliminary to creating a new world in which there will be no place for those who seek to appease them.

Kissinger admits that he shared the common American illusions about the Hanoi regime – until he met its representatives. He then found them to be very different from the misunderstood nationalists of his imagination. They were 'dedicated Leninists who saw themselves as the inexorable spokesmen of an inevitable future, absolute truth, and superior moral insight'; men who were not prepared to compromise or accept anything less than total and immediate American withdrawal and the dismantling of the Saigon regime – the humiliation which Kissinger, if only in the interest of his *Weltpolitik*, was determined to avoid. But he could only avoid it by making Hanoi prefer peace by negotiation to military victory; and that meant setting on military victory a price they would be unwilling to pay. How could this be done when Congress had made clear its intention of winding down the war anyhow? Only by 'Vietnamization'; equipping the South Vietnamese to defend themselves and so reversing the disastrous policies of the Johnson administration. But this would take time, and meanwhile, how could Hanoi be deterred from exploiting its advantages, except by the use of American air power?

Strategic air bombardment is so murderously indiscriminate as a weapon of war that it can be morally justified only when there is no alternative which would not in the long run cause even greater suffering. Those who opposed the bombing of Hanoi have not convincingly shown how else the North Vietnamese could be brought to negotiate. Those who have attacked the bombing of Cambodia quietly assume it to be acceptable that the North Vietnamese alone should be permitted to violate the neutrality of that desperately unfortunate land. The crude reductionism that attributes all the subsequent miseries of Cambodia to that American intervention is a remarkable illustration of the American illusion of omnipotence compounded by the common Anglo-Saxon guilt complex: if anything goes wrong anywhere in the world, it must be our fault. It is neither surprising nor discreditable that Kissinger should have made last-minute revisions in his text to take account of the ferocious attacks which his critics focused on this aspect of his policy to the exclusion of all his other achievements.

But in a way he brought these attacks upon himself. It was not just the fact of the bombings that infuriated his critics; it was the deliberate and elaborate deception in which they were cloaked. The American people were not only kept in the dark; they were lied to. A clandestine foreign policy is one thing; a clandestine war is quite another, and if it is to be resorted to at all it has got to succeed. The Americans' shock when they discovered what had been done behind their backs and in their name was entirely justifiable. This was not their war. It was Henry Kissinger's; a clandestine instrument of his clandestine policy. He must bear for it a peculiar responsibility, as he must be accorded a peculiar credit for his break-through to China, his handling of the Soviet Union and his initiatives in the Middle East.

Die Weltgeschichte ist das Weltgericht. Had Kissinger succeeded in Vietnam, his *Kabinettkrieg* in Cambodia might have been forgiven him. As it was, he failed, and the tragedy of Cambodia compounds that of Vietnam as a whole, a net debit to be set against the credits on his account. But was it his fault that he failed? Was he wrong to make the attempt? Caught between the cold implacability of Hanoi and the public determination of Congress to wind down the war, what other courses were open to him? These are the questions that must be answered if we are to sit in moral judgment on a man who assumed so crushing a responsibility, and the dogmatism of the judgment is usually in inverse ratio to the time spent in examining the facts. One can but remark with some amazement on the amount of obloquy the American liberals have heaped on the man who eventually got them out of Vietnam as compared with their sympathetic attitude to those who got them in.

There is still a great deal more to be said on this subject, not least by Dr Kissinger himself. Another volume is promised to follow, dealing with his years as Secretary of State, and he would not be human if he did not hope for another opportunity to play Merlin to another King Arthur. One cannot help feeling, however, that if he ever did return he would find the world sadly changed. The concept of the balance of power may not have been outdated in the 1960s, but it was obsolescent, because the nature of power itself was changing. Great states, either individually or in concert, were losing their capacity to control events. Military strength and alliances were increasingly irrelevant to a world where change was being determined by social, economic and ideological developments beyond the power of any state to affect more than marginally. If Dr Kissinger returns to power he will not this time be able to ignore the Third World; nor will 'leverage' help him much in dealing with the fundamental problems besetting developed societies. The model of Metternich and Bismarck has served him well, but he will need to look for another.

Henry Kissinger's second volume, *Years of Upheaval*, takes something over 1,200 pages to cover the eighteen months from February 1973 to August 1974. It is a huge, self-indulgent monster of a book. One suspects that it grew larger with each revision, instead of being judiciously trimmed and pruned into manageable shape. But there is no padding. The immense detail, though often unnecessary, is never irrelevant. The documentation is always subsumed into a narrative which, if sometimes ponderous, is never unreadable. Only a churl would grudge Kissinger his length. For the best part of a decade he was one of the most important, if not the most powerful men in the world; and though we may hope that he will one day once more be given employment commensurate with his talents, he is unlikely to dwell on peaks quite so exalted again. He was plucked from obscurity at the whim of a despot (albeit an elected one) and although his political skills enabled him to survive the fall of his patron, the domestic circumstances that gave him such immense authority are not likely to be recreated. All the more reason why he should write an account in lavish detail of what a less realistic if not a less modest man might have called 'The Years of Power'.

Such length has its drawbacks. One must work very hard at this volume to derive from it any sense of shape. It is not that Dr Kissinger does not interpolate at frequent intervals his reflections on the nature of international politics, the problems of international negotiations and the proper objectives for American foreign policy. He does, and very sage they usually are. Nor does he fail to divide his material into coherent sections, so that we can follow separately the course of negotiations with the North Vietnamese, the Russians, the Israelis and the West Europeans, even when they were being carried on, as in a multiple chess game, at the same time. But all these negotiations are given exactly the same weight. A visit to Algiers or Damascus is described in as much detail as one to Moscow or Peking. There is little feel for priorities. As Secretary of State, Kissinger seems to have delegated nothing to his subordinates. Everything received his own meticulous and demanding attention. This absence of shading, one might almost say of balance, makes for a jumble of a book. Perhaps it made for a jumble of a policy as well, in spite of Dr Kissinger's efforts to impose intellectual cohesion on it.

On careful reading, however, the jumble resolves itself into four constituent elements: two central, two regional. The central ones are American relations with the Soviet Union and those with Western Europe. The regional are the negotiations with North Vietnam (with China in the background) and with Israel and her Arab adversaries. Both of these last are described in a detail that indicates the degree of attention Kissinger himself devoted to them. But these four pillars of US foreign policy rested on a domestic foundation which grew steadily more insecure and ultimately collapsed entirely. It was in February 1973, as Kissinger was switching the focus of his attention from Vietnam to the Middle East, that in another room in the White House Nixon was receiving his first briefings from John Dean about the growing ramification of the Watergate affair. From then onwards Watergate provided a continuous ground base to Kissinger's diplomacy, rising in a crescendo that eventually drowned out with its discords the harmonies that he was trying so hard to create in the outside world.

If there is a unifying theme in this book, indeed, it is this contrast between the power of the American Presidency abroad and its progressive paralysis at home. (The book might appropriately have been called 'The Watergate Years'.) But for Watergate, implies Dr Kissinger, everything might have been very different. Watergate distracted the President, who could no longer bring to foreign affairs the sustained attention that had characterized his first term of office. It eroded the credibility of American leadership with both adversaries and allies, who became increasingly sceptical of the will and capacity of the American government to deliver on any of the promises that Dr Kissinger might make. Watergate indeed, as he interestingly explains, gave Kissinger an authority he might not otherwise have possessed. Without the backing of a strong President his position as Presidential Adviser lacked any political muscle; if he was to be effective he had to be given the full power of Secretary of State – something that Nixon did very ungraciously indeed. And once Secretary, he could do very much as he pleased, subject to an unpredictable President occasionally rousing himself from his torpor to take an initiative or make a gesture designed to reassert his authority and gain a little domestic credit.

But Kissinger protests altogether too much about Watergate. It was a negligible factor, for instance, in his failure to settle the Vietnamese imbroglio on the honourable terms for which he had been striving ever since 1969. The basic problem here was that the North Vietnamese were implacable, the American people heartily sick of a war whose object they had never fully understood, and Congress unwilling to provide the military muscle needed to compel Hanoi to stick to its agreements. Nor did Watergate impede Kissinger's sustained and largely successful efforts to sort out the tangle in the Middle East after the Yom Kippur War. In relations with the Soviet Union Watergate was certainly an embarrassment, but one that the Russian leadership did curiously little to exploit. The problem over relations with Moscow did not lie with the Russians, who in their desire to avoid trouble accepted humiliation after humiliation in the Middle East, but with an American public opinion quite unable to appreciate the delicate nuances of Kissinger's *détente* policy. What mattered was not the erosion of Presidential authority through Watergate but Kissinger's inability to manage a Congress that regarded any agreement with Moscow as a sell-out unless it resulted in a clear-cut American victory.

As for Europe, the suggestion that Watergate was in any

degree responsible for the worsening of transatlantic relations simply will not wash.

With the European allies Kissinger showed, in spite of his excellent personal relations with many of their leaders, an astonishing unsureness of touch. Admittedly they were being more difficult than usual. Italy was wracked by internal difficulties. Willy Brandt was anxiously tending the first shoots of his new *Ostpolitik*, with all its complex implications for domestic as well as foreign policy. Britain and France were adjusting to a new and difficult relationship within the enlarged European Community. The diplomatic circuits were overloaded enough already. It was not a good moment for Kissinger to try to revive the great days of Marshall and Acheson with noble exhortations for rededication to high moral purpose, with anachronistic demands for a new Atlantic Charter.

The whole idea of 'A Year of Europe' seemed to most Europeans a pious and pointless irrelevance. It awoke no enthusiasm whatever, and it is a pity that Kissinger's many European friends were too polite to tell him so. Certainly M. Jobert treated poor Dr Kissinger very badly indeed, but his bad behaviour reflected a widespread sense of exasperation among European leaders that the United States should have chosen this moment to demand new commitments and assurances when they would rather have been left alone to sort out their own problems in their own way. It is paradoxical that, whereas Kissinger seemed to so many of his own countrymen to embody the old European diplomacy at its worst, to his European allies he seemed at times the reincarnation of Woodrow Wilson, proclaiming grandiose goals that bore little evident relation to the needs of the moment.

It was all the more regrettable that, after some nine months of bickering over 'The Year of Europe', the Alliance should have been tested at its weakest point by the Yom Kippur War. No one showed up very well during that crisis. The Europeans were cantankerous and self-regarding: that is the nature of states, as Dr Kissinger should know better than most. But his expectation that they should passively accept American leadership while Washington and her Israeli clients involved them not just in a damaging conflict with the oil-producing countries but in a confrontation with the Soviet Union arising from an 'out-of-area' crisis was oddly unrealistic, and his argument that the United States should have accepted French and British leadership during the Suez crisis of 1956 does not improve his case. Evidently Dr Kissinger's view of the Alliance is a surprisingly romantic one. The argument that its terms did not, and do not, extend to the Middle East he dismisses as 'legalistic'. But the fact is that the North Atlantic Treaty did not and does not cover the Middle East. There as elsewhere in the world the states of the Alliance have divergent interests and perceptions that have to be carefully managed if they are not to conflict. Again it is a paradox that Kissinger, who so impressed such adversaries as the Russians and the Chinese with his acute appreciation of their fears and interests, should have shown such impatience with those of his allies.

There were in fact two Kissingers. One was the diplomat, immensely intelligent, hard-working, well-briefed, acute in his perceptions, with a capacity for 'laying himself alongside' his interlocutor that was almost uncanny. In this capacity he rendered outstanding service to his country and the world. He talked as no other Western statesman had ever talked to Mao Tse-tung and Chou En-lai, skilfully coaxing China out of her self-imposed isolation. He dealt with the Soviet leaders not as alien ideologues but as intelligent adults with whom a substantial area of common interest could be found. He established relations of equal confidence – even of intimacy – with those apparently irreconcilable adversaries Golda Meir of Israel, President Assad of Syria, and President Sadat of Egypt. His descriptions of his negotiations with all these leaders and his reflections on them deserve to become classic guides to diplomatic practice.

But associated with this charming and patient negotiator was Kissinger the demiurge; the intellectual who believed that international politics could not be carried on without some overarching concept, some grand strategy, that all could and must be moulded to some grand design. He complained of the US Foreign Service that it had always seen its role simply

as a negotiating instrument, not as a designer of foreign policy, more as solving concrete issues as they arose than as conceiving a strategy and shaping events.

As a critique of a purely passive and reactive policy this is justifiable. The statesman has to anticipate events, not simply respond to them, and must judge how best they can be resolved in the interests of his nation and those of the international community as a whole.

But there are limits beyond which this conceptualizing cannot be pressed in so diverse and unpredictable a world. The most valuable contribution that an intellectual can bring to politics is *insight* rather than concepts: an appreciation, based as much on instinct as on analysis, that a situation may be ripe for change, that an adjustment of the accepted framework has become possible and perhaps necessary; an insight to be checked against analysis but rarely deducible from it. It was this kind of insight that enabled Kissinger to react so quickly to the hints and initiatives of others; to pick up the first faint signals that the People's Republic of China might be interested in rejoining the community of nations, to realize what Brezhnev meant when he suggested *détente*, to appreciate the enormous importance of Sadat's first subtle overtures. Kissinger's brilliance, like that of the early Bismarck, lay in discerning and grasping opportunities and following where they led him. He was able to recognize an opportunity when he saw one because he had an instinctive feel for the shape of international politics. It was only when he tried to conceptualize this, to conceive of a 'grand strategy' and take bold initiatives in pursuit of it that his efforts ran into the sand.

It was both Kissinger's good fortune and his misfortune that he should have had to conduct the foreign policy of the United States.[1] It was good fortune in that the task gave him

1. We may speculate interestingly (as he no doubt often has himself) as to what would have happened had he never left his native Germany but had remained to become Chancellor or at least Foreign Minister of the

such unexampled scope. It was bad, because anyone who has to conduct the foreign affairs of the American people can expect little but trouble. Kissinger has analysed the problem many times, and has done so nowhere better than in this volume:

Two schools of thought developed [in the United States]. The liberal approach treated foreign policy as a subdivision of psychiatry; the conservative approach considered it an aspect of theology. Liberals equated relations among states with human relations. They emphasized the virtues of trust and unilateral gestures of goodwill. Conservatives saw in foreign policy a version of the eternal struggle of good with evil, a conflict that recognized no middle ground and could end only with victory. Deterrence ran up against liberal ideology and its emotional evocation of peace in the abstract; coexistence grated on the liturgical anti-communism of the Right.

This is a chronic condition of American politics. Under Richard Nixon it became acute. The conservatives were, as ever, sulky and suspicious. The liberals, determined to deny Nixon and Kissinger any credit for implementing even a policy they approved, attacked *détente* with the Soviet Union as condonation, if not actual cooperation, in the suppression of human rights. The two combined in an unholy alliance under Senator Henry 'Scoop' Jackson, whose persistent attacks on Kissinger's *détente* policy came close to defeating it. The entire American body politic was still in a feverish condition after Vietnam, the conservatives resentful and revengeful, the liberals baying for blood; but even if the temperature had been normal it would still have taken exquisite skill and dogged hard work to mobilize opinion behind Kissinger's flexible and imaginative policy.

We in the Nixon Administration [he wrote] felt that our challenge was to educate the American people in the balance of power.

It was indeed; but one can only say they chose a very odd

Federal Republic. On this smaller but no less vital and far more manageable stage, might he not have secured no less significant but perhaps more lasting results?

way of doing it. What was needed for so daunting a task was a subtle and persistent wooing of Congress, a continual, patient dialogue with the media, and persuasive appeals to grass-roots opinion on the lines of Franklin Roosevelt's campaign to coax America out of its isolation in 1939–41. Instead the Nixon Administration virtually declared war on Congress, alienated the media, and ignored public opinion. As a result Kissinger was able for a few years to conduct foreign policy as if he were a Richelieu or a Kaunitz, responsible only to a monarch whose moods and objectives he perfectly understood. His complaint about Watergate is a revealing one: 'It eroded Presidential authority.' It certainly did that. But the real trouble was that the President tried to use that authority in a particular way, secretive, arbitrary, absolute; exactly what Kissinger needed for the conduct of an intelligent, if idiosyncratic, foreign policy, but disastrous for the proper functioning of a democratic republic.

Kissinger returns in this volume to the charge over Cambodia, and takes up much space in rebutting the wild and largely unjust accusations levelled against him by William Shawcross in his book *Sideshow*. But the fact remains that operations in Cambodia, whatever their political or military justification, were carried on largely without the knowledge, and certainly without the consent, of the United States Congress and the American people. In authorizing them Kissinger was stretching Presidential authority far beyond acceptable limits, and he has been deservedly excoriated for it.

Kissinger's Vietnam policy, however well-meant, was an unrelieved disaster. His European policy was a humiliating flop. In both these theatres he set his sights too high, expecting in the first instance more of his countrymen, in the second more of his allies, than they could reasonably be expected to provide. But his breakthrough to China was historic, and the dialogue he established with the Soviet Union was perhaps the greatest contribution to the normalization of Superpower relations – one is tempted to say, 'to peace' – made by any statesman since the end of the Second World War. It is perhaps no coincidence that in both these cases he was dealing with despotisms whose leaders did not have to reckon with public opinion and who were as coolly calculating of their countries' interests as he was himself. In talking to Brezhnev and to Chou En-lai Kissinger was at home in the nineteenth-century world he was trying to recreate, the world of Talleyrand and Alexander and Metternich, of Friedrich Gentz and the intelligent manipulation of the balance of power. If only his European and Japanese allies, if only his bloody-minded fellow-countrymen would fit into this pattern, how much more manageable the world would be!

Finally, there was the Middle East. If the situation there over the last eight years has turned desperately sour it is through no fault of Kissinger's. He brilliantly exploited the divisions among the Arab states without alienating any significant one of them. He won Egypt to the side of the West, and eliminated the Soviet Union as a serious actor in the region altogether. He set on foot the process of reconciliation that President Carter was to carry a stage further at Camp David; and if Israel has now fallen into the hands of extremists for whom the whole concept of reconciliation is and always has been meaningless, not even a William Shawcross can lay the blame for that at Kissinger's door. If a criticism is to be made, it is that he allowed the Middle East to become an obsession with him. Here Kissinger the diplomat took over almost compulsively. He spent ten days on the Cairo shuttle in January 1974; a further week in the region at the beginning of March; and the entire month of May, over four weeks, was passed commuting between Jerusalem and Damascus. Were the details of the Golan frontier really so important as to warrant quite so much of the personal attention of the US Secretary of State? Or did he find in this intricate filigree work, of which he was such a master-craftsman and which demanded so much patience and concentration, a blessed distraction and escape from the Europeans who had humiliated and his own people who had misunderstood him? Washington in the spring of 1974, with Watergate reaching its climax, was an excellent place not to be. But an aircraft shuttling between Damascus and Jerusalem was hardly the ideal locale for the conduct of American foreign policy – let alone the education of the American people in its more complex realities.

But when all is said and done, the record is impressive. Like all great public figures Kissinger has had his failures, but they have been the result of misplaced boldness – never of weakness and incompetence. Under his leadership the United States was able to carry on a creative, a constructive and a coherent foreign policy commensurate with its power; a policy not always successful, not always well-judged, but always worthy of respect. History will certainly rank him among the major figures of the late twentieth century: and not only because he will have written so much of it himself.

Acknowledgements

'The Causes of War' was the Creighton Lecture in the University of London, November 1981

'War and the Nation State' was delivered as an Inaugural Lecture as Chichele Professor in the History of War in the University of Oxford, November 1977

'The Strategic Dimension in International Relations' is reprinted from *The British Journal of International Studies* 2 (1976)

'Ethics and Power in International Politics' was delivered as the Martin Wight Memorial Lecture at Chatham House, January 1977

'Social Change and the Defence of the West' was written for the Brussels Conference of the Georgetown Center for International Studies, September 1979

'The Relevance of Traditional Strategy' is reprinted from *Foreign Affairs*, January 1973

'The Forgotten Dimensions of Strategy' is reprinted from *Foreign Affairs*, Summer 1979

'Surviving a Protest: A Reply to E. P. Thompson's Polemic' is reprinted from *Encounter*, November 1980

'On Fighting a Nuclear War' was delivered as the Bernard Brodie Memorial Lecture in the University of California, November 1980

'War in the Making and Unmaking of Europe' was delivered at the University of Sussex, February 1979

'The British Way in Warfare: A Reappraisal' was delivered as the Neale Lecture in English History, at University College, London, 1974

'The Use and Abuse of Military History' was delivered at the Royal United Services Institution, London, 1961. It was printed in their *Journal* in February 1962 and reprinted in *Parameters*, March 1981

'Liddell Hart' is reprinted from *Encounter*, June 1970

'Montgomery' is reprinted from *Encounter*, August 1976

'Kissinger' is reprinted from *The Times Literary Supplement*, 21 December 1979, and from *Encounter*, November 1982.